New York Sluggers
The First 75 Years

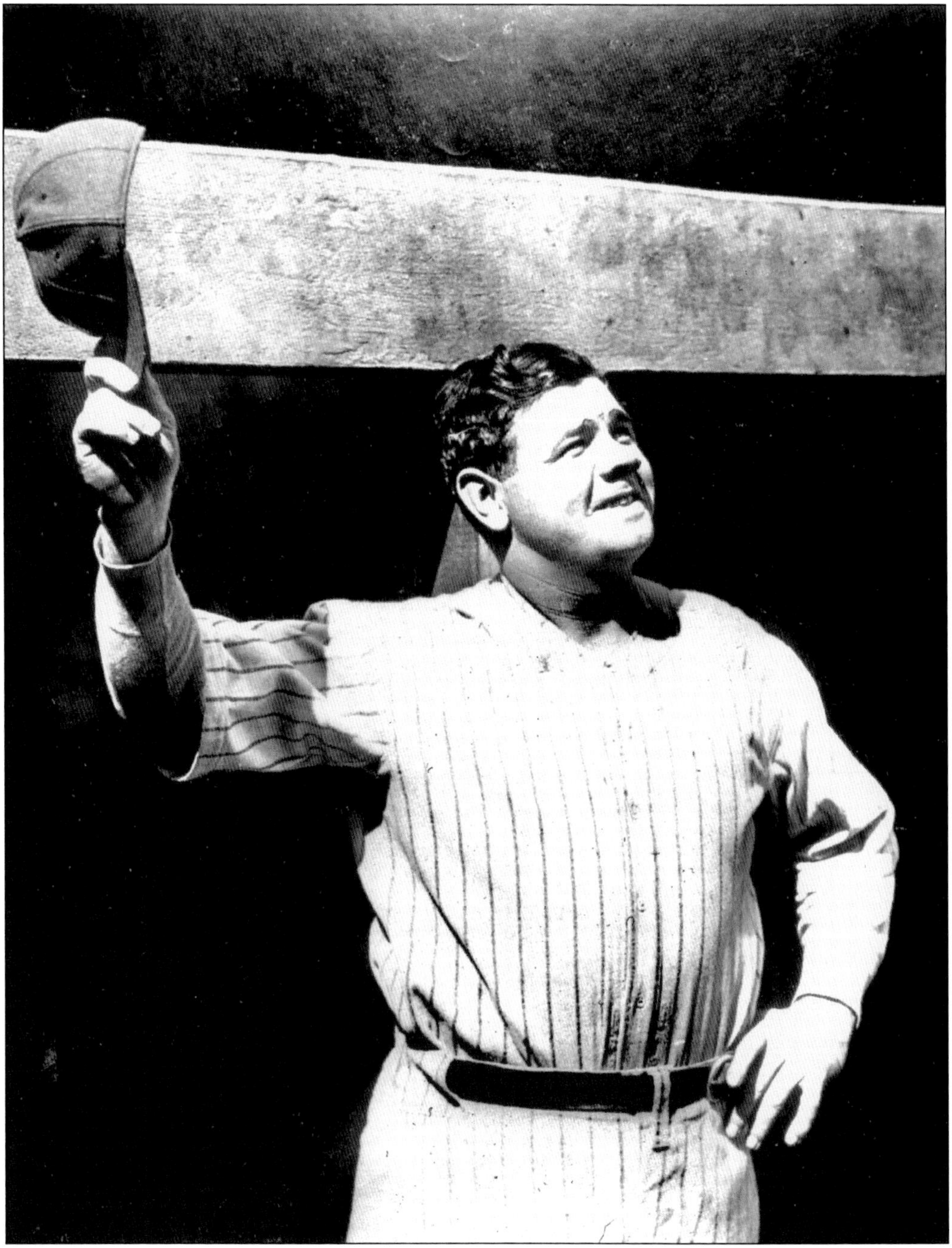

Babe Ruth was a symbol of rags-to-riches fortune through baseball in the Roaring Twenties.

NEW YORK SLUGGERS
THE FIRST 75 YEARS

Mark Rucker

ARCADIA
PUBLISHING

ISBN 978-0-7385-3785-6

Published by Arcadia Publishing,
Charleston, South Carolina

Printed in the United States of America

Library of Congress Catalog Card Number: 2005922084

For all general information, contact Arcadia Publishing:
Telephone 843-853-2070
Fax 843-853-0044
E-mail sales@arcadiapublishing.com
For customer service and orders:
Toll-free 1-888-313-2665

Visit us on the Internet at www.arcadiapublishing.com

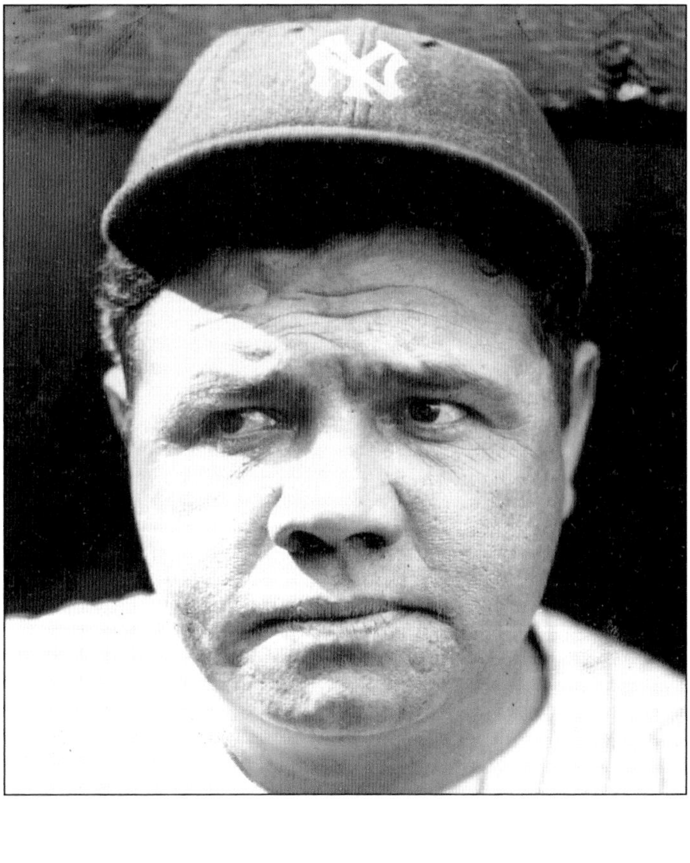

The most recognizable
face in baseball history.

CONTENTS

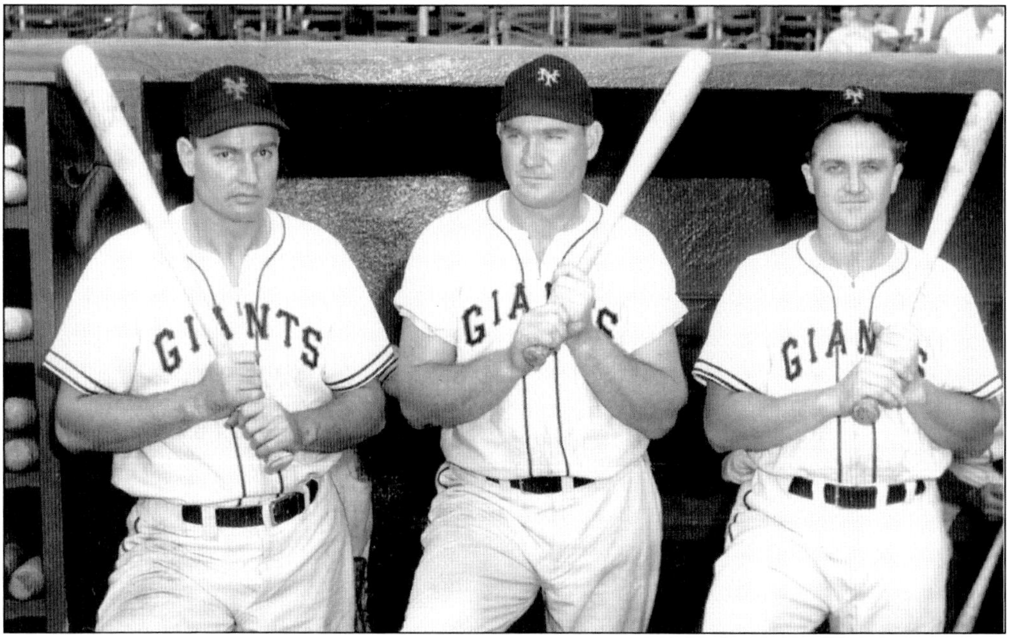

These two 1940s slugging trios played for the New York Giants and the Yankees. In the 1947 photograph above are Walker Cooper (left), Johnny Mize (center), and Willard Marshall. Below, Joe DiMaggio (left), Charlie Keller (center), and Johnny Lindell line up for a spring training shot in 1946. Both teams sent hitters to the plate that fans would remember for a lifetime.

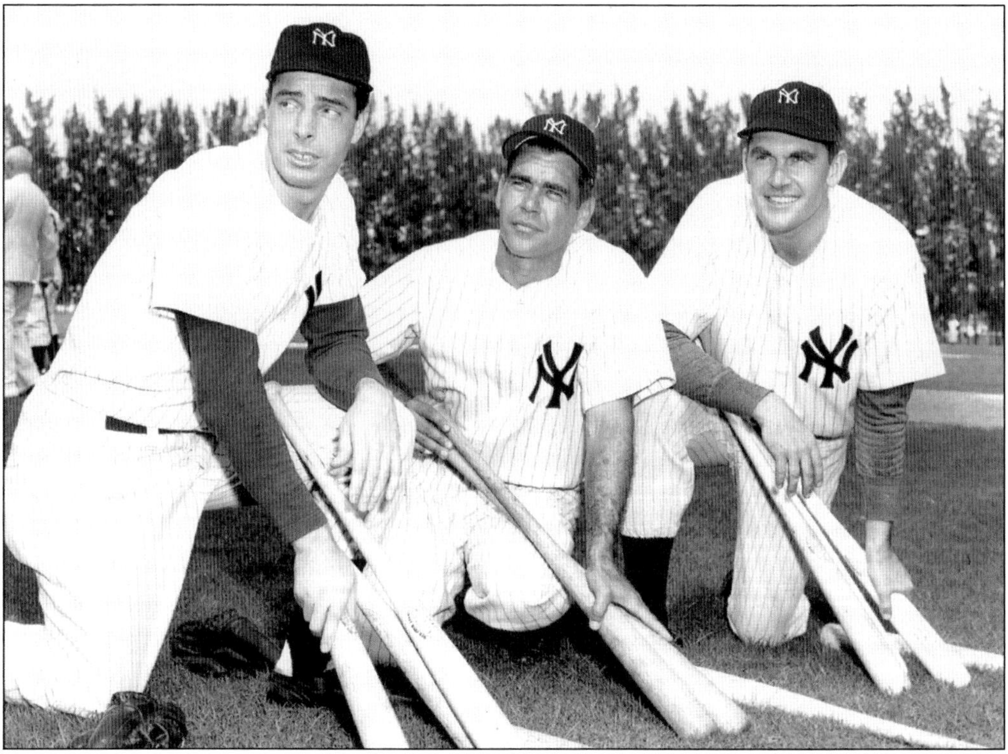

INTRODUCTION

When fans think about players who could hit a baseball—or, better yet, smash or crush a baseball—the first team to come to mind is always the New York Yankees. Slugging was actually invented by the Yankees, and was most prominently demonstrated by Babe Ruth. When Lou Gehrig joined the team in 1923, a one-two punch of home runs and extra-base hits was established, setting a standard seldom equaled in major-league history. Meanwhile, across the East River in New York, the Giants also manufactured lots of hitting. And although they were never the powerhouse the Yankees were, the New York Nationals could rattle the walls in the Polo Grounds against any comers.

New York City was the original hotbed of baseball, so it is not surprising that fans in the five boroughs are very knowledgeable about the game. It did not take long after the game was established in New York City in the late 1850s for heavy hitters to rise in popularity. News reports of contests during this period remarked on long drives to the outfield or hard striking by the local boys. The pleasure of seeing a ball hit right on the nose is among the most enjoyable moments for spectators. But to a hitter, cutting a fastball in half off the sweet spot of the bat is an ecstatic moment like no other.

Relying on the long ball to win games was something new to baseball in the late 1910s. Before that, strategic systems were employed to score runs. New Yorkers understood strategy, baseball intelligence, and working as a team. But they were not averse to new developments when something eye-opening came onto the scene. And Babe Ruth was certainly an eye-opener, a player who single-handedly changed the game. No one before the Babe had swung always from their heels, and Babe got more of his upper body to provide power than any player before him. After his follow-through, Ruth's body would look like a wrung towel.

With the Babe's success, sluggers of many varieties began to appear in the major leagues. Within a few years, the Giants had sluggers of their own. John McGraw's hustling squad added Rogers Hornsby to the mix for a few years, and then Mel Ott, and then Johnny Mize—all long-ball artists. A tradition was established during the 1920s that teams needed home run hitters, both to entertain the crowds and to increase scoring. For the Yankees, no sooner was the Ruth-Gehrig era waning than Joe DiMaggio arrived from San Francisco. DiMaggio's strength and grace enthralled fans for almost a decade and a half. Then, as DiMaggio's career was fading away, along came Mickey Mantle from Oklahoma. It was as if the Yankees could manufacture slugging superstars whenever they were needed, generation after generation.

But knocking balls over the wall is not all you need to win ball games. For the Giants and Yankees, there was a constant parade of good hitters moving on and off their rosters. But all hard hitters were not home run threats. Mugsy McGraw, the manager of the Giants for 30 years, built his teams with doubles-hitters and singles-hitters to go with his top-level pitching. They could usually score enough runs to win. Still, the big drama and the big bang was with the Yankees, and they outdrew the Giants at the box office almost every year.

Simultaneous to segregationist white America enjoying its National and American League action, the Negro Leagues were in full flower. The New York Lincoln Stars, the Lincoln Giants, the New York Black Yankees, and the New York Cubans were among the teams that played in the city, exciting their audiences every season. Stars like Pop Lloyd, Ghost Marcelle, Bill Holland, Mule Suttles, Turkey Stearnes, Chino Smith, Clint Thomas, Martin Dihigo, Dick Lundy, and Luis Tiant Sr. were on the field annually for their Negro League fans, and they would have been impressing crowds across the nation were it not for institutionalized racism. They often leased major-league stadiums when white teams were away on road trips.

The talent that passed through New York ballparks—both black and white—was staggering, and the fanatics, whether rooting for their Negro League clubs or for the their Giants or Yankees, were thoroughly appreciative. We can thank the camera for bringing us a visual record of these wonderful years.

One

1875–1900

'Orator' Jim O'Rourke

Career 1876–1904 New York 1885–1892

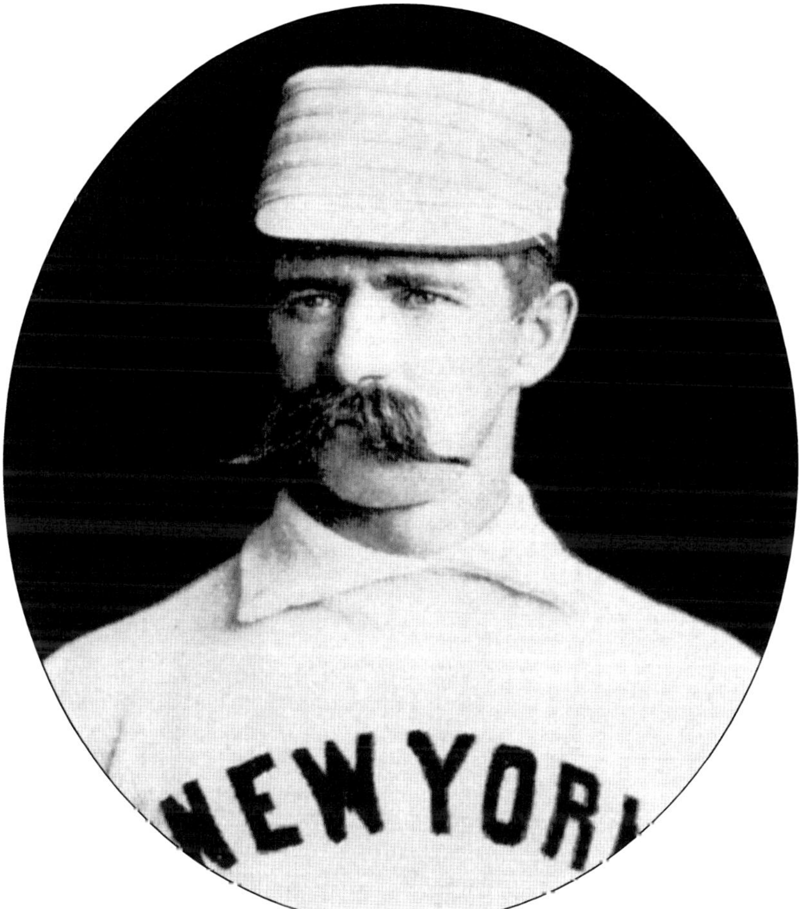

Jim O'Rourke played outfielder and catcher for his seven major-league teams. He hit for a high average, ending his 19-year career with a .310 mark, and led the league in home runs three times (with totals that never reached double figures). His league-leading .347 average for the 1884 Buffalo Base Ball Club made O'Rourke particularly attractive to the Giants, and after moving to New York in 1885 he led the Giants and the league in doubles with 16. In New York he contracted with both the Giants and with New York's entry in the Players League for the one year of its existence. The incessant talker, known as Orator, became a Hall of Famer in 1945 for his work both on the field and in the front office after his retirement.

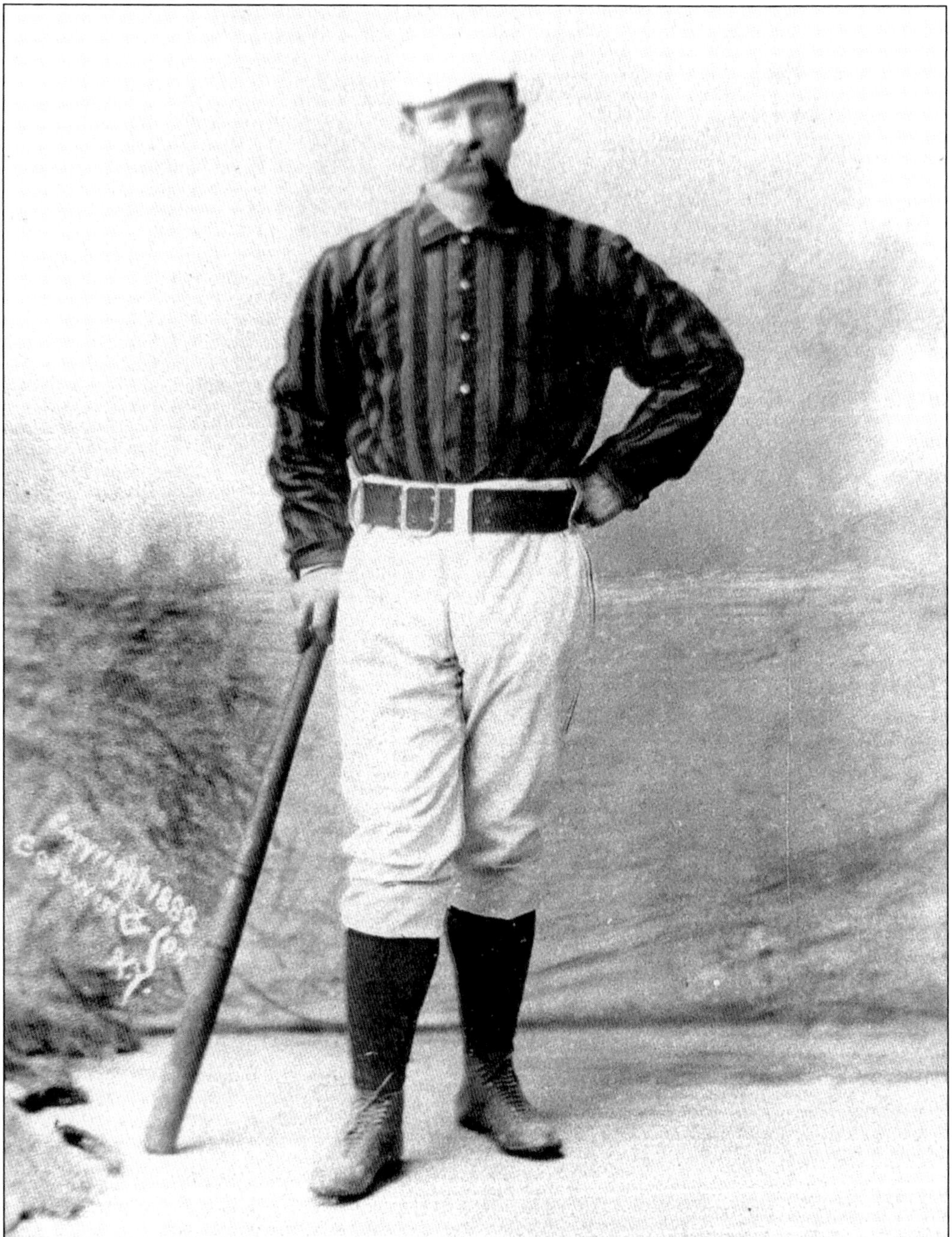

Jim O'Rourke knew how to win wherever he served, and played for seven pennant-winning teams, including one title with Providence, five with Boston, and one with New York. Among his most memorable moments was getting the first-ever base hit in National League play quite early on opening day, April 22, 1876. On the other end of his career, O'Rourke, in a planned stunt, returned to the Giants lineup in late 1904 and played a complete game at the age of 52. After retiring from the field, O'Rourke became a minor-league manager, which led to his service as president of the Connecticut State League and then the Eastern Association.

MONTE WARD

CAREER 1878–1894 NEW YORK 1883–1889, 1893–1894

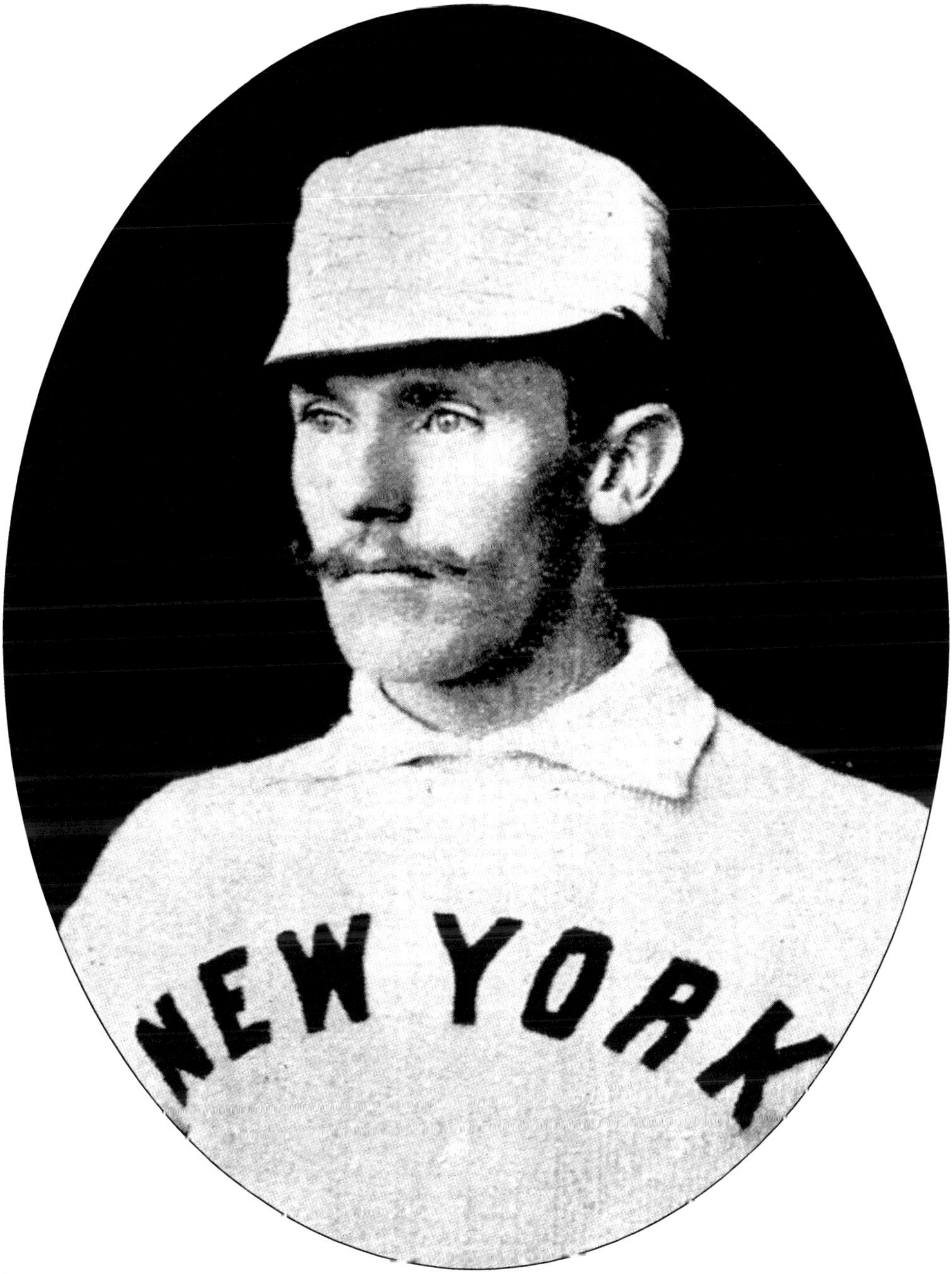

John Montgomery "Monte" Ward was a ballplayer, a manager, a coach, an executive, a league founder, a lawyer, a writer, and a labor organizer. If he had not been stellar at playing baseball, much of his life's work could never have been achieved. He was a successful pitcher in his first years in professional ball in Providence, sometimes playing another position on his off days. His pitching arm did not hold up, so Monte moved to shortstop.

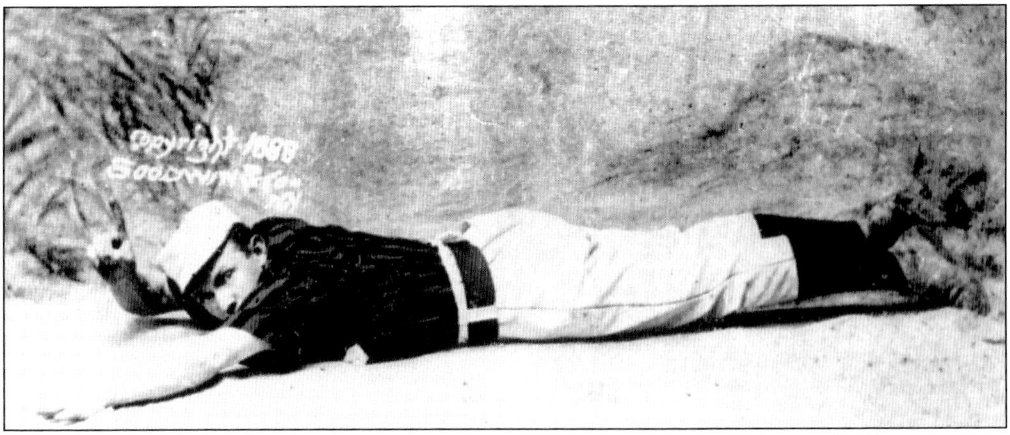

Monte Ward had a great baseball mind, which he employed on the field and off. As captain and later manager of the Giants, Ward could strategize a win as easily as he could hit and run the bases for a victory. His staggering record of 111 stolen bases for New York in 1887 stood well into the modern era, while his .338 batting average was among the league leaders. His longstanding fight with baseball owners over the reserve clause, which bound players to their teams without recourse, led to the formation of the first players' union and eventually to the establishment of the union-controlled Players League in 1890. Ward not only oversaw the new league's operations, but also played like a man possessed that season. He hit 12 triples that year, knocked in 60 runs (his second-highest total), and batted .335 with a .426 slugging percentage. But his work and his personal exploits could not save the league, and the following year Ward was back in the National League with Brooklyn. He helped organize a revitalized Giants club in 1893 and 1894, and they won it all the latter year, taking the Temple Cup, or World Series, from Baltimore, which had finished the regular season three games ahead of the Giants. After 17 years in the big leagues, Ward retired in the winter of 1894 to become a full-time lawyer. He kept his hand in the game, if only by representing ballplayers who had been wronged. Ward traveled around the world during an 1888–1889 baseball tour and visited Egypt along the way. Below, Ward sits at far left in this photograph taken at the base of the Great Pyramid at Giza. (The other men are not identified.) In the image above, Ward demonstrates a head-first slide.

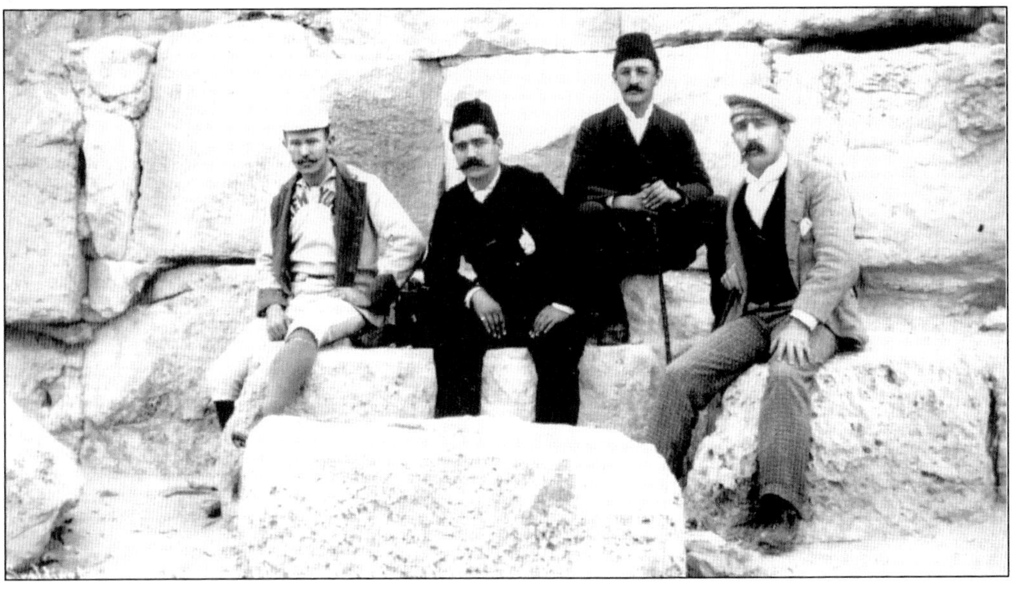

Roger Connor

Career 1880–1897 New York 1883–1891, 1893–1894

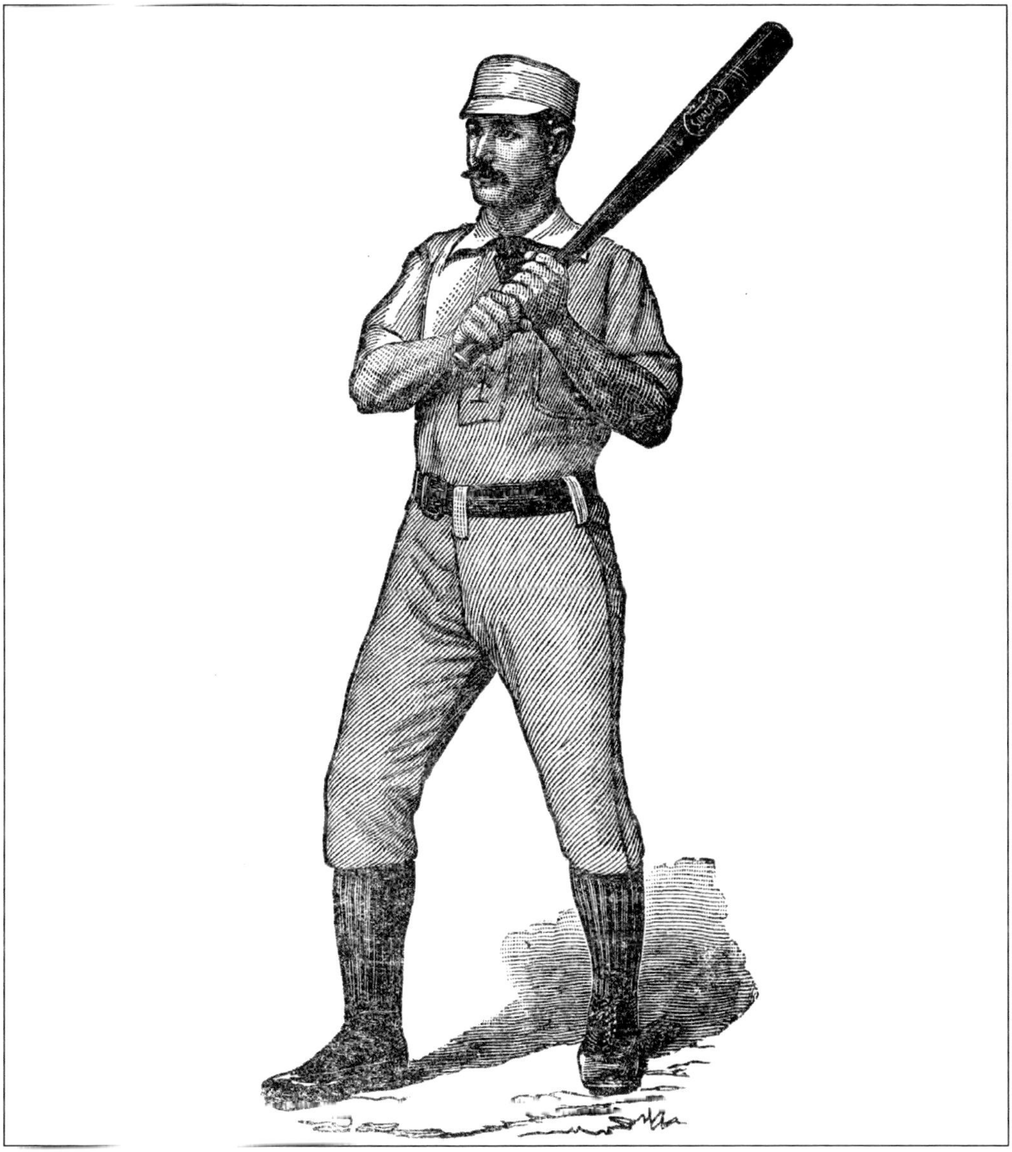

Roger Connor was the holder of the all-time home run record until Babe Ruth shattered it. Connor was literally a giant in his time, standing 6 feet 3 inches tall and weighing 220 pounds, and he used his size and strength to pound balls all over the park. He started in the National League with Troy, and when the franchise moved to New York City he became a Giant. At one time or another during his 18-year career, Connor led the National League at least once in hits, doubles, triples, homers, RBIs, walks, batting average, slugging percentage, and on-base percentage. He collected a grand total of almost 2,500 hits. In the season that he led all others in circuit clouts, he was a member of the New York entry in the short-lived Players League (he was a friend and business associate of fellow Giant Monte Ward). After hanging up the uniform at the close of the 1897 season, Connor tried managing for a year, and then was done.

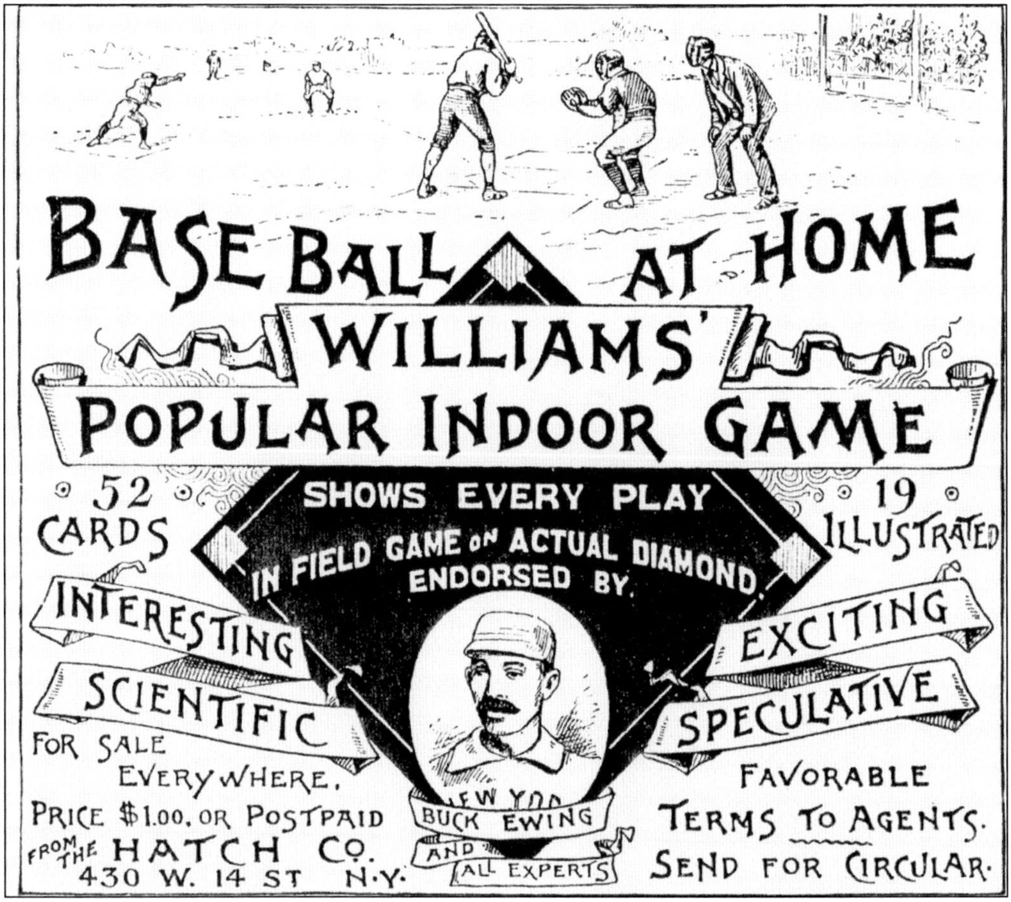
BASE BALL AT HOME
WILLIAMS'
POPULAR INDOOR GAME
52 CARDS
19 ILLUSTRATED
SHOWS EVERY PLAY
IN FIELD GAME ON ACTUAL DIAMOND
ENDORSED BY
INTERESTING
SCIENTIFIC
EXCITING
SPECULATIVE
NEW YORK
BUCK EWING
AND
ALL EXPERTS
FOR SALE EVERYWHERE.
PRICE $1.00, OR POSTPAID FROM THE HATCH CO. 430 W. 14 ST N.Y.
FAVORABLE TERMS TO AGENTS.
SEND FOR CIRCULAR.

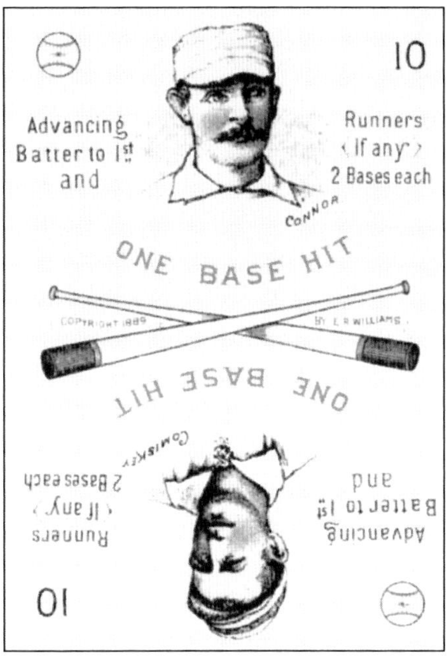
10
Advancing Batter to 1st and
Runners (If any) 2 Bases each
CONNOR
ONE BASE HIT
COPYRIGHT 1889
BY E.R. WILLIAMS
ONE BASE HIT
COMISKEY
10

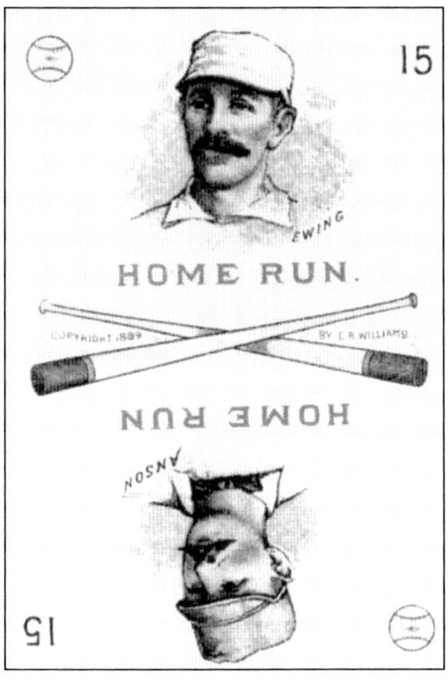
15
EWING
HOME RUN.
COPYRIGHT 1889
BY E.R. WILLIAMS
HOME RUN
ANSON
15

Buck Ewing

Career 1880–1897 New York 1883–1892

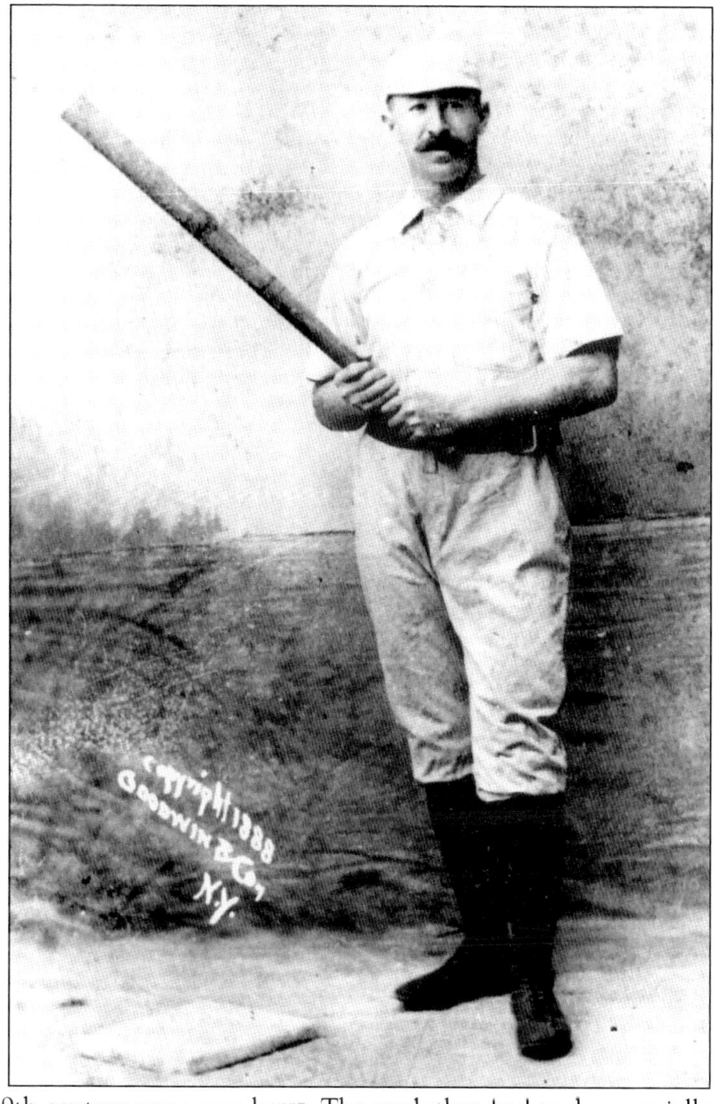

A baseball catcher in the 19th century was a rare beast. The work they had to do, especially before the invention of protective equipment, was brutal. Few were willing to stand up against a high-speed fastball with nothing but their hands and body to block it. (There was one catcher who had all the bones in both hands and his face broken at one time or another in his career.) So it is not surprising that Buck Ewing was a national hero. Fans around the country knew what a painful job catching could be, but they also knew that without capable catchers there would be few victories. Besides being the finest backstop in the country for nearly a decade, Ewing was a strong hitter. His best years in baseball were his 10 seasons in New York, where he hit over .300 in all but one season. At the bottom of the opposite page are two 1887 game cards, the Victorian version of rotisserie baseball leagues. Buck Ewing is on the right and Roger Connor is on the left. The advertisement at the top of the page featured Ewing's portrait, indicating just how popular the Giants catcher was at that time.

GEORGE GORE
CAREER 1879–1892 NEW YORK 1887–1892

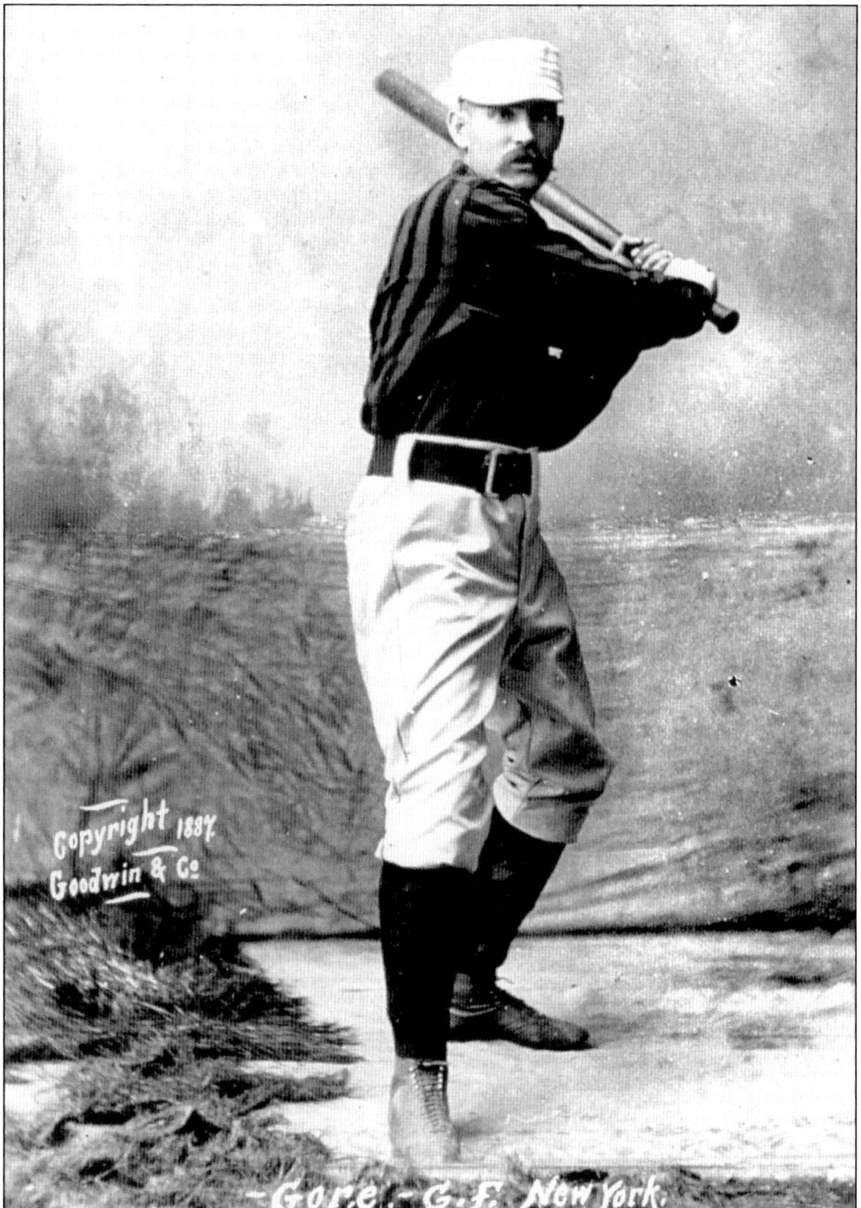

George Gore was a rookie in 1879, but the next year he put up some league-leading numbers. In 1880 he was the batting-average champion and also topped all others with a .463 slugging percentage. After hitting .300 or higher every year for the Chicago White Stockings, Gore was picked up by the Giants for the 1887 season. In the photograph above, he is wearing the Giants' handsome red-and-black-striped uniform. He continued his hard hitting in New York, knocking a career-best 10 home runs during the 1890 season. Over his career, Gore scored more runs than the number of games he had played, making him one of only three players in baseball history to do so.

MIKE TIERNAN

CAREER 1887–1899 ALL IN NEW YORK

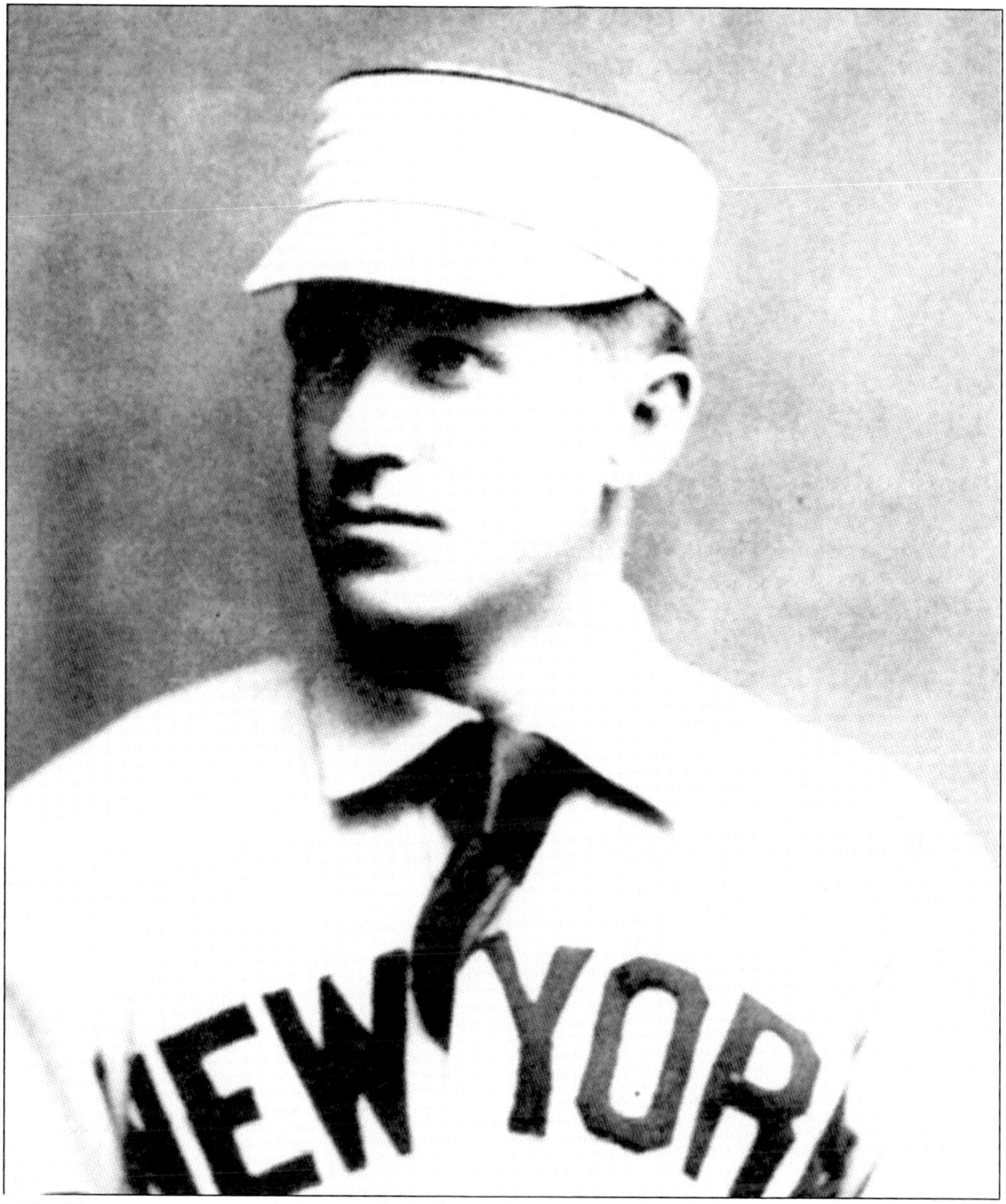

Mike Tiernan was one of those early ballplayers who never gained much fame, but he was a pioneer slugger in the game. He led the National League in home runs in 1890 with 13, and again in 1891 with 16—big numbers in those days. In 1894, Tiernan's .495 slugging percentage was the best in the league. He played the outfield in New York for his entire professional career, and was surrounded in the lineup by players such as Monte Ward, Roger Connor, Jim O'Rourke, and Buck Ewing. In the mid-1890s, the first- and second-place teams in the National League played a postseason set of games. Tiernan played on two pennant-winning squads and in two World Series for the Giants.

George Van Haltren

Career 1887–1903 New York 1894–1903

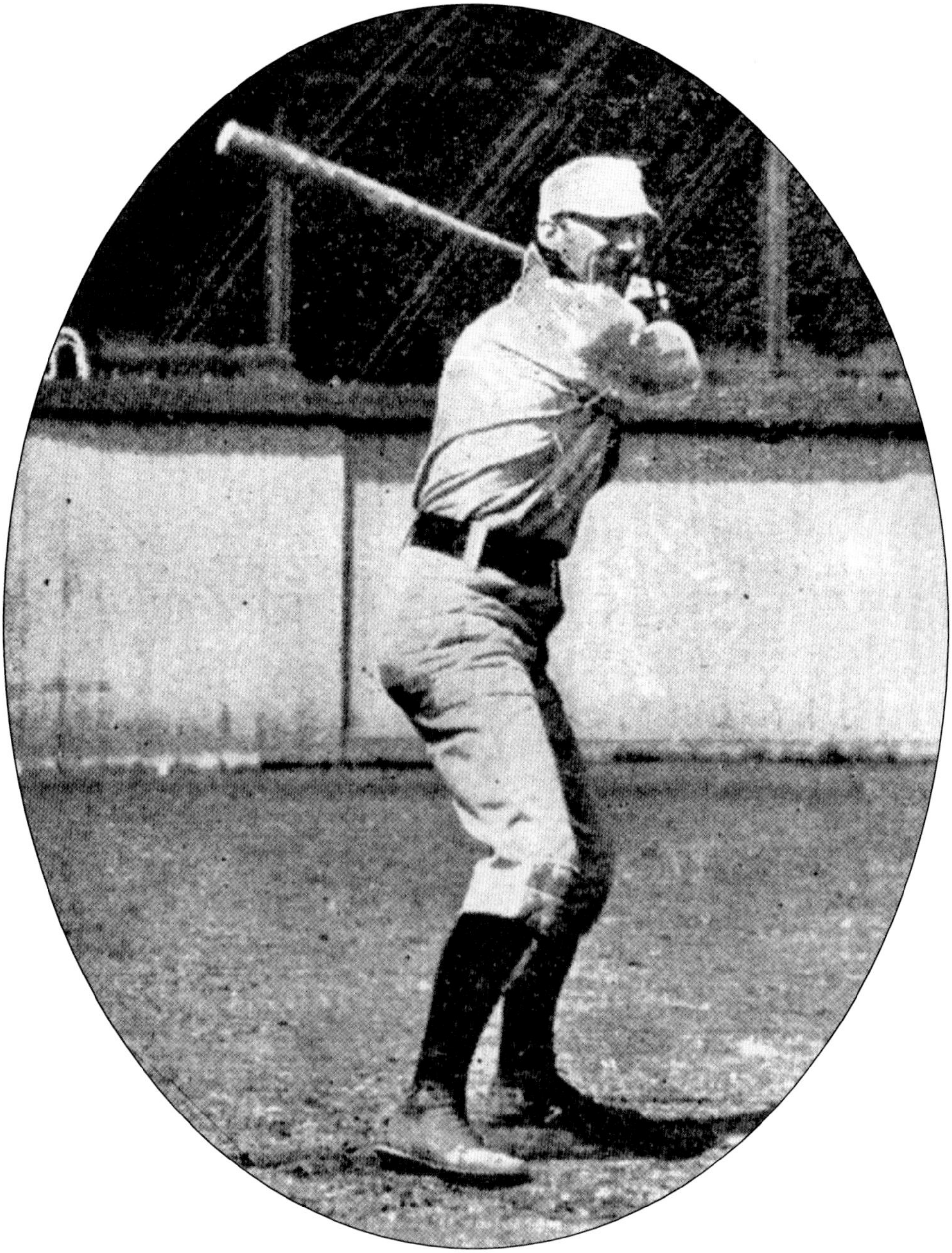

Was George Van Haltren called Rip because of the way he stroked 69 home runs, 161 triples, and 285 doubles among his 2,532 lifetime hit total? Who cares? All you have to know is that Van Haltren, a consistent performer from 1888 to 1901, has been on the Hall of Fame's doorstep for decades. He batted over .300 for four straight years and then again for nine straight seasons, finishing with a .316 lifetime average. The photograph above was taken in 1892 at the Polo Grounds and was published in Frank Leslie's weekly newspaper.

Two

1901–1920

KIP SELBACH

CAREER 1894–1906 NEW YORK 1900–1901

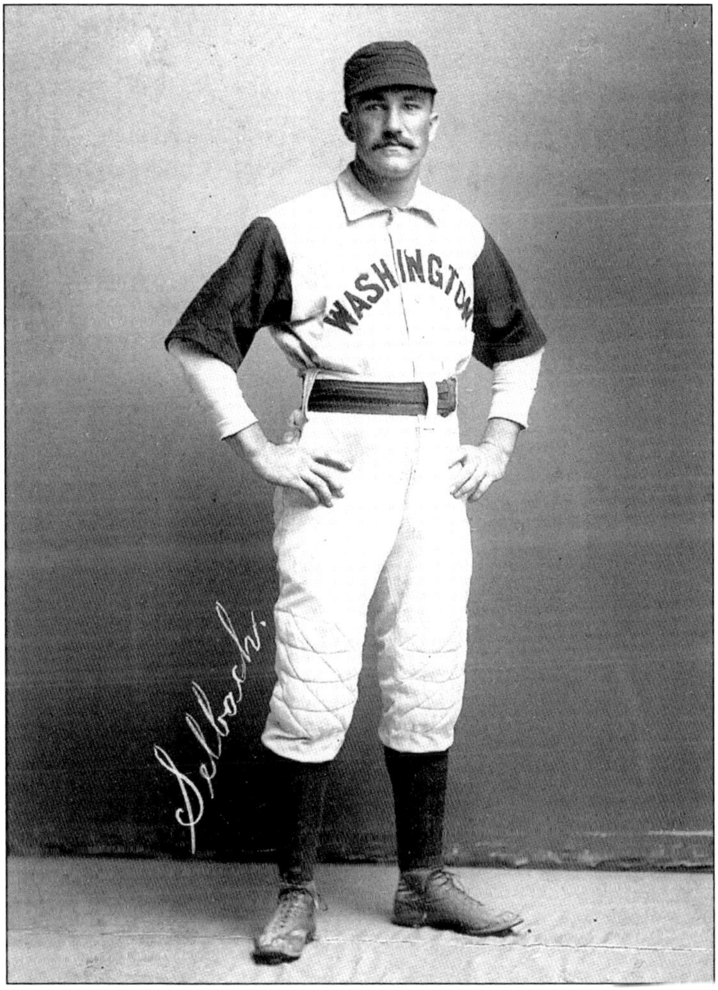

Another star with a long career was Kip Selbach, posing above in his 1893 Washington uniform. He played for only two seasons in New York, in 1900 and 1901. Selbach was a speedster, stealing more than 30 bases five times and collecting a total 334 steals before his career was done. In 1895 he led the National League in triples with 22 for Washington. Selbach's career with the Giants started out well in 1900; he hit .337, with 29 doubles and 68 RBIs. But he was injured in 1891, and with all his numbers down, he left New York for Baltimore.

Mike Donlin

Career 1899–1914 New York 1904–1911, 1914

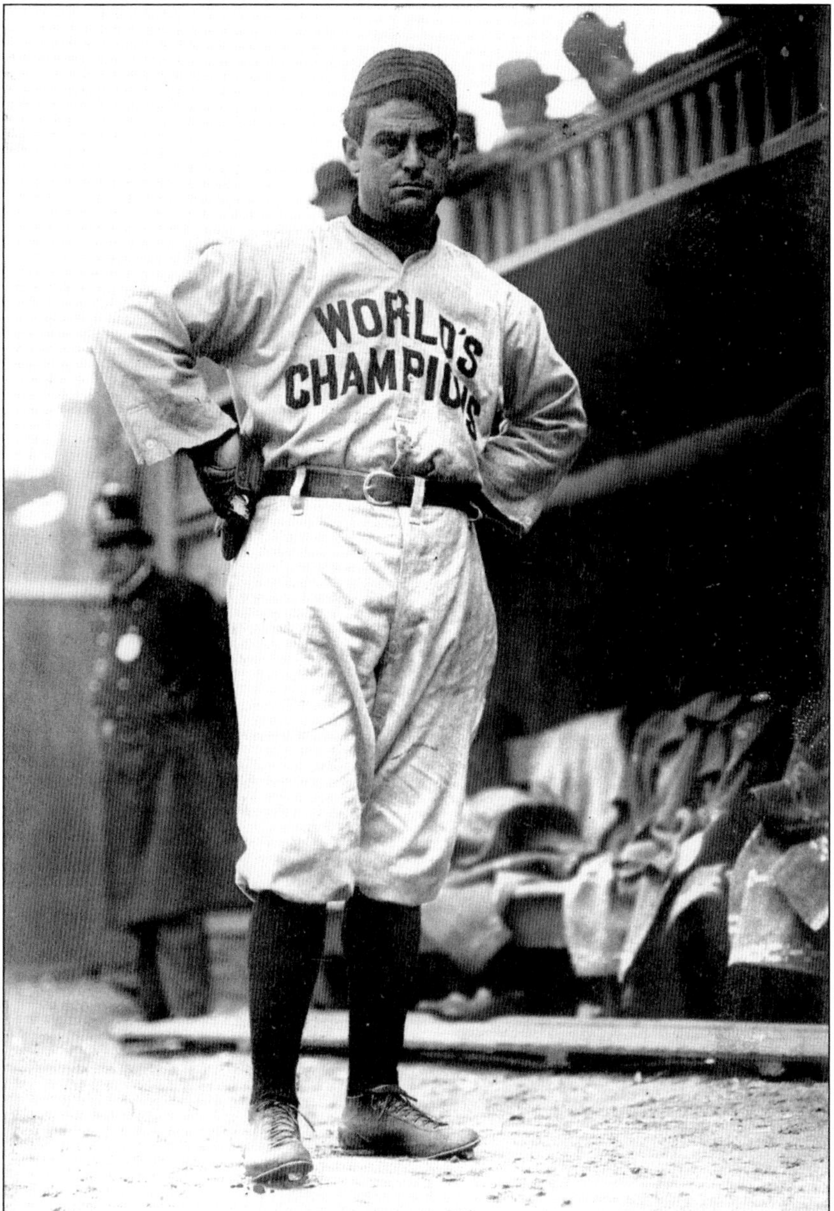

"Turkey" Mike Donlin averaged one hit for every three at-bats over his 12-year career. He had some great seasons with the Giants. He batted at least .315 for five straight years in the Polo Grounds, and led the team and the league in runs scored with 124 in 1905. Donlin was speedy in the outfield and on the base paths, stealing more than 20 bases seven times. He lost a considerable number of at-bats due to injury and contract disputes, but he had more interests than baseball to attract him. After the 1909 season, Donlin temporarily retired to headline on Broadway and in movies.

BILL DAHLEN

CAREER 1891–1911 NEW YORK 1904–1907

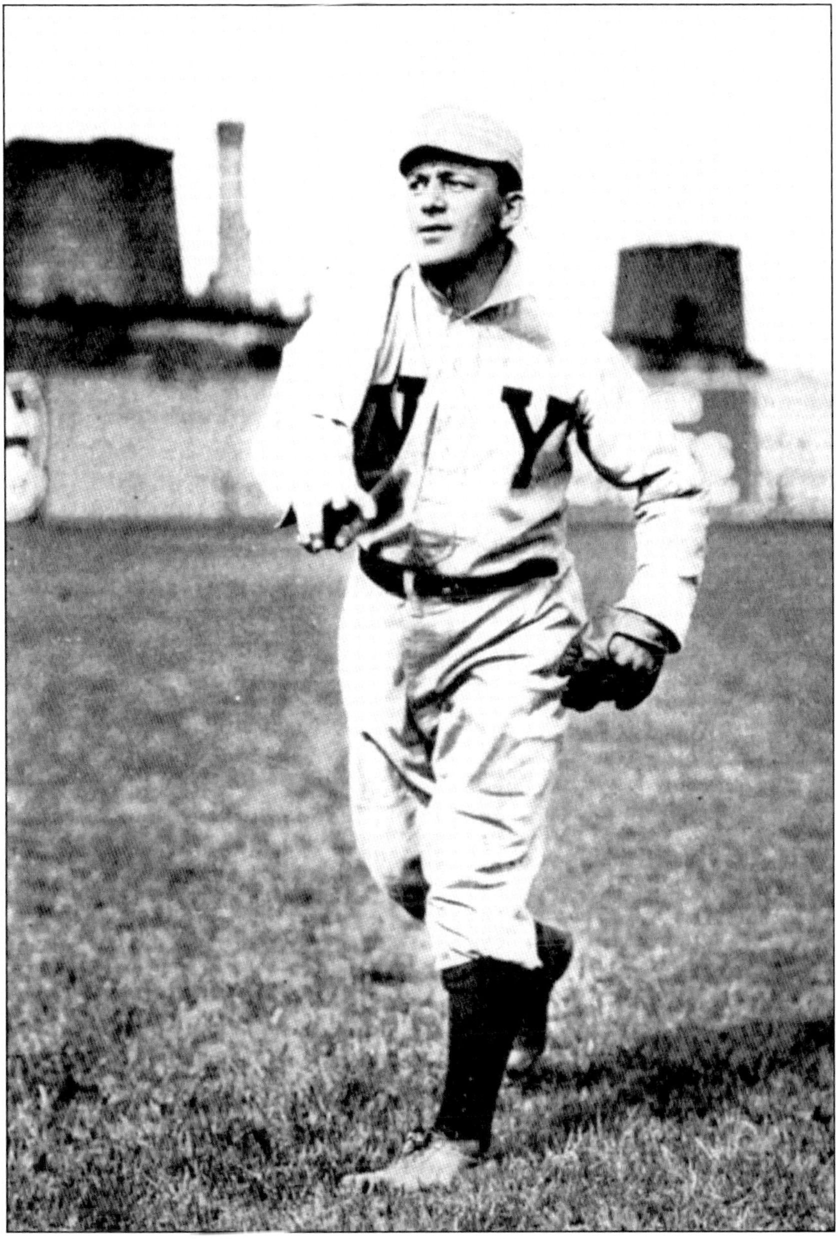

Slick-fielding Bill Dahlen also knew how to handle a bat. In 1894, he set the National League record for hits in consecutive games; and after one off day, he proceeded to hit in another 28 straight games, bringing his hitting record to 70 of 71 games. That year was Dahlen's best overall: he hit 15 homers, knocked in 107, batted .357, scored 149 runs, and had a slugging percentage of .566. While in New York, he led the National League in RBIs with 80 in 1904. The Giants won the pennant that year, but there was no World Series due to front-office politics. Dahlen closed out his playing days with a total of 2,457 hits over 21 seasons.

Deacon McGuire

Career 1884–1912 New York 1904–1912

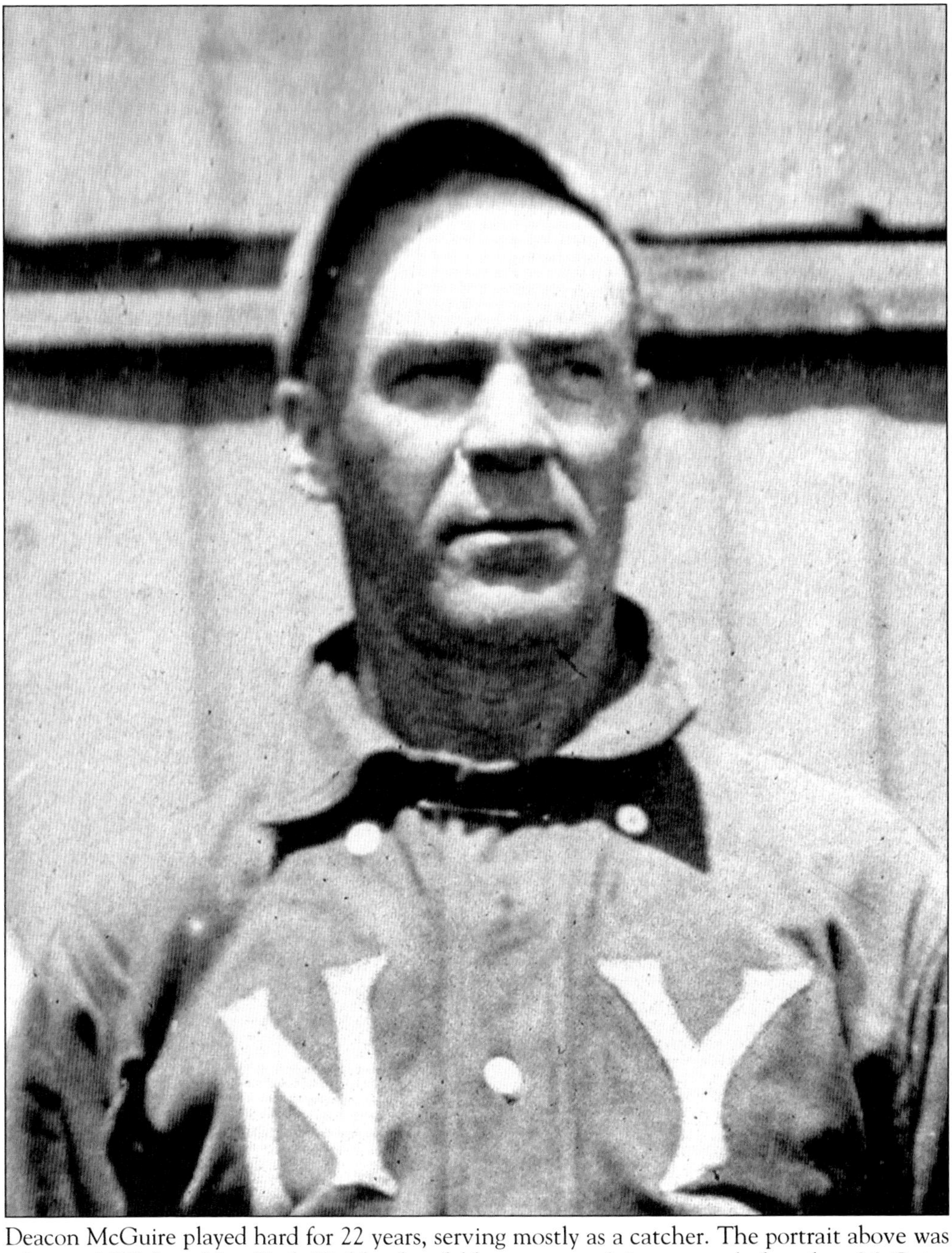

Deacon McGuire played hard for 22 years, serving mostly as a catcher. The portrait above was taken in 1907 for a New York Highlanders fold-out postcard. In seasons before that, McGuire had been the No. 1 catcher in Hilltop Park following a career solely in the National League. His best years were during baseball's dark ages, in the mid-1890s, when he covered home plate for Washington.

George Stacey Davis

Career 1890–1909 New York 1893–1901

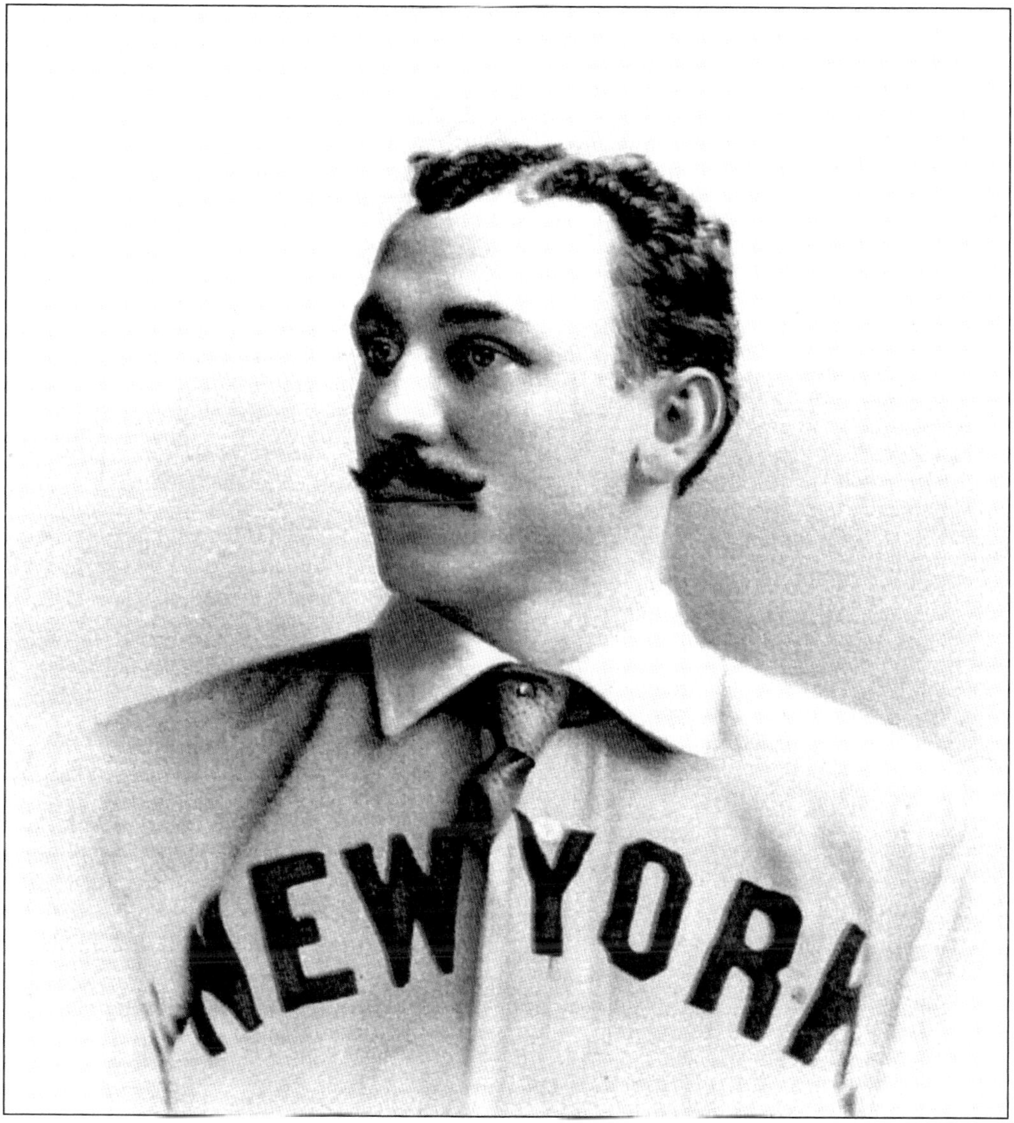

The most productive years in George Davis's career were spent in New York. He came to the Giants in 1893 in a trade with Cleveland for catcher Buck Ewing, and immediately secured the job at third base, before moving to shortstop four years later. Davis knocked in more than 100 runs three times for the Giants, and he led the league in 1897 with 136 RBIs. He stole 616 bases over his career, and set his personal record of 65 steals during the 1897 season. In 1893, his first year in the Polo Grounds, Davis whacked 27 triples, but he did not lead the league. His season averages of .355 in 1893, .352 in 1894, and .353 in 1897 were the most consistently high of any of his fellow Giants. Davis was the centerpiece of a tug-of-war between labor and management when he elected to move his contract from New York to Chicago. He was enjoined from doing so, which set off court battles involving John "Monte" Ward. By August of 1903 all was settled, and Davis played out the rest of his career in Chicago unindicted.

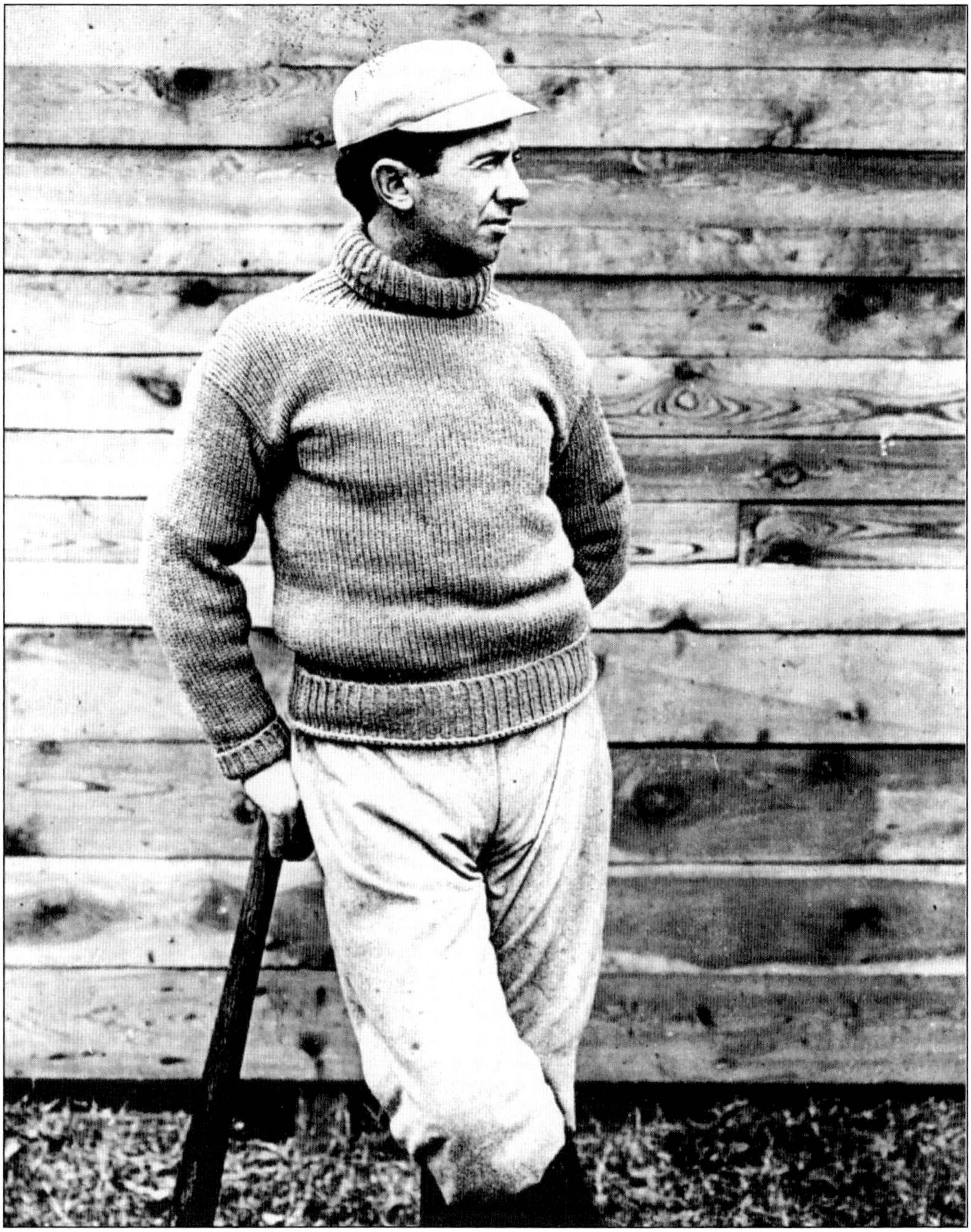

The diminutive William Keeler manned the outfield for five teams along the East Coast. The author of the old baseball saw, "Hit 'em where they ain't," Keeler was able to put the ball out of fielders' reach 239 times in 1897, 216 times in 1898, and 204 times in 1900, all numbers that led the league. "Wee Willie" played on five championship teams with Baltimore, where he helped develop the famed Baltimore chop, a maneuver that involves hitting a pitch straight down off hard-packed earth and then running like wildfire. This mighty mite hit .424 in 1897 and completed his career in 1910 with an amazing .341 lifetime average. Keeler and John McGraw provided the one-two punch for the Orioles, but Keeler never played for McGraw after he became a manager in New York.

WEE WILLIE KEELER

CAREER 1892–1910 NEW YORK 1903–1910

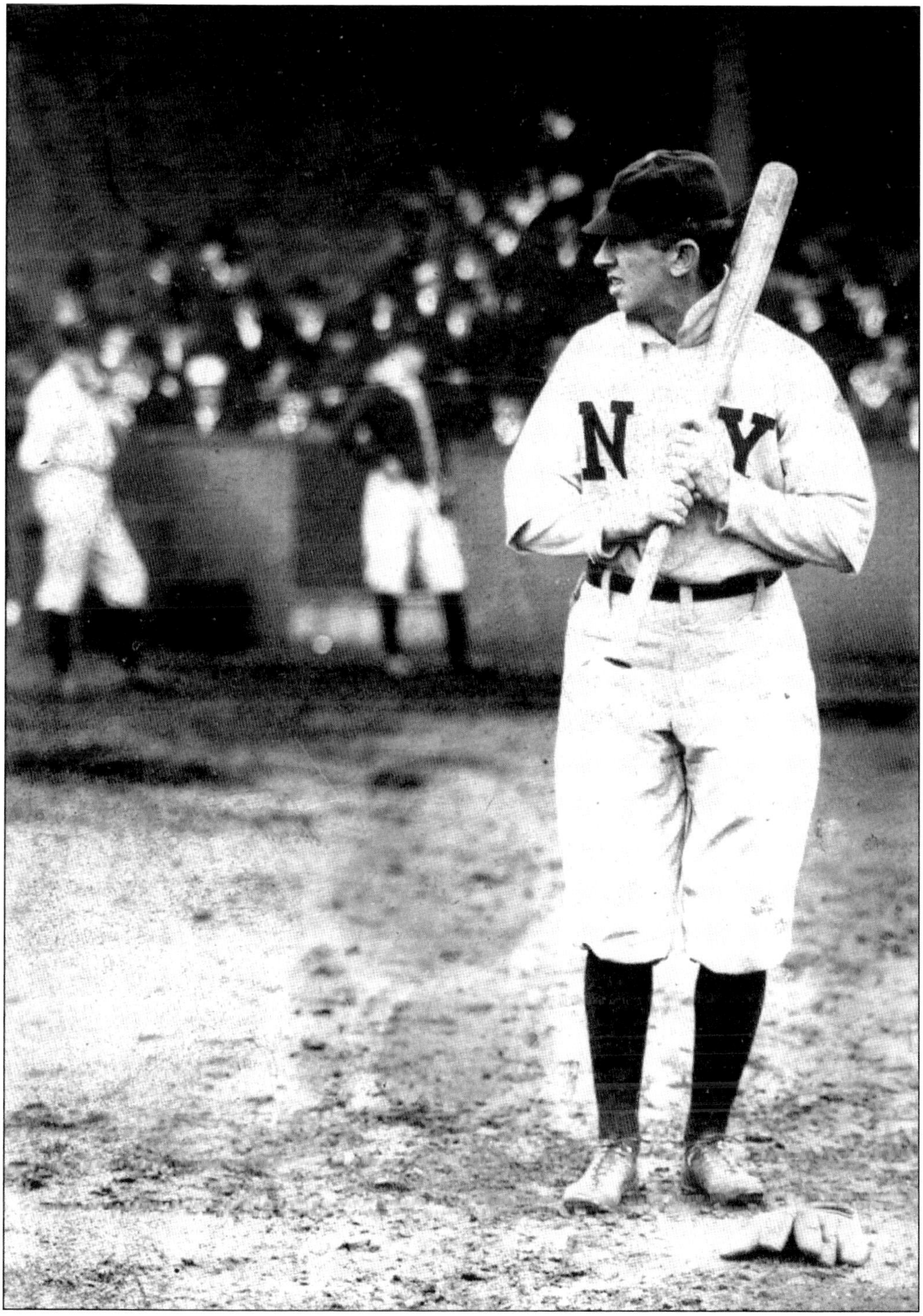

Sammy Strang

Career 1896–1908 New York 1901, 1905–1908

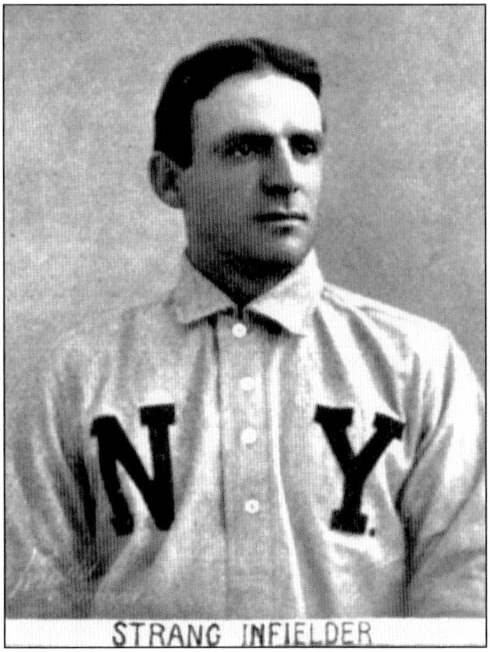

Cy Seymour

Career 1896–1913 New York 1896–1900, 1906–1910

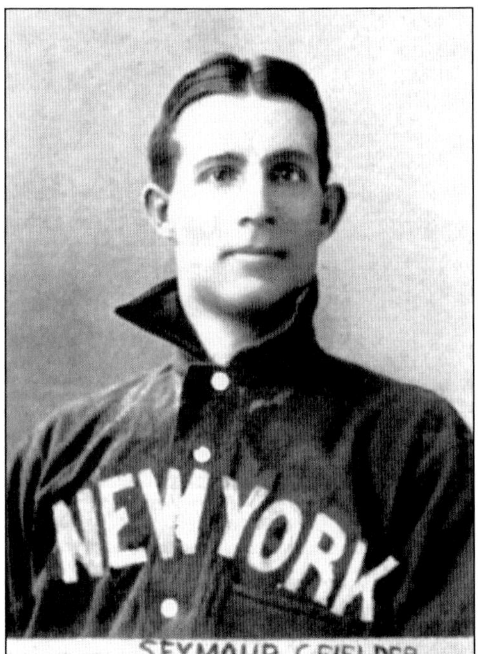

Dan McGann

Career 1896–1908 New York 1902–1907

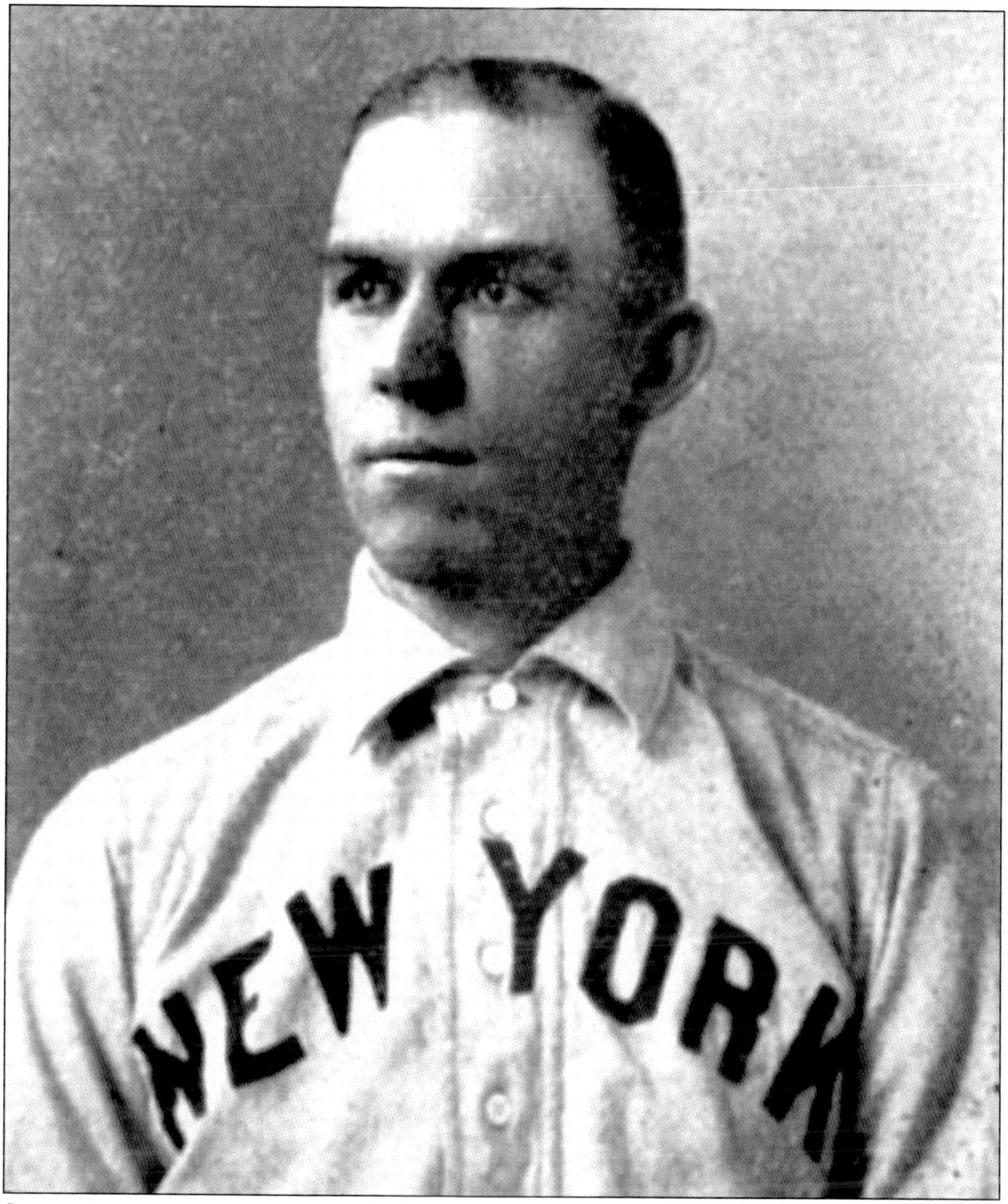

Sammy Strang (opposite page, top) played in 137 games in his first full season with New York in 1901. But it was after his return to the Giants four years later that he had his greatest impact, leading the league in pinch hits with eight. Cy Seymour (opposite page, bottom) started out with the Giants as a pitcher, but by 1901 he was moved to the outfield. After a five-and-a-half-year tour of other cities, Seymour returned to the Giants to drive in runs for John McGraw. Dan McGann (above) was one of McGraw's favorites. He moved with McGraw from Baltimore to New York, where he played first base from 1902 to 1907. In 1904, he stole five bases in one game, the first player to do so in the 20th century.

George Browne

Career 1901–1912 New York 1902–1907

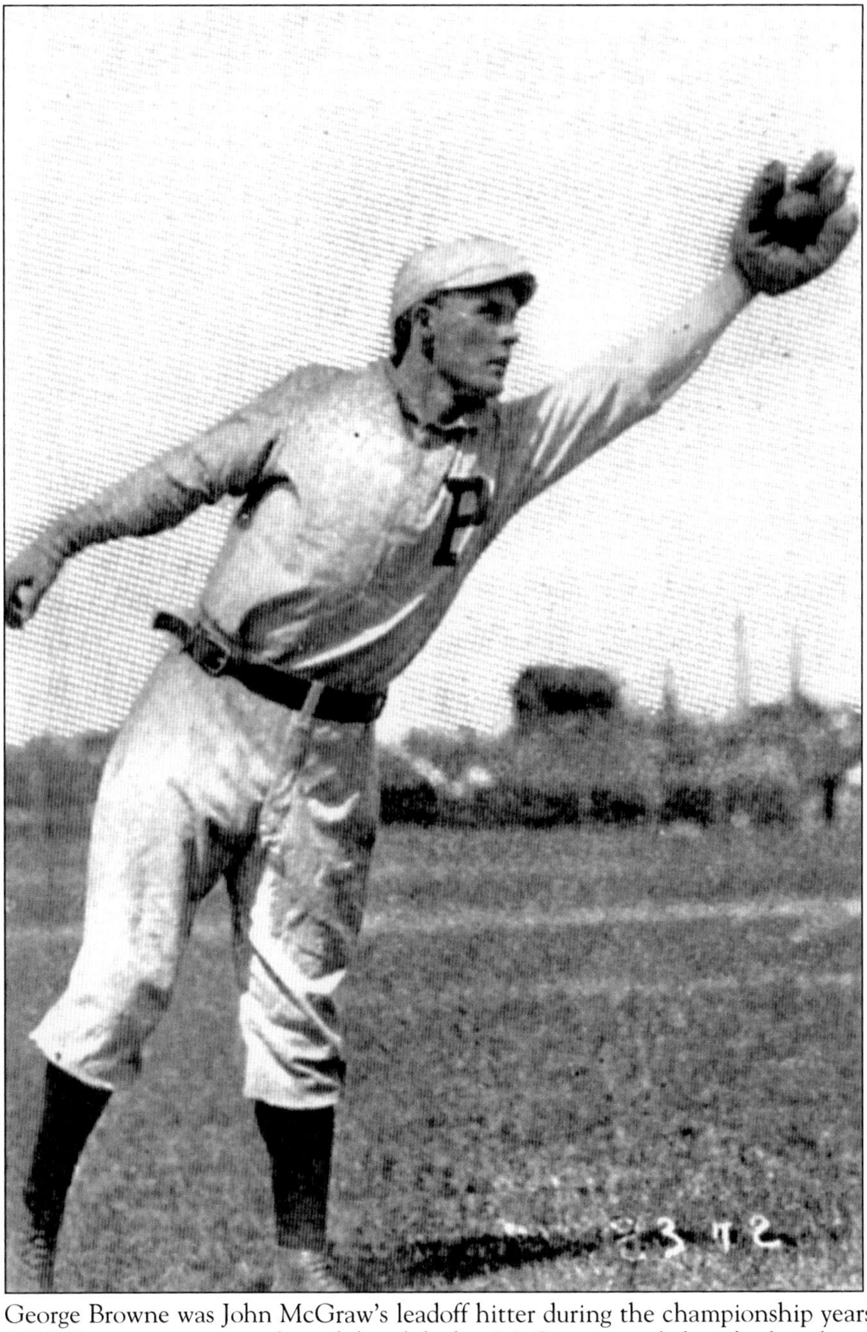

George Browne was John McGraw's leadoff hitter during the championship years of 1904 and 1905. Browne was a member of the club that McGraw regarded as the best he ever managed. Browne's 99 runs in 1904 helped his team win the flag, and he played in five games in the 1905 World Series. He played full seasons for New York from 1903 to 1907, and hit .300 twice for the Giants. Browne died at the young age of 44, eight years after he retired from baseball.

Sam Mertes

Career 1896–1906 New York 1903–1906

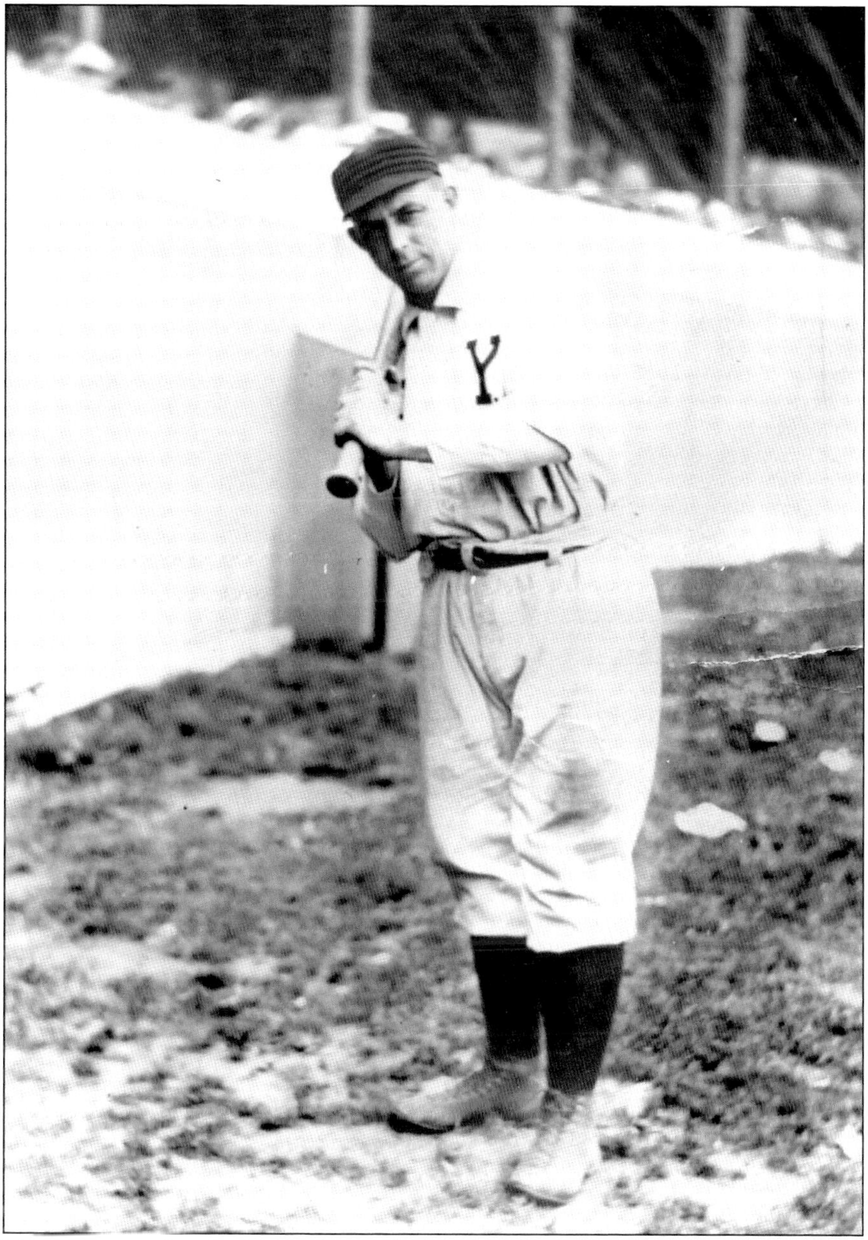

Stocky Sam Mertes was nicknamed "Sandow" after the famous Prussian bodybuilder of the Victorian era. After six seasons with Philadelphia and Chicago, Mertes lit up his first year in New York with league-leading numbers of 32 doubles and 104 runs batted in. Two years later he was just as good, piling up 27 doubles, 17 triples, and 108 RBIs. His stolen-base numbers were impressive every year; his best mark was 52 steals in 1905. Mertes's speed also helped him score 81 runs in 1905 and helped the Giants earn the National League flag. His last four productive years were with New York. Mertes closed out his career by playing half a season in St. Louis.

Wid Conroy

Career 1901–1911 New York 1903–1908

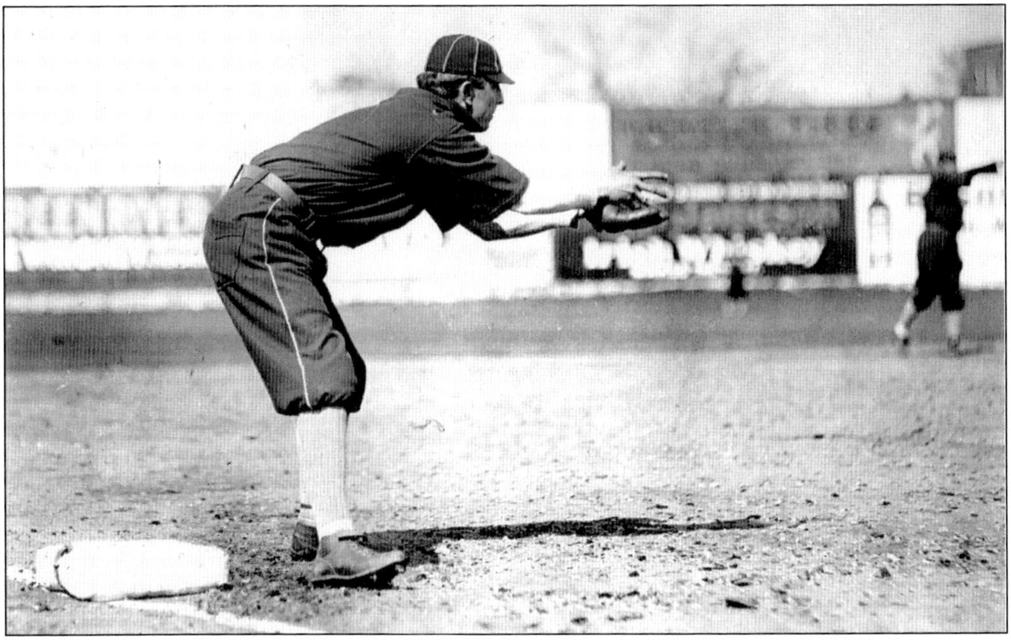

Dave Fultz

Career 1898–1905 New York 1903–1905

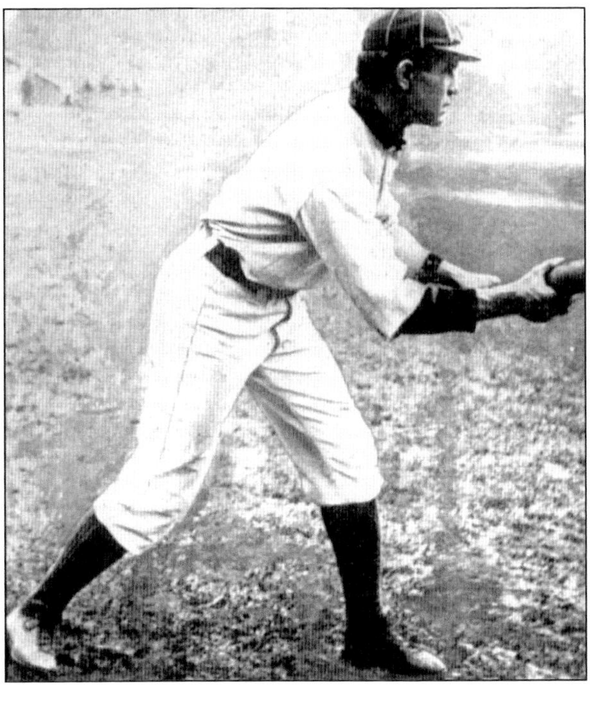

Wid Conroy (above) was a third baseman who put together a fine career in New York. From 1903 to 1908, Conroy was a regular in the Highlanders lineup. He stole between 20 and 40 bases for seven years in the major leagues, and he legged out 10 or more triples in five seasons. Dave Fultz (left) was a well-educated ballplayer who must have had a pure love for the game, because he certainly could have made more money in another line of work. During his stay with the Highlanders, Fultz recorded the franchise's first-ever extra-base hit. Perhaps underutilized in Clark Griffith's scheme, Fultz never regained his form after the 1902 season, when he scored 109 runs for the Philadelphia Athletics, tops in the American League.

ROGER BRESNAHAN

CAREER 1897–1915 NEW YORK 1902–1908

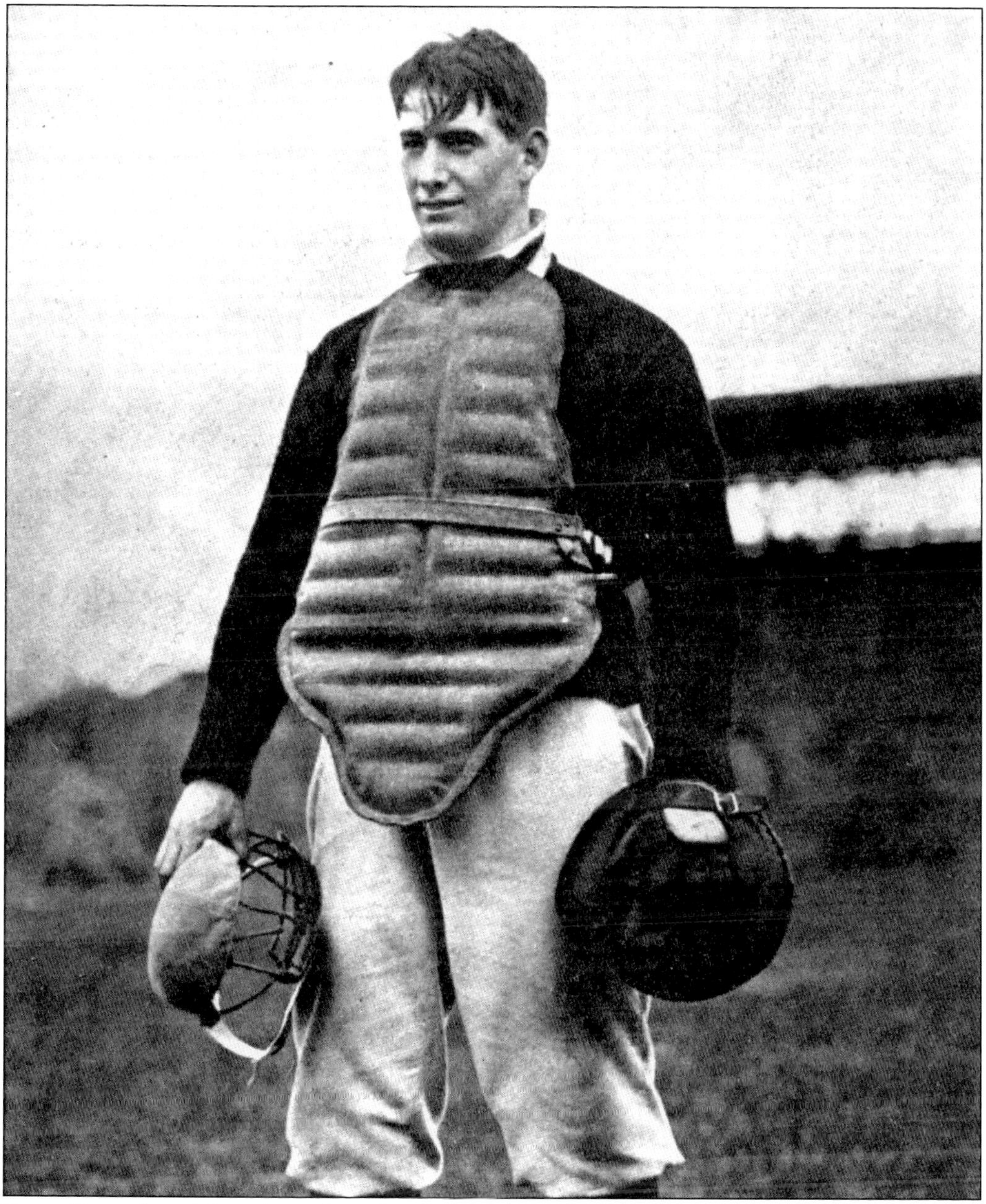

Roger Bresnahan (above) was fiercely competitive with teammates and officials while playing behind the plate. Managers loved him and umpires hated him. He always demanded the best from himself and those around him, a trait that would later make him an effective manager. Bresnahan arrived in New York halfway through the 1904 season, his fourth year in the bigs. By 1905, he was installed as full-time catcher for the Giants. He hit for a respectable average every year and was always among the statistical leaders for catchers both offensively and defensively. This photograph was taken shortly after Bresnahan became a Giant.

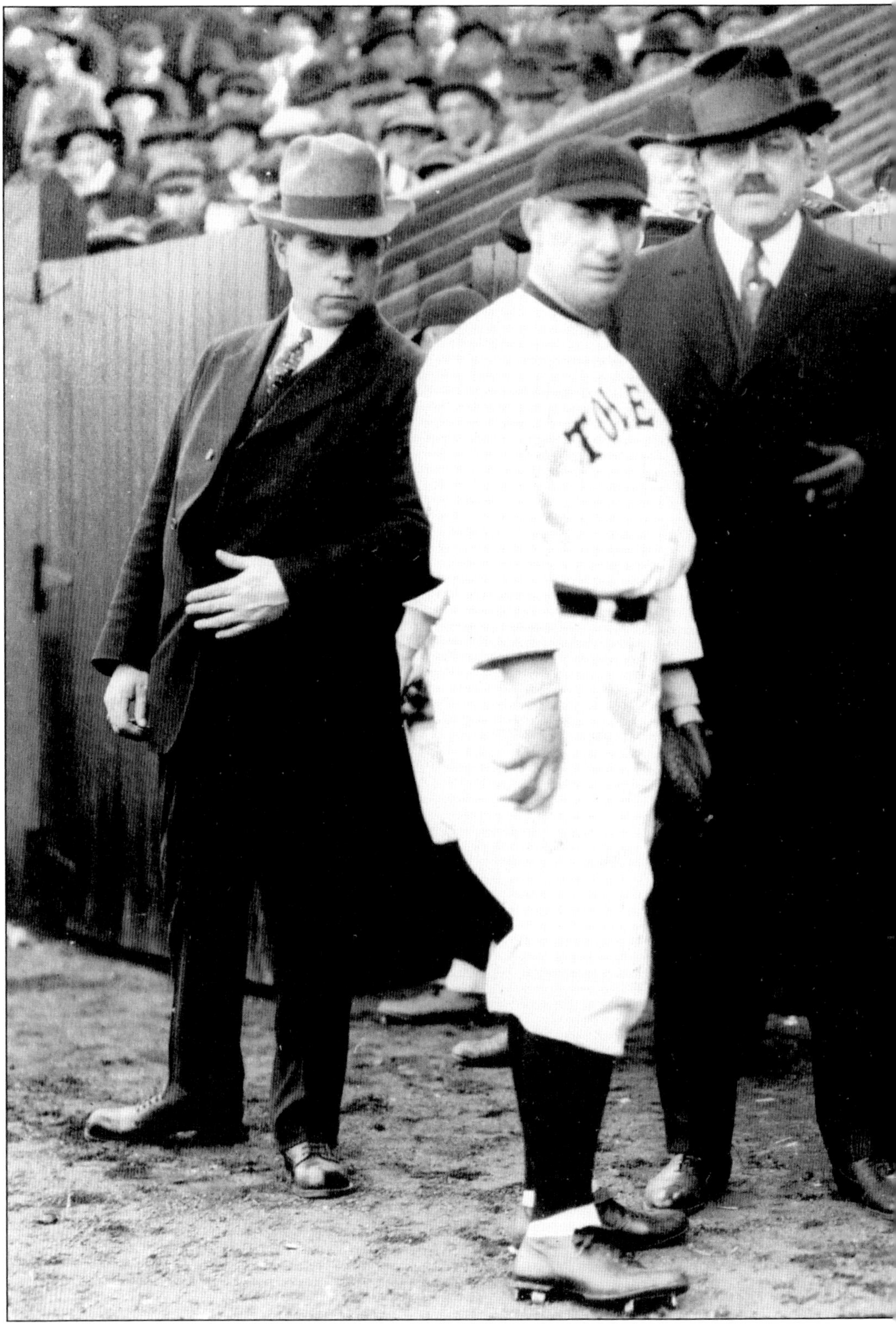

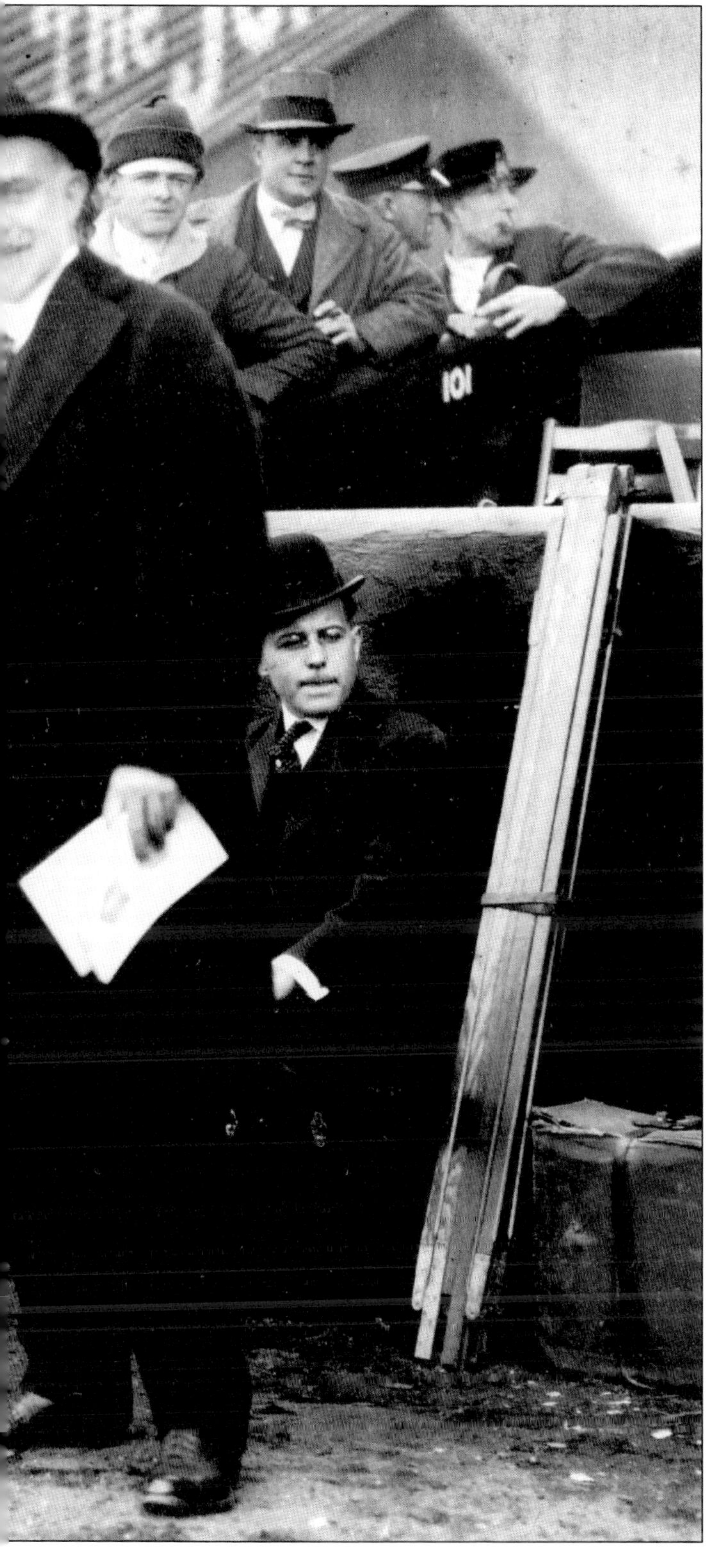

This *c.* 1920 photograph of Roger Bresnahan as manager of Toledo is too good to go unpublished. It is unclear what kind of conversation uniformed manager Bresnahan is conducting, but it appears conspiratorial.

BUCK HERZOG

CAREER 1908–1920 NEW YORK 1908–1909, 1911–1913, 1916–1917

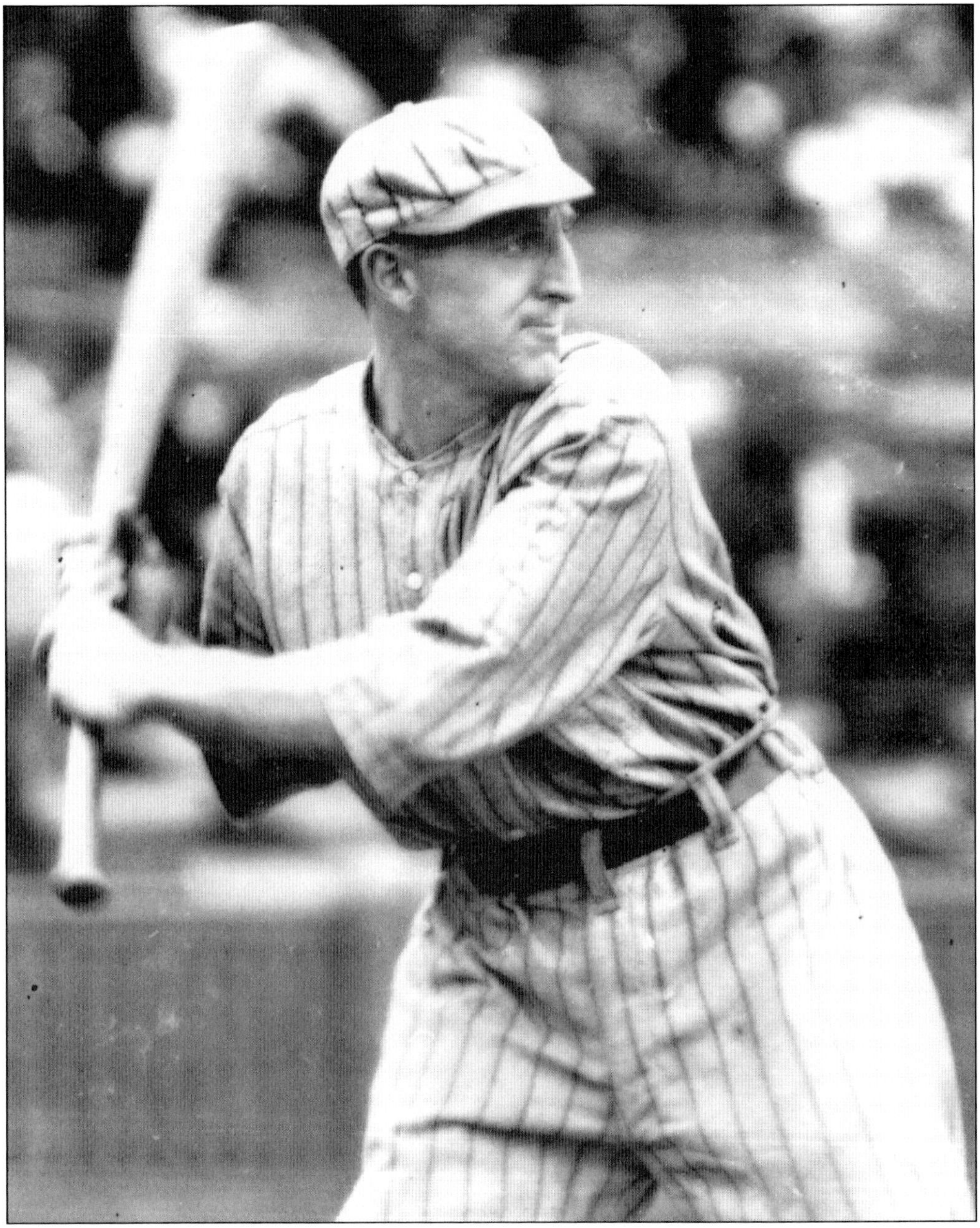

Buck Herzog came and went from the New York Giants three different times. John McGraw always wanted him back, and the manager was rewarded with fantastic World Series play by Herzog in 1912, when he went 12 for 30 and led the team in batting. In the next World Series Herzog did not do so well, so he was shipped out again . . . only to return in the middle of 1916. Herzog started at shortstop or second base and produced about 100 runs a year (a combined total of runs batted in and runs scored).

Fred Snodgrass

Career 1908–1916 New York 1908–1914

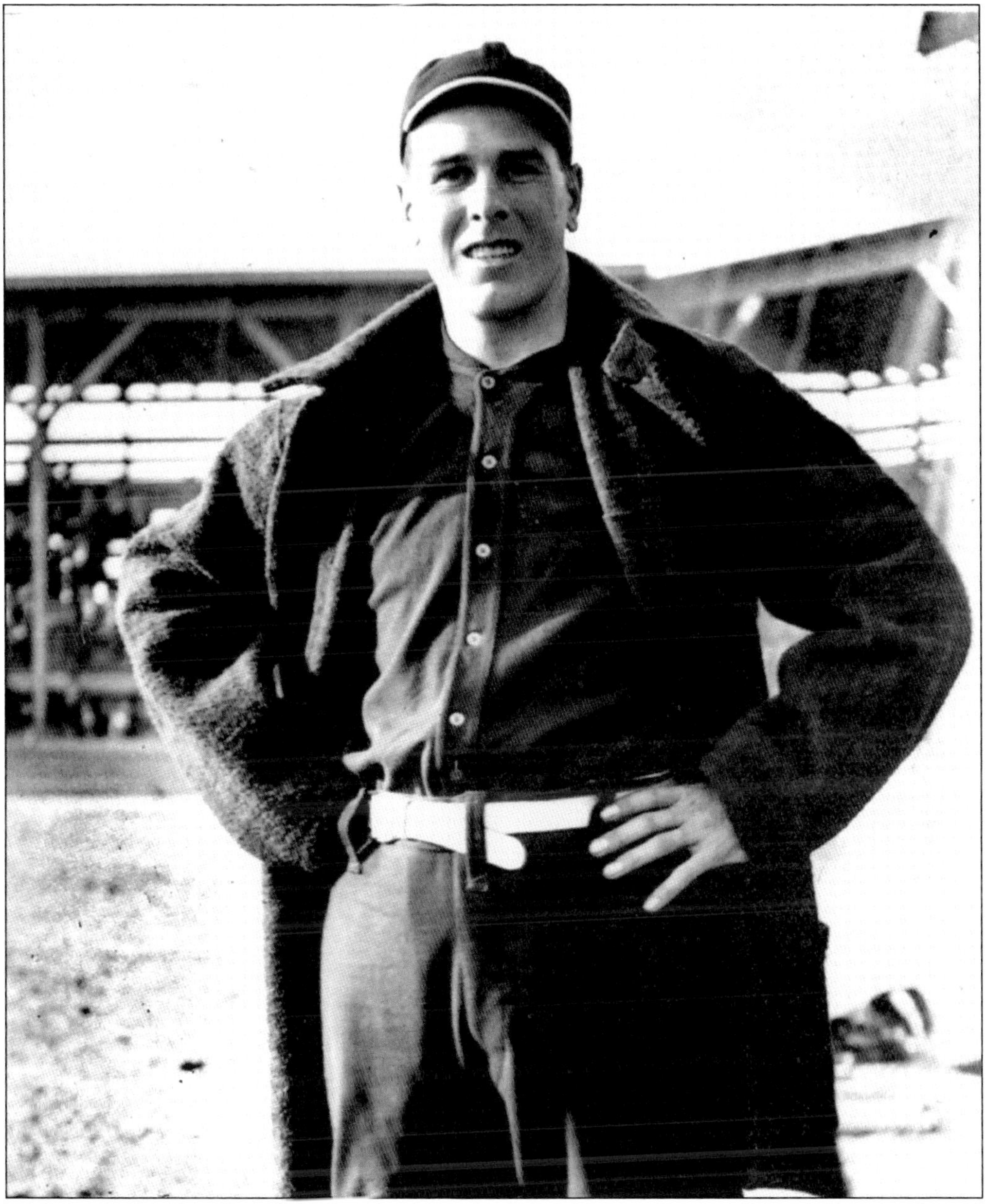

Fred Snodgrass played outfield for John McGraw's Giants, using his speed on the base paths and in the garden. Snodgrass's batting prowess allowed him to score runs at a goodly rate every year in New York. He was a member of the Giants' pennant-winning teams for three straight years, from 1911 to 1913. But it was the 1912 World Series that changed Snodgrass's life and legacy forever. In the 10th inning of Game 7 against the Red Sox, Snodgrass made one great catch and one very memorable error. The easy fly ball he dropped allowed the Sox to score the run that won the Series. Ever since, the play has been known as "Snodgrass's muff."

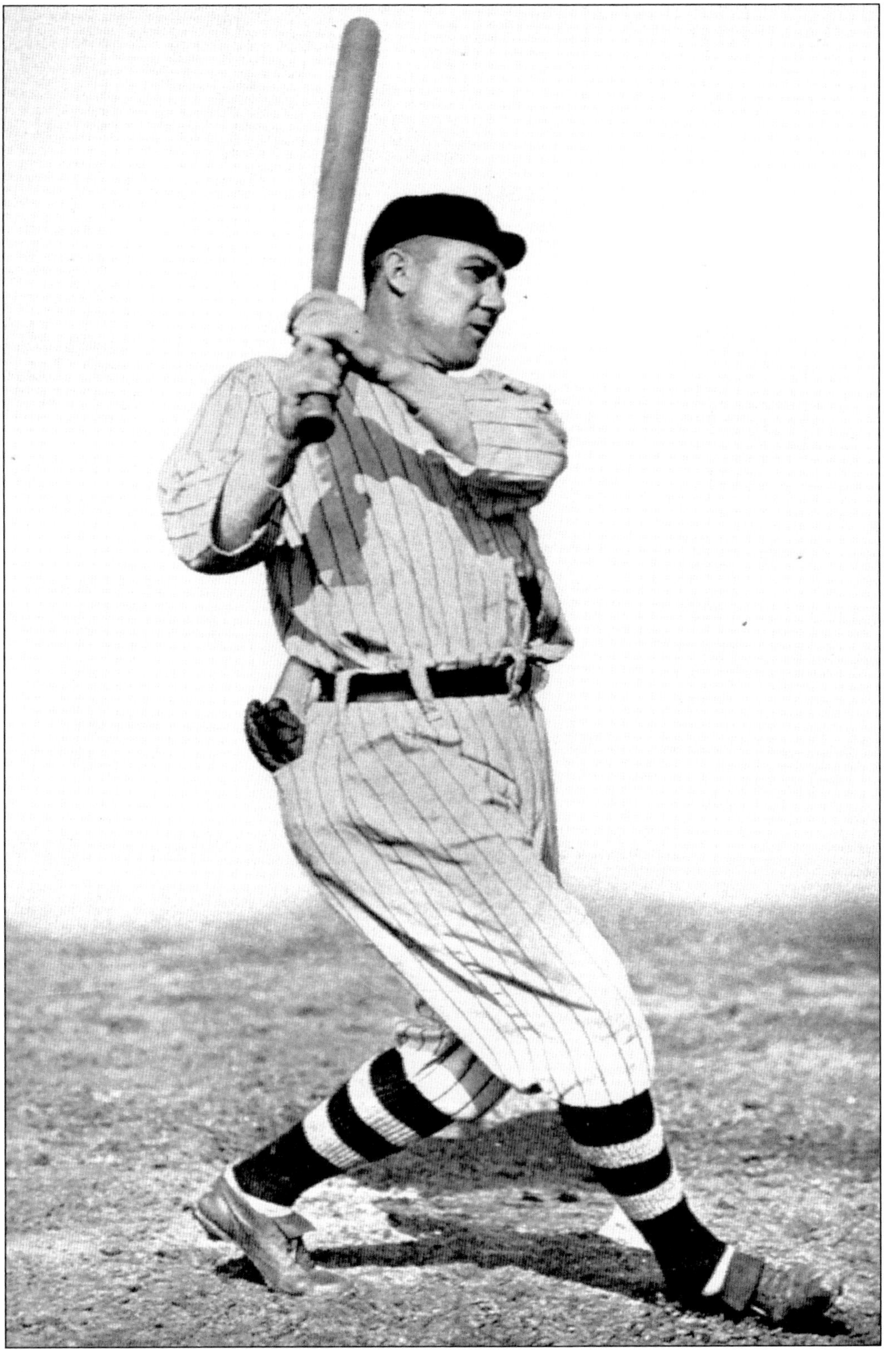

Larry Doyle

Career 1907–1920 New York 1907–1915, 1918–1920

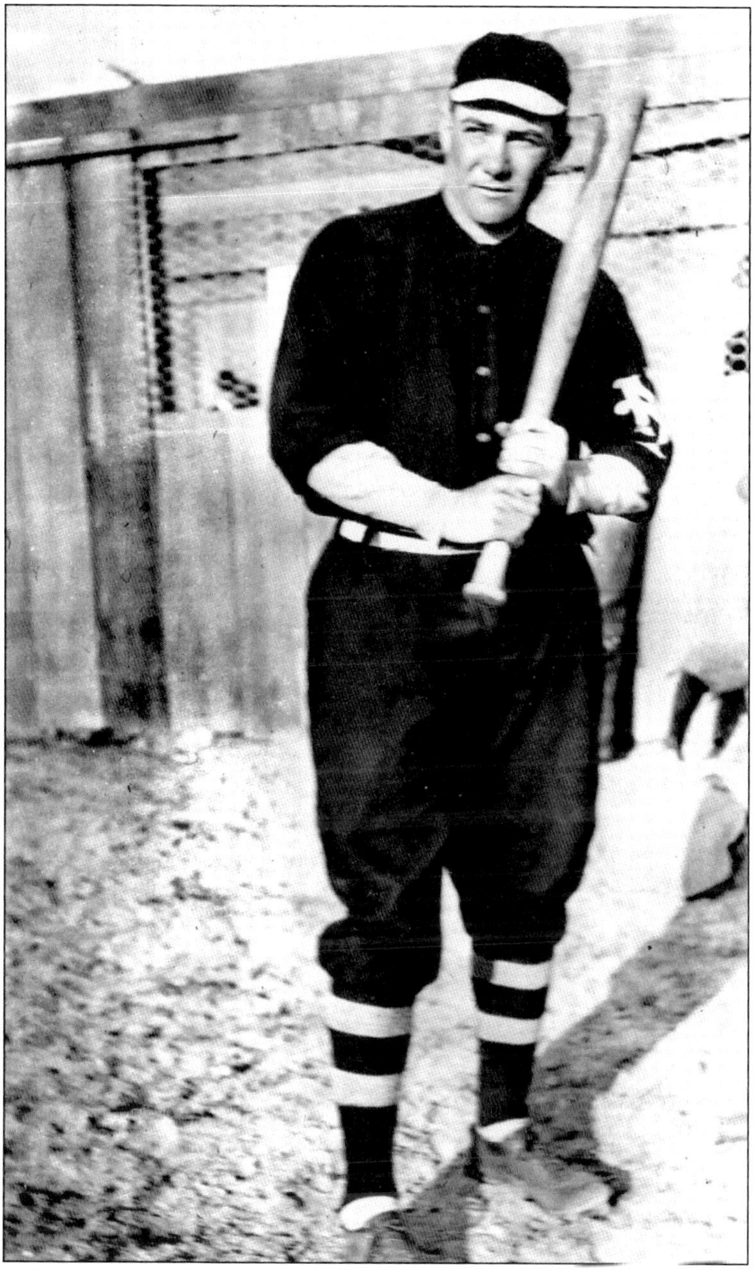

Laughing Larry Doyle was the captain and often the public face of the New York Giants during the early 20th century. If there was a promotional event of any kind in the big city, it would be Christy Mathewson and Larry Doyle who would be pictured. Doyle led the team and the league twice in hits, once in doubles, and once in triples. With his powerful performance in the 1915 season, he led the National League in hitting at .320. Doyle's all-time high was .330 in 1912. Among his 298 stolen bases were 12 steals of home.

Art Devlin

Career 1904–1913 New York 1904–1911

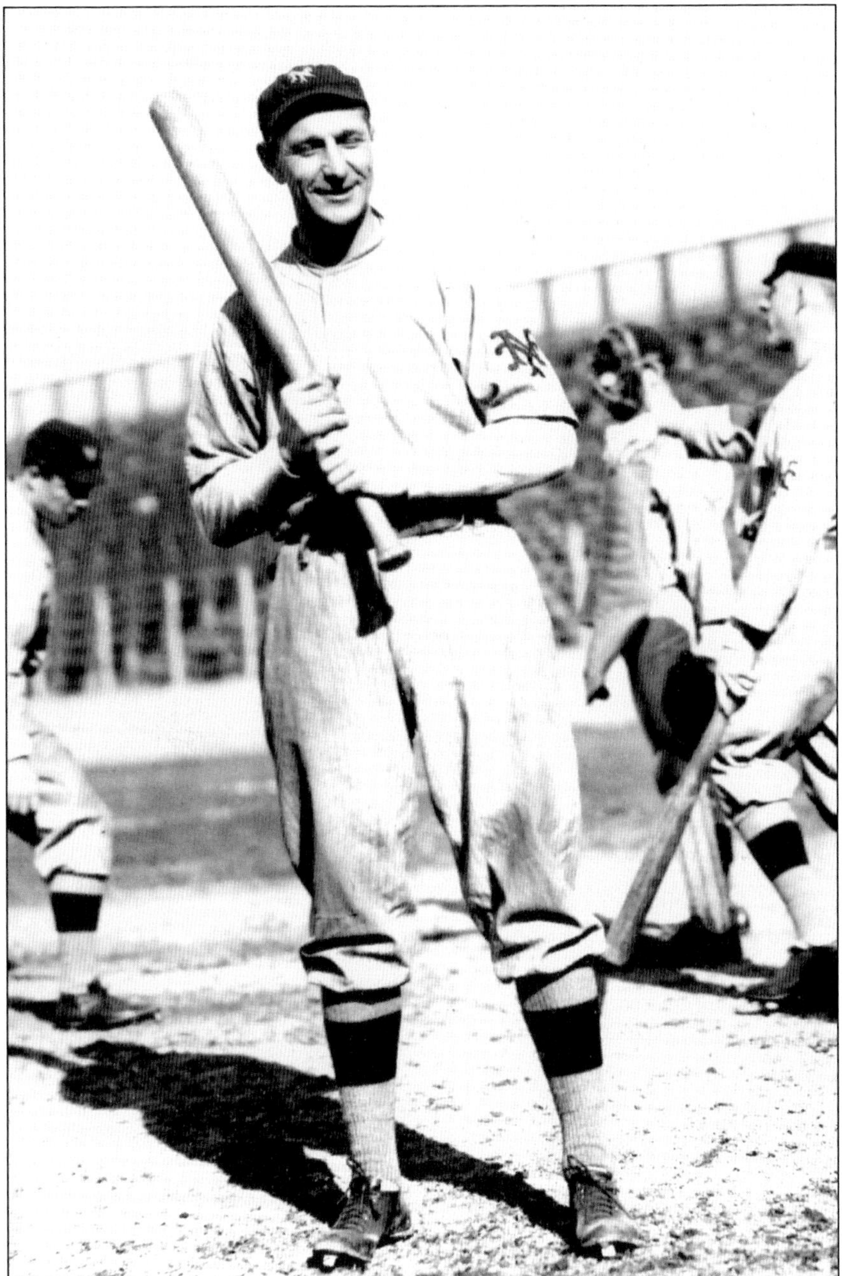

In his first major-league at-bat, Art Devlin hit a grand slam. However, it was hardly a harbinger of his batting future—Devlin would only hit one or two homers a year for the balance of his career. His best season at the plate was 1906, when he hit .299, with 23 doubles and 65 runs batted in. His only league-leading offensive statistic was a stolen-base crown in 1905. That same year Devlin saw his only World Series action as the Giants wiped out the Athletics in five games.

Heinie Zimmerman

Career 1907–1919 New York 1916–1919

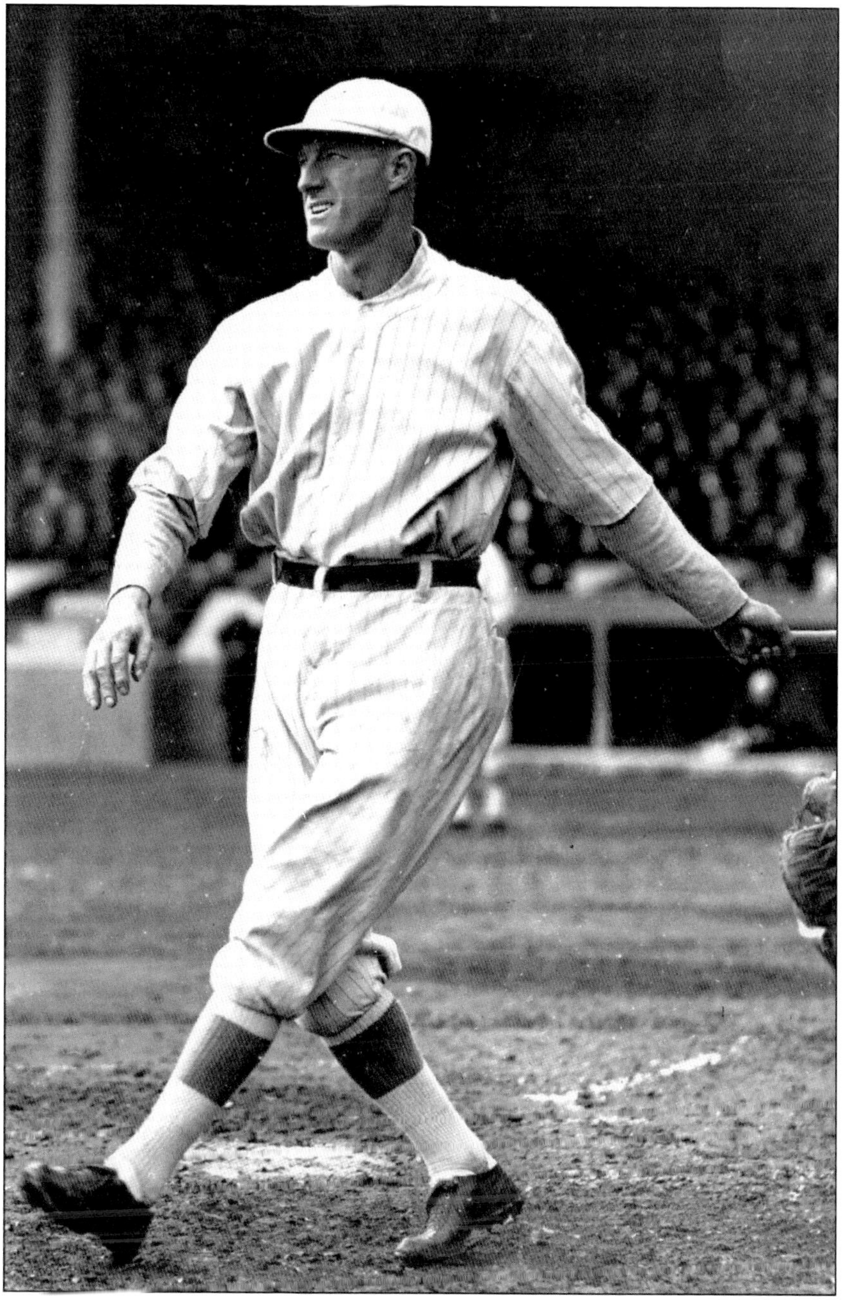

Henry "Heinie" Zimmerman played third base for the Giants after leaving the Cubs at midseason in 1916. He proceeded to lead the National League in RBIs, driving in 83 total in 1916 and 105 the following year. Zimmerman helped New York battle the White Sox in the 1917 Series, his only post-season appearance with the Giants. He wrapped up a 13-year career in the majors with a solid .295 lifetime batting average.

Hal Chase

Career 1905–1919 New York 1905–1913, 1919

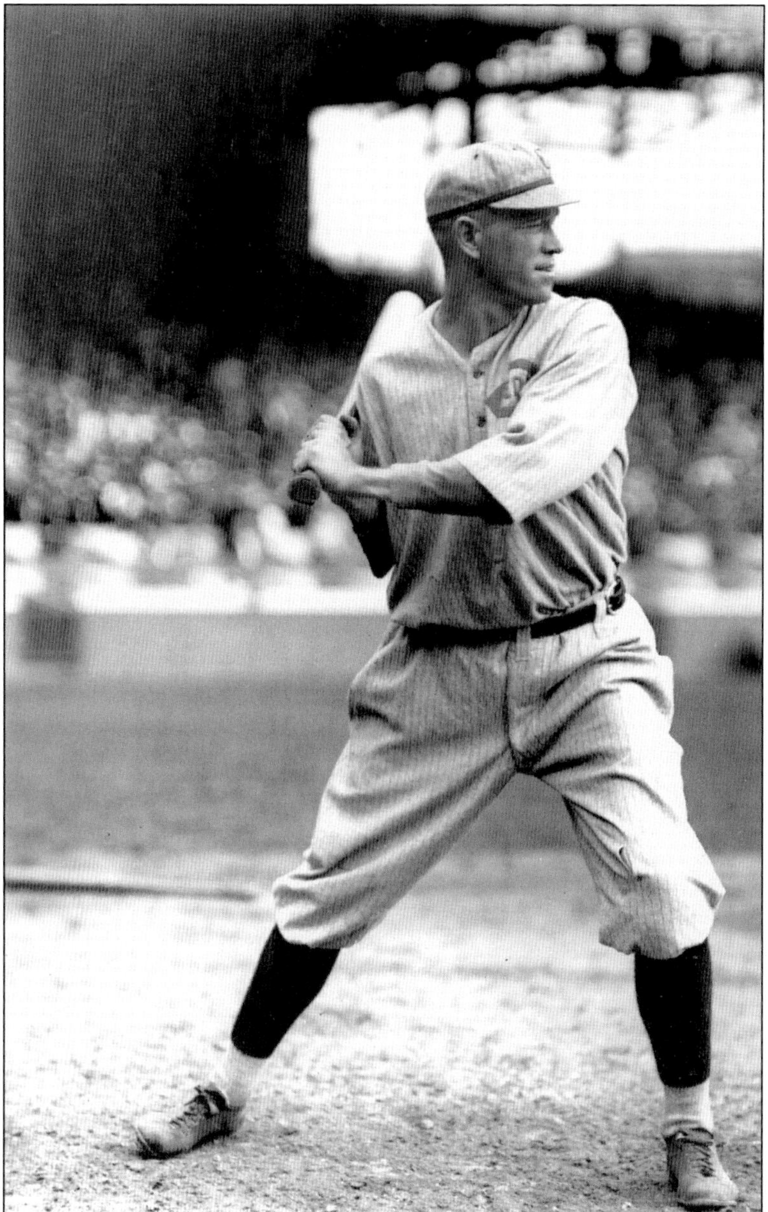

"Prince" Hal Chase was as handsome and dashing to female fans as he was graceful and skilled at first base and at bat. So good was he with a glove that Chase was almost never photographed with a bat in his hands. The shot above was taken when he played for the Reds at the end of his 15 years in the majors. Chase hit .300 twice for the Highlanders, scoring between 50 and 80 runs a season. His career was besmirched with accusations about gambling and throwing games, and Chase was eventually banned from baseball. When he managed the Yankees in 1910 and 1911, the club's record spiraled downward. Few wondered why.

JOSH DEVORE

CAREER 1908–1914 NEW YORK 1908–1913

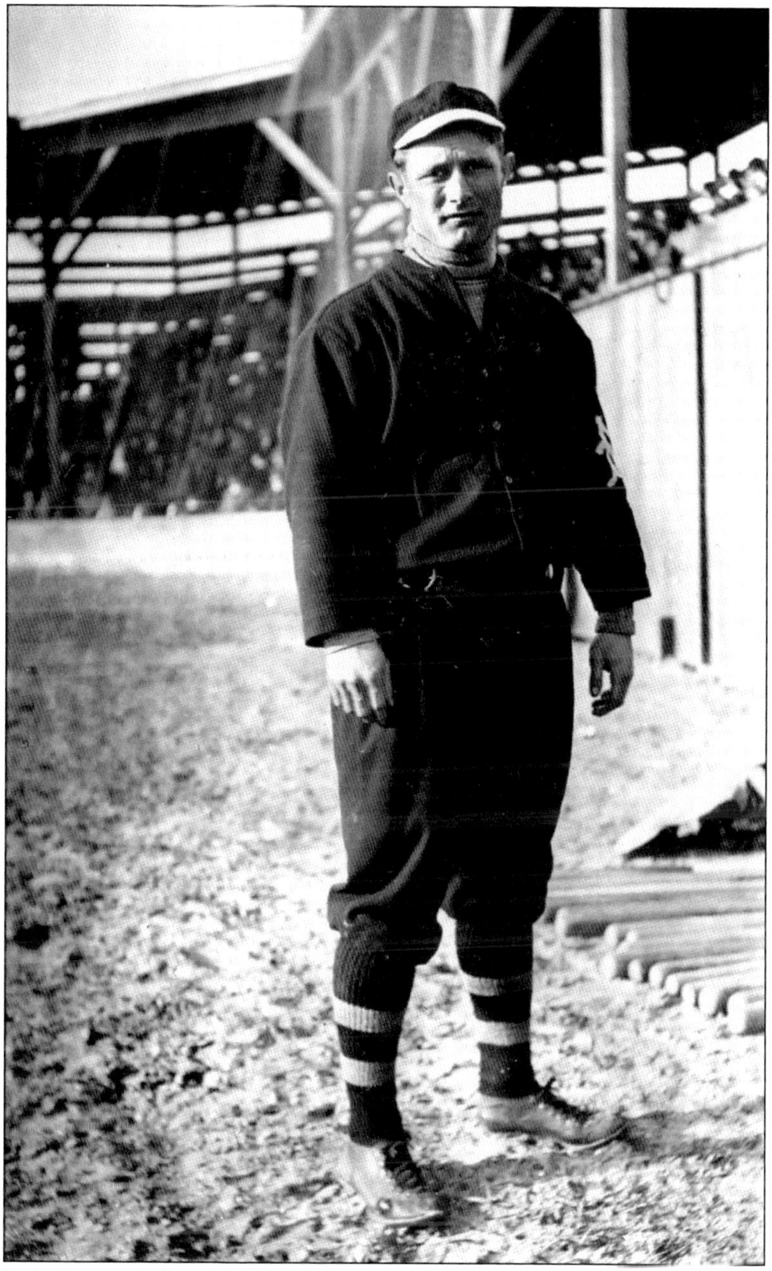

The 1908 season was Josh Devore's first in the major leagues and his first with the Giants. Though he hit only 11 home runs in his career, his speed and skill with the bat produced runs every year for New York. He scored 92 runs in 1910, and the next season scored 96 runs while stealing 61 bases. In the 1912 World Series, Devore made a game-saving catch near the outfield wall, preserving a 2-1 win over the Red Sox. He played in one more World Series in 1914 with the Braves, after leaving the Giants in 1913.

Fred Merkle

Career 1907–1926 New York 1907–1916, 1925–1926

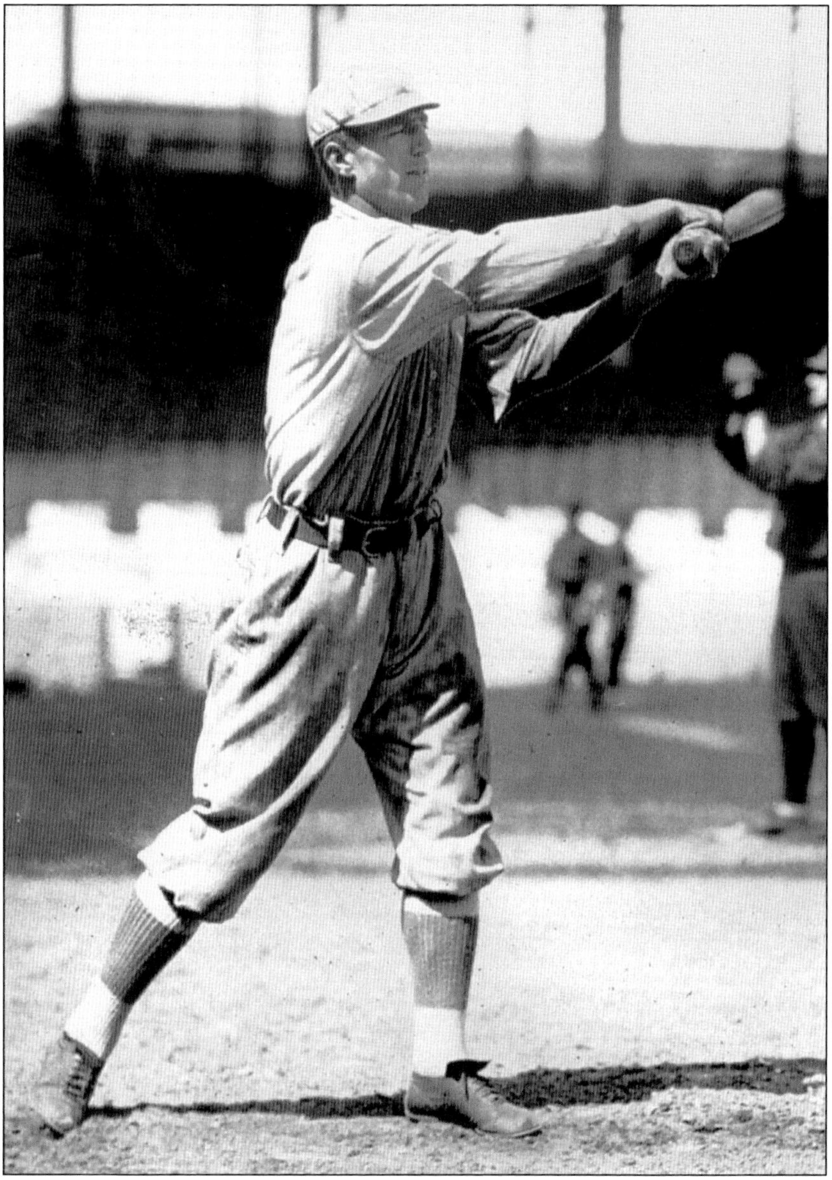

Poor Fred Merkle. Everyone has forgotten his more than 1,500 major-league hits, his 290 lifetime doubles, his 272 stolen bases, and his 733 runs batted in. But no one has forgotten his base-running mistake at the end of the Giants' playoff game against the Cubs on September 23, 1908. After a single had driven home the Giants' winning run, Merkle, who had been on first base, did not move to second and touch the base, but instead returned to the dugout. A clever Johnny Evers, the Cubs second baseman, fought the crowd that had taken over the field, found the ball, dragged an umpire with him to second base, and touched the bag to record the third out. The game thus ended with a tie, and a rematch was scheduled. The Giants lost that game, and Merkle's reputation was never the same.

Chief Myers

Career 1909–1917 New York 1909–1915

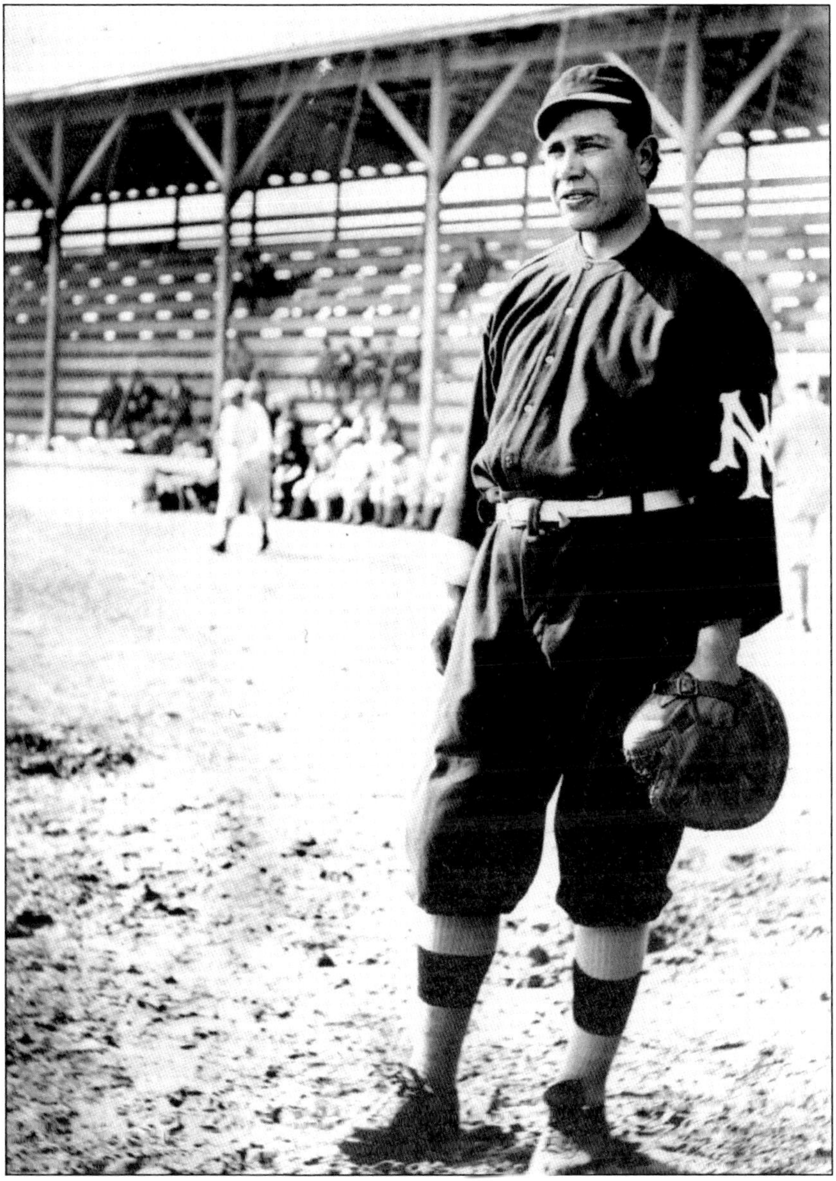

After John McGraw found young catcher John Meyers, a member of the Cahuilla tribe, Roger Bresnahan became dispensable. Meyers was given the nickname "Chief," but the Dartmouth-educated Native American found the appellation abhorrent. His seven full seasons in the majors were all played in New York; in three of those years he batted over .300. His highest average was .358 in 1912; it was the second-highest average in the National League that year. The Giants' World Series years from 1911 to 1913 were strong ones for Meyers. In the 1911 Series he hit .300, and in the 1912 Series he batted .357 and caught in every game. Playing in so many games eventually wore down his body. After retirement, Meyers worked with the Native American population for the U.S. Department of the Interior.

Birdie Cree

Career 1908–1915 all in New York

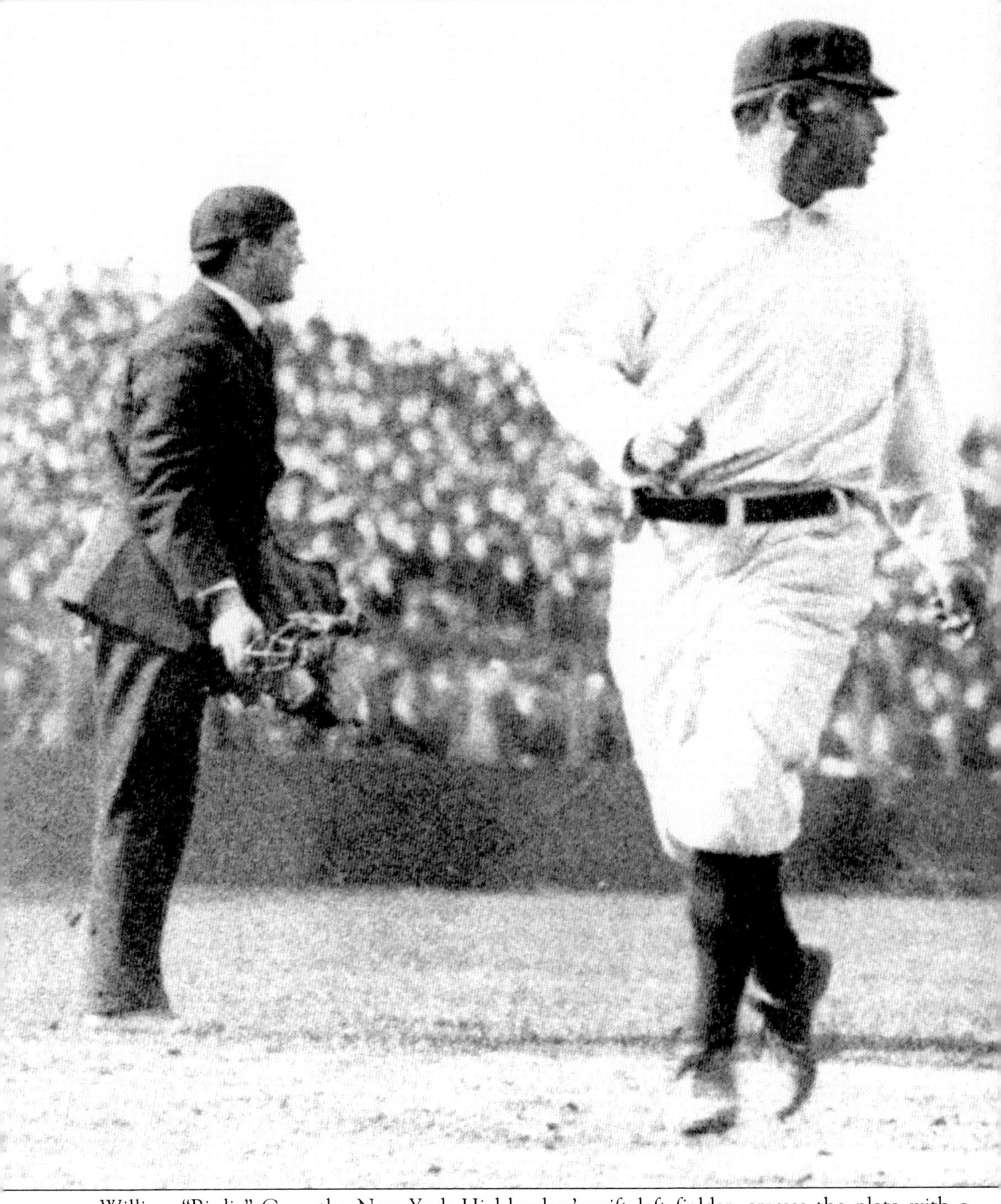

William "Birdie" Cree, the New York Highlanders' swift left fielder, crosses the plate with a teammate hot on his heels. He played almost four complete seasons with the American-Leaguers.

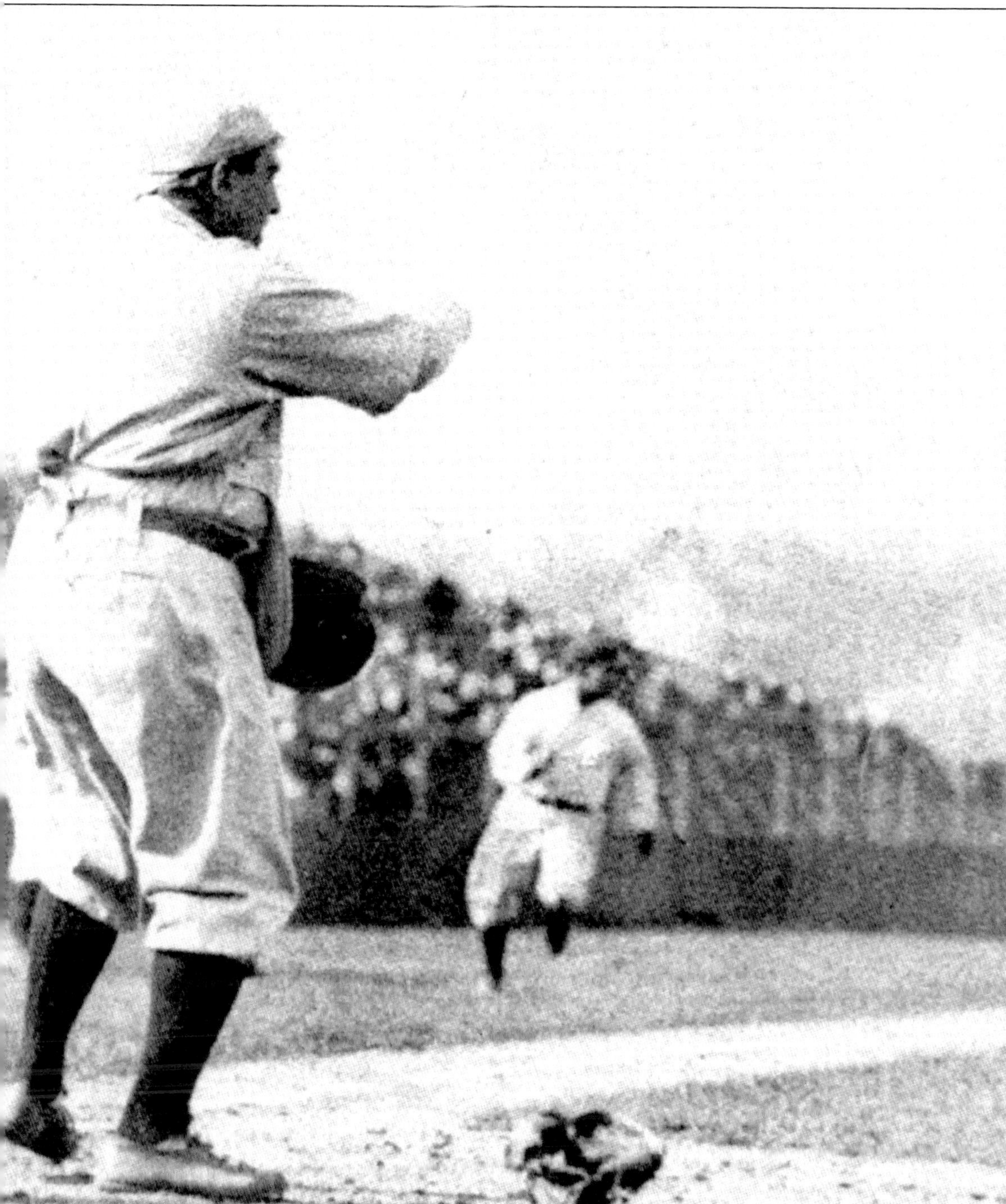

Cree's best year came in 1911, when he hit .348, drove in 88 runs, and scored 90 runs. His average was above .300 in 1912 and again in 1914.

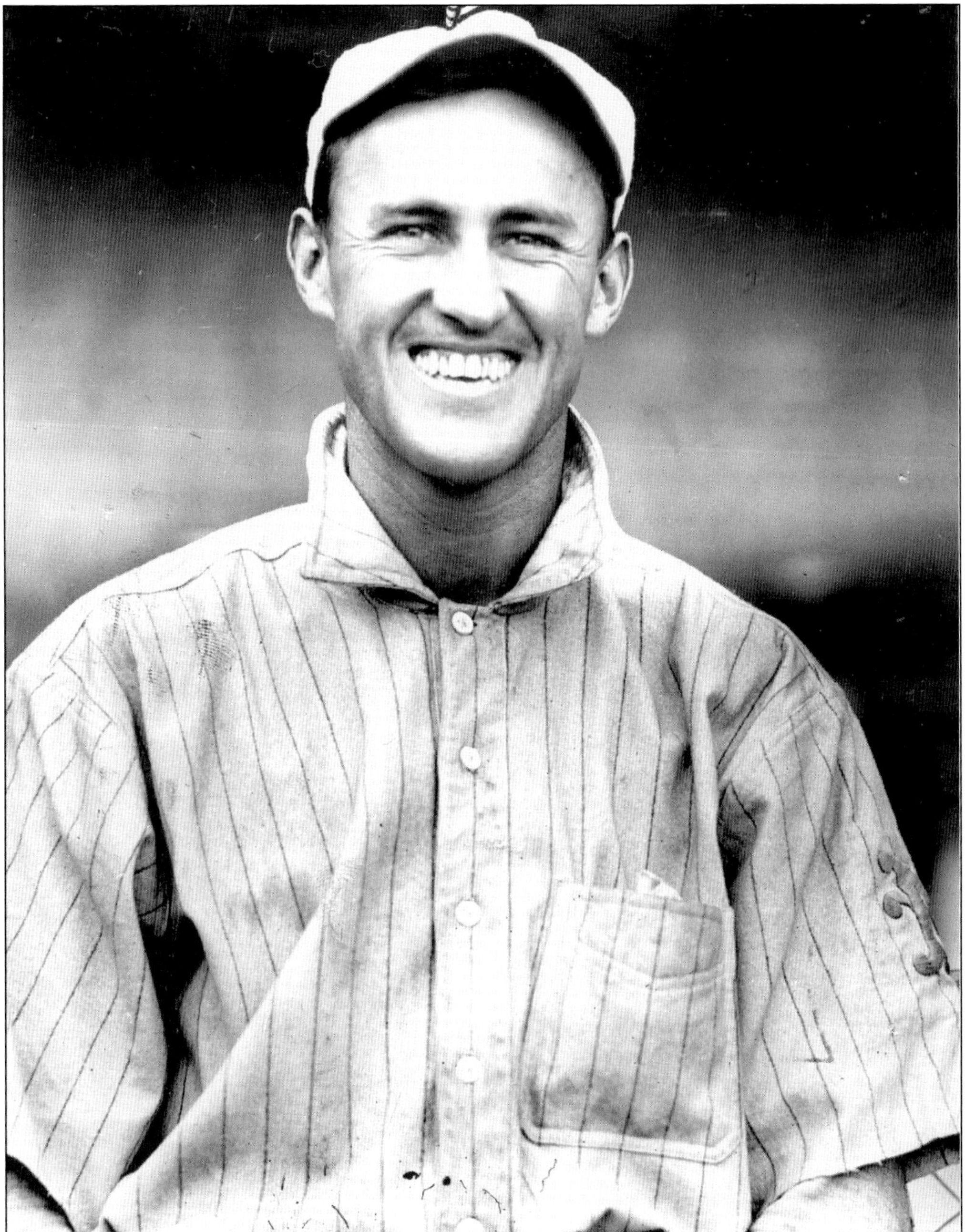

On these two pages, Art Fletcher appears in different New York uniforms. Above, he is seen as a player in 1913, posing in his Giants shirt. On the opposite page, he is a coach wearing the Yankees uniform. Fletcher was John McGraw's shortstop for all but 2 of Fletcher's 13 years in the majors. He was a solid and productive hitter. Though he only hit .300 once, his average never went below .260 in full seasons. He came to the Giants in 1909 and was installed as starting shortstop by 1911. In 1920, Fletcher was traded midseason to the Phillies. He became Philadelphia's manager the year after he retired.

Art Fletcher

Career 1909–1922 New York 1909–1920

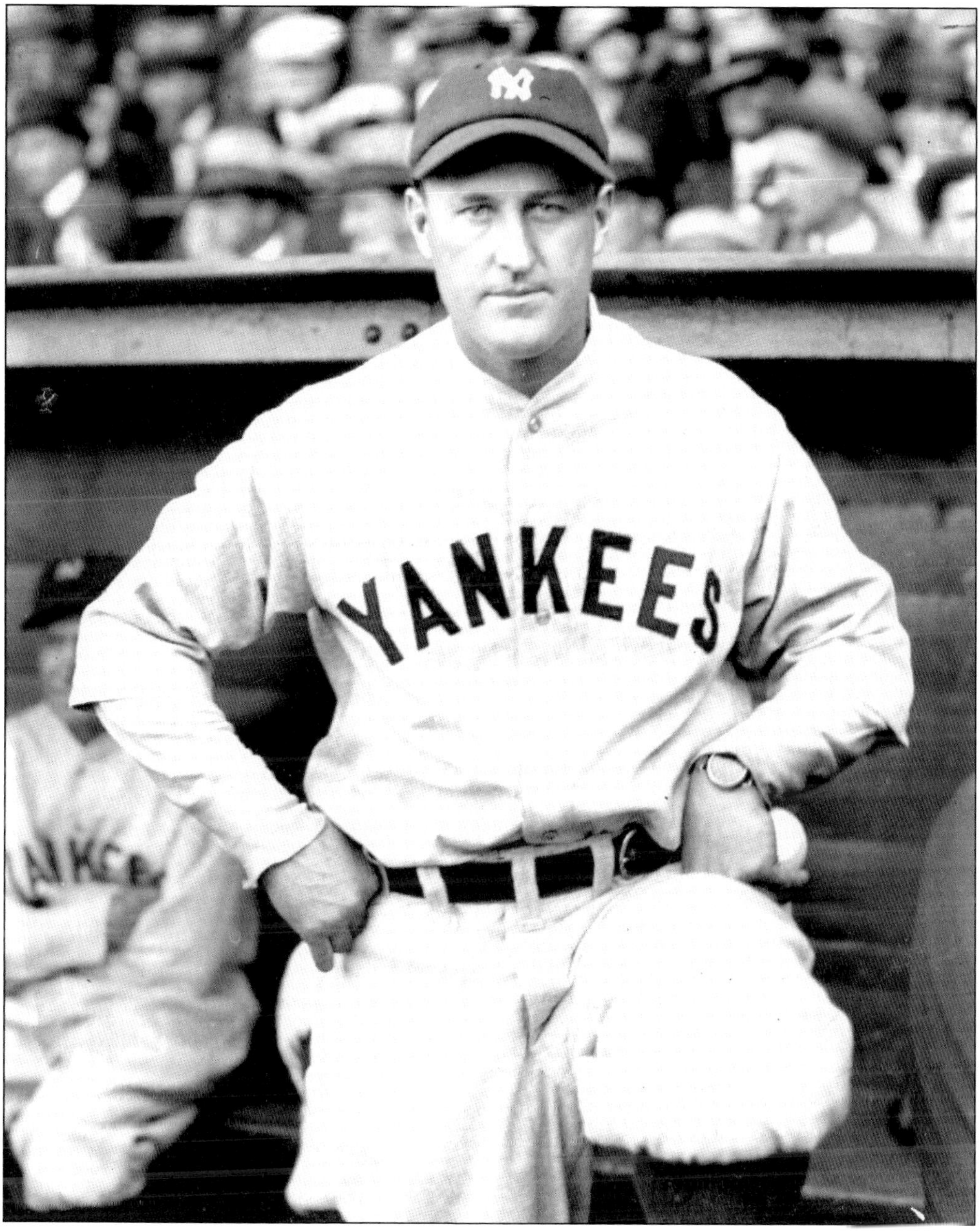

Frustrated with his thankless job as manager of the Phillies, Art Fletcher returned to New York to become the No. 2 man in the Yankee dugout under Miller Huggins. Fletcher drew upon his experience in the Polo Grounds, where he had served John McGraw as his on-field team leader. Fletcher received a job offer from the Bronx and arrived in Yankee Stadium in 1927, and stayed on until 1945. He was manager of the Yankees for a brief period after the death of Huggins, but Fletcher no longer wanted the responsibility of the job.

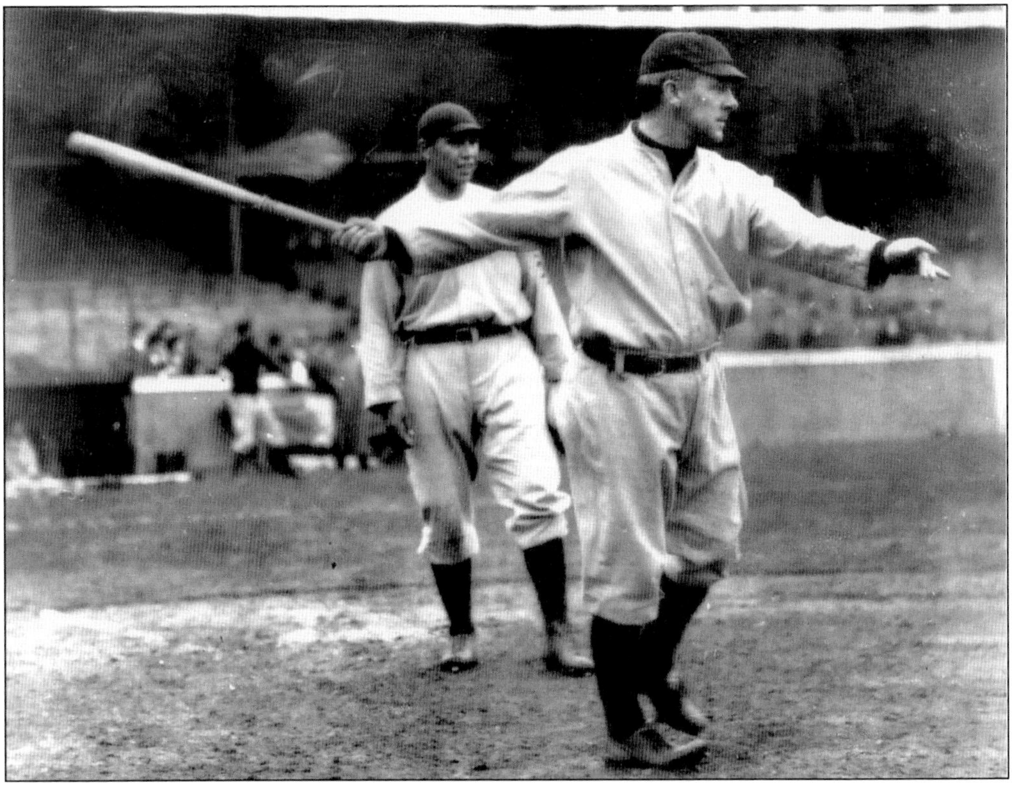

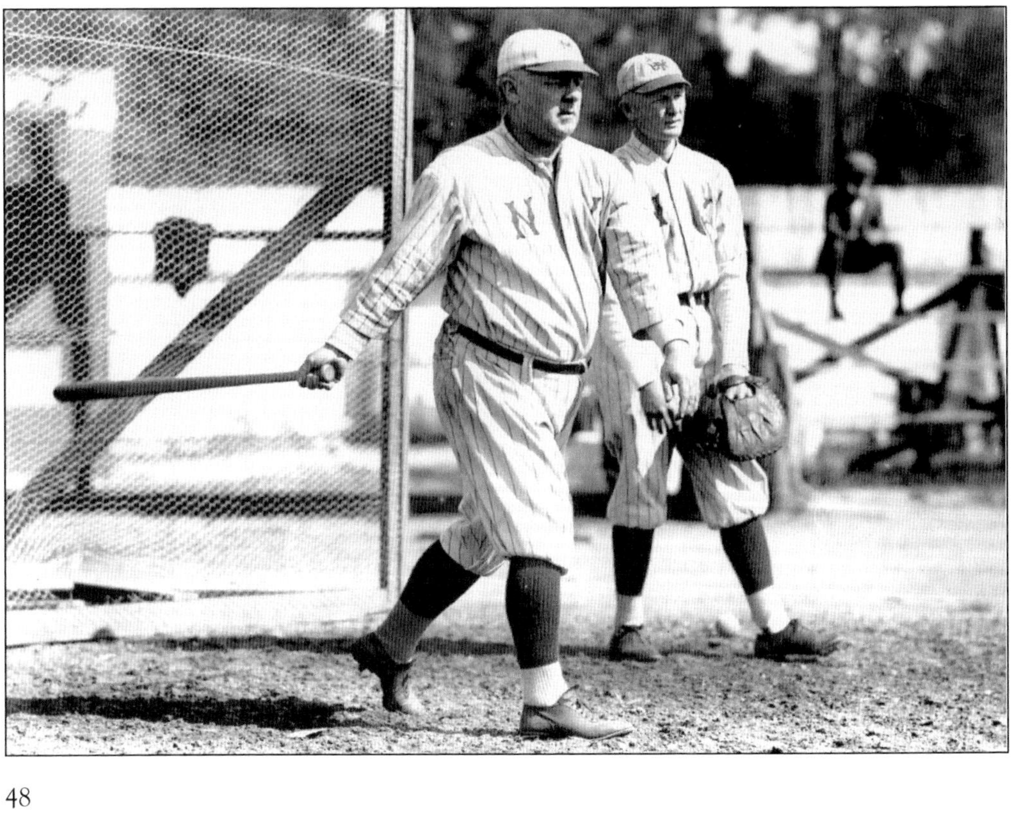

N

John McGraw

Playing Career 1891–1906 New York 1902–1906

Managerial Career 1899–1932 New York 1902–1932

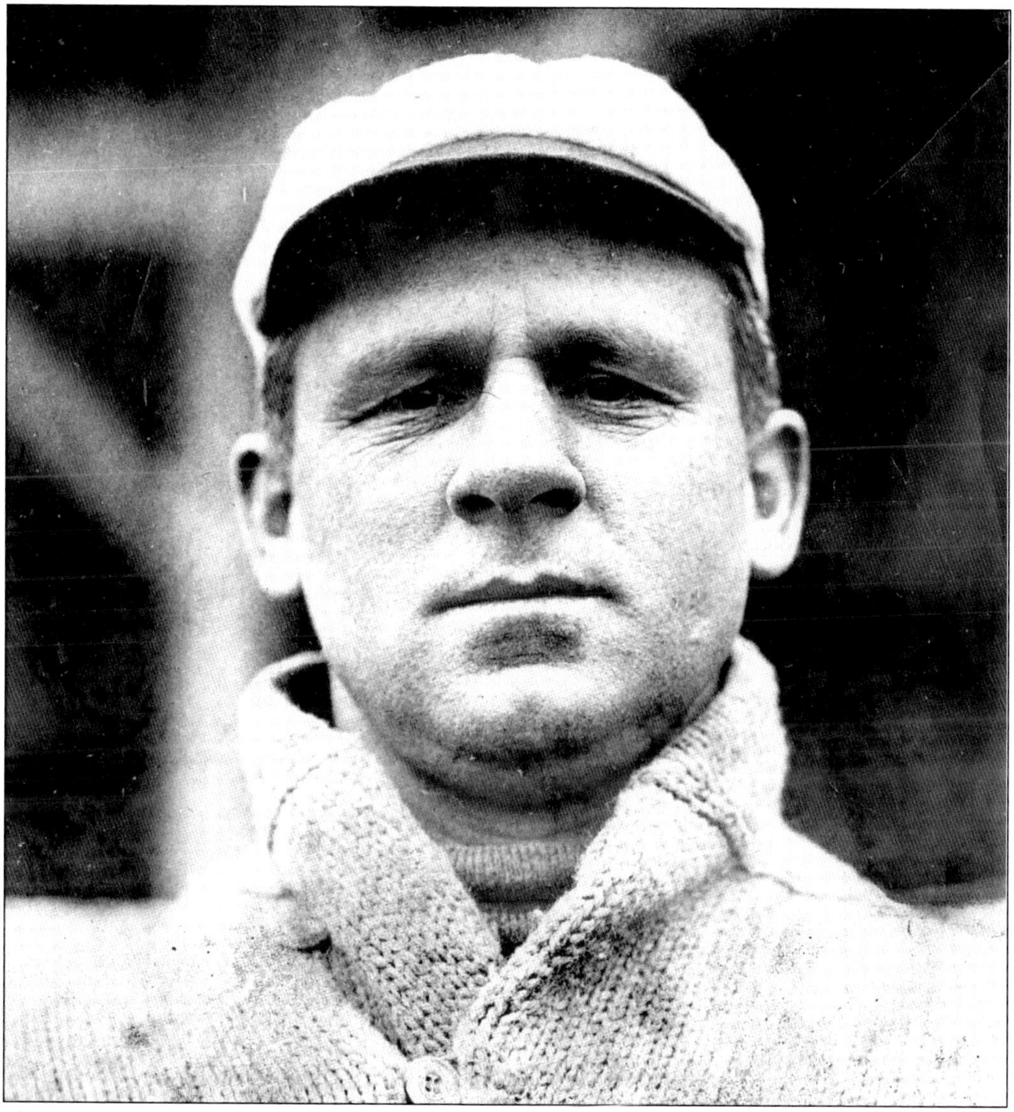

If John McGraw was not the toughest man in baseball, he was certainly among the toughest. A no-nonsense disciplinarian, McGraw wanted a 100 percent commitment from his players. But McGraw was not seeking just raw physical talent—he wanted "head work" from his charges. He wanted to win above all, but he preferred winning with brains rather than brawn. A veteran who didn't play with intelligence would not last long with the Giants. McGraw made his mark as a player, arriving in Baltimore in 1891 at the age of 18, and starring at third base there for nine years. After leaving Baltimore, he played a total of 59 games for the Giants and then retired as a player. His pugnacious demeanor on the field was replicated when he became a manager. On the facing page, McGraw is pictured hitting batting practice at different points in his managerial career—above, in 1908, and below, in 1918.

Roger Peckinpaugh

Career 1910–1927 New York 1913–1921

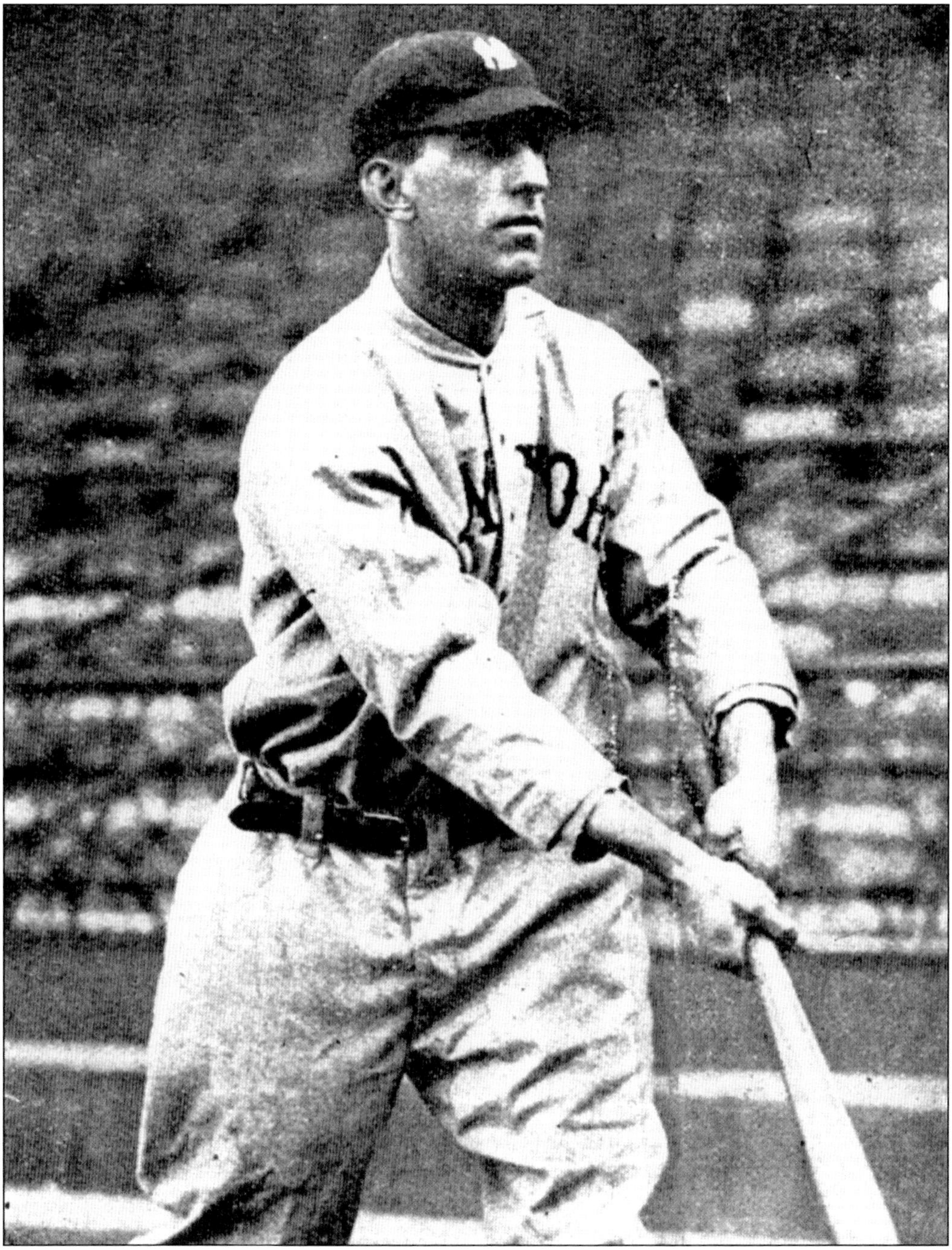

The nonpareil shortstop of the American League during his heyday, Roger Peckinpaugh produced hits and runs for the Yankees from 1913 to 1921. He twice broke the century mark in runs scored, amassing 109 in 1920 and 128 in 1921. His combined skills at batting and fielding brought him the Most Valuable Player award in 1925, when he was a member of the Washington Senators.

GEORGE BURNS

CAREER 1911–1925 NEW YORK 1911–1921

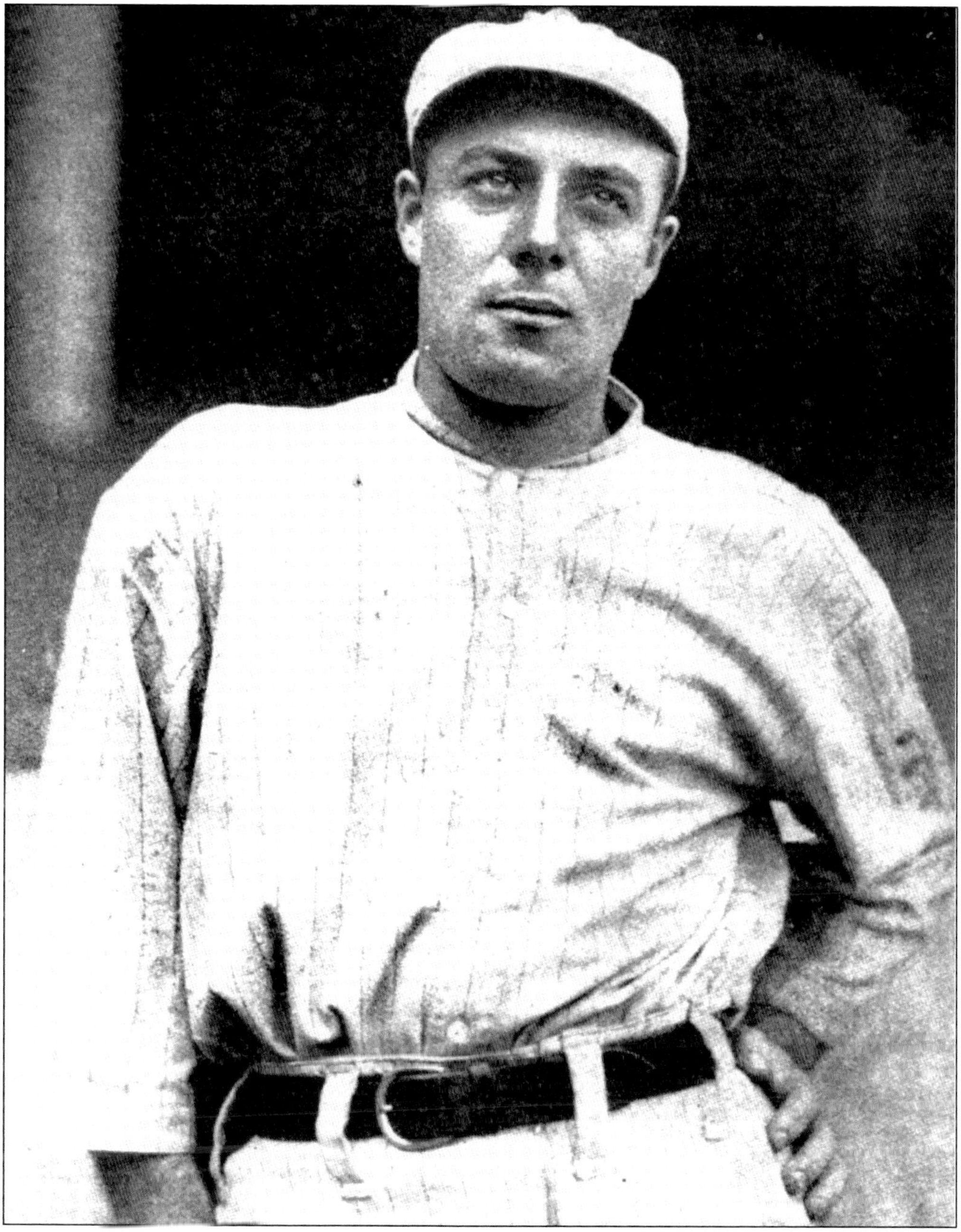

The popular George Burns patrolled left field in the Polo Grounds for more than a decade, and the stands behind him were called "Burnsville." In five separate years he led the National League in runs—those numbers were aided by his league-leading walk totals. Burns ended his career with a .287 lifetime average and just over 2,000 base hits. He was traded to Cincinnati in 1921 for fellow outfielder Heinie Groh.

Wally Pipp

Career 1913–1928 New York 1915–1925

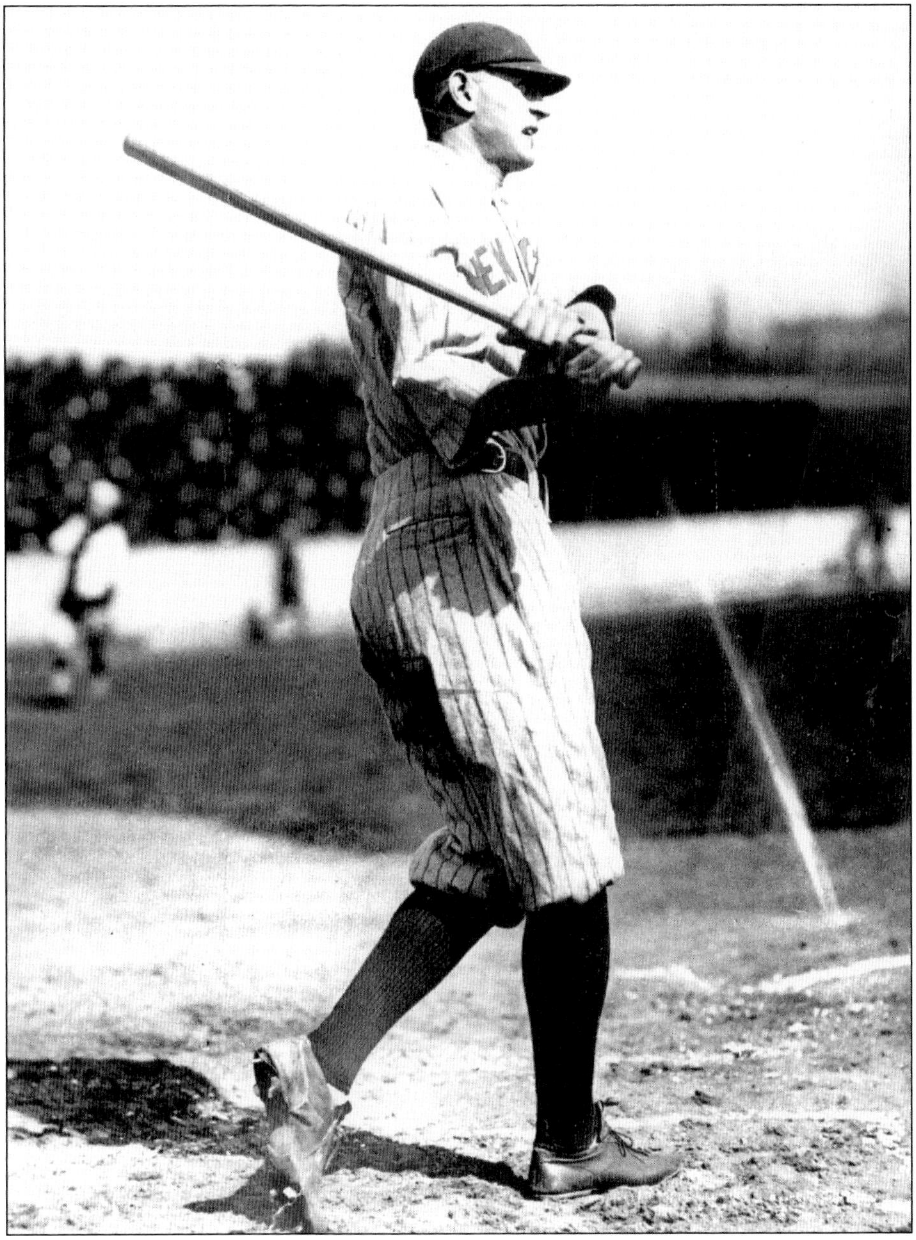

Wally Pipp played 15 games for Detroit during his rookie season in 1913 before becoming a Yankee. He stayed on for 11 years in the Bronx, where he played first base nearly every day until 1925, two years after Lou Gehrig had arrived. Pipp had an unfortunate experience when he took a day off to treat an injury and was replaced in the infield by Gehrig—and wound up losing his position for good. Pipp was then traded to the Cincinnati Reds. He was a true slugger in his youth, leading the American League in home runs in 1917 and 1918. He twice drove in more than 100 runs, and four times knocked in more than 90.

George Kelly

Career 1915–1932 New York 1915–1926

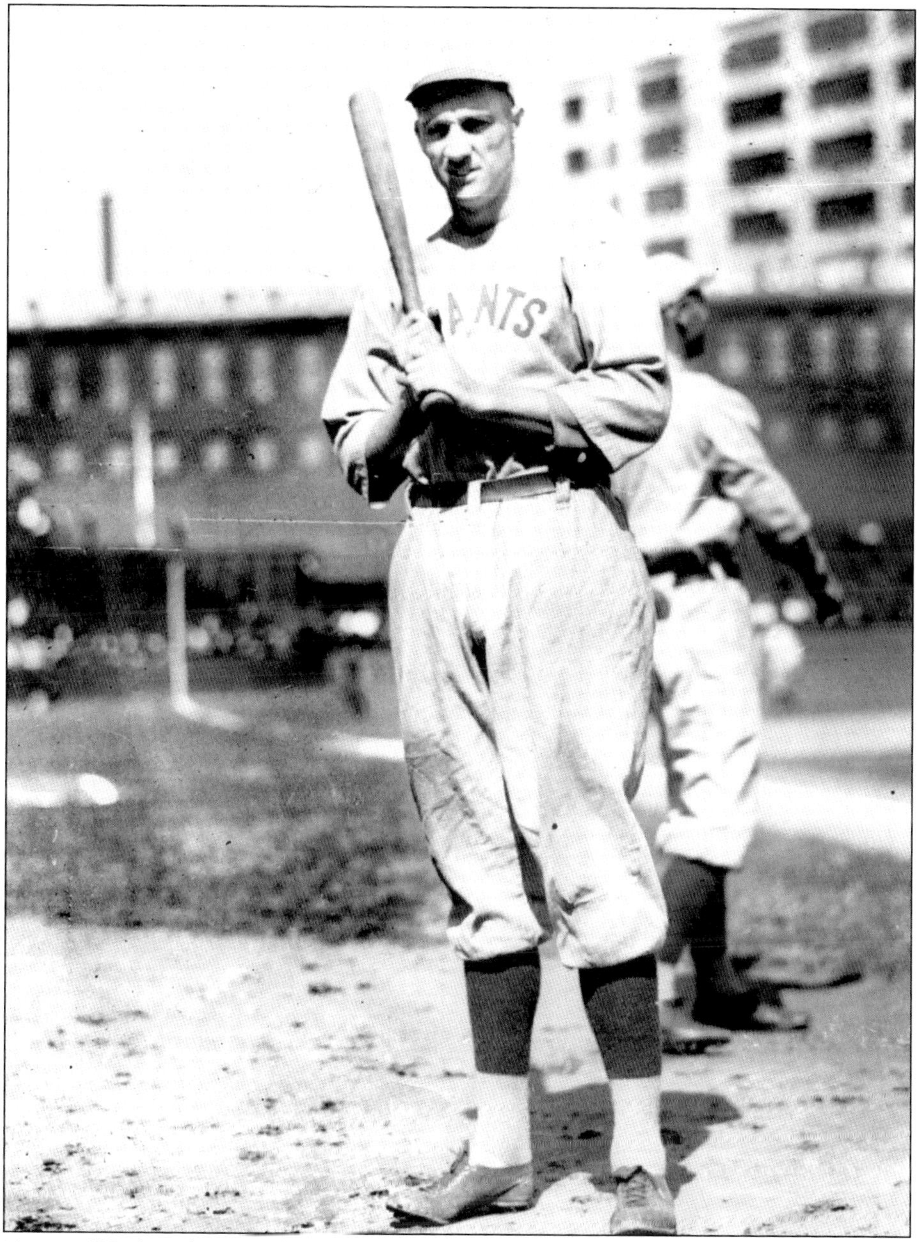

The tall George "Highpockets" Kelly was first baseman in an infield alignment that included Dave Bancroft, Heinie Groh, and Frankie Frisch. The quartet formed what was considered the Giants' best infield of all time. Kelly was a steady hitter, but he had streaks of brilliance. From 1921 to 1926, he finished each season with a batting average over .300, and for four years in a row he drove in more than 100 runs. McGraw believed Kelly to be the finest clutch hitter on his squad, even though he did not always hit for power. Kelly left the Giants in 1926 for Cincinnati, where he played for four more years.

Jim Thorpe

Career 1913–1919 New York 1913–1915, 1917–1919

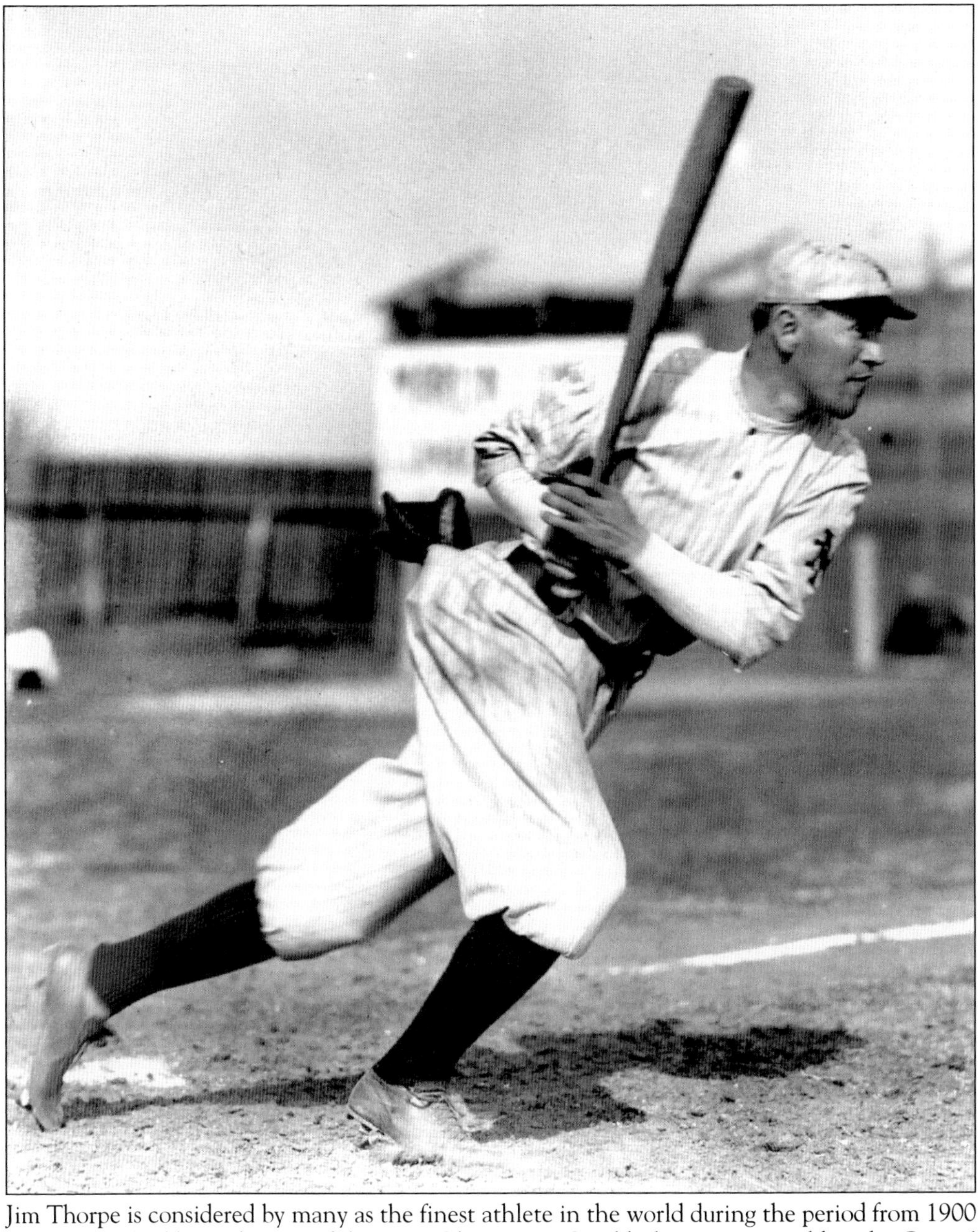

Jim Thorpe is considered by many as the finest athlete in the world during the period from 1900 to 1950. He had been the star of the 1912 Olympics in Stockholm, winning gold in the Games' most grueling events—the pentathlon and the decathlon. He may have been hired as a drawing card for the Polo Grounds, but he ended up playing as a fourth outfielder, and only once had more than 300 at-bats in a season. He was more famous as a football player, and was named an All-American twice while attending the Carlisle Indian School in Pennsylvania. He later played professional football, and was talented enough to be elected to the Football Hall of Fame.

Benny Kauff

Career 1912–1920 New York 1912, 1916–1920

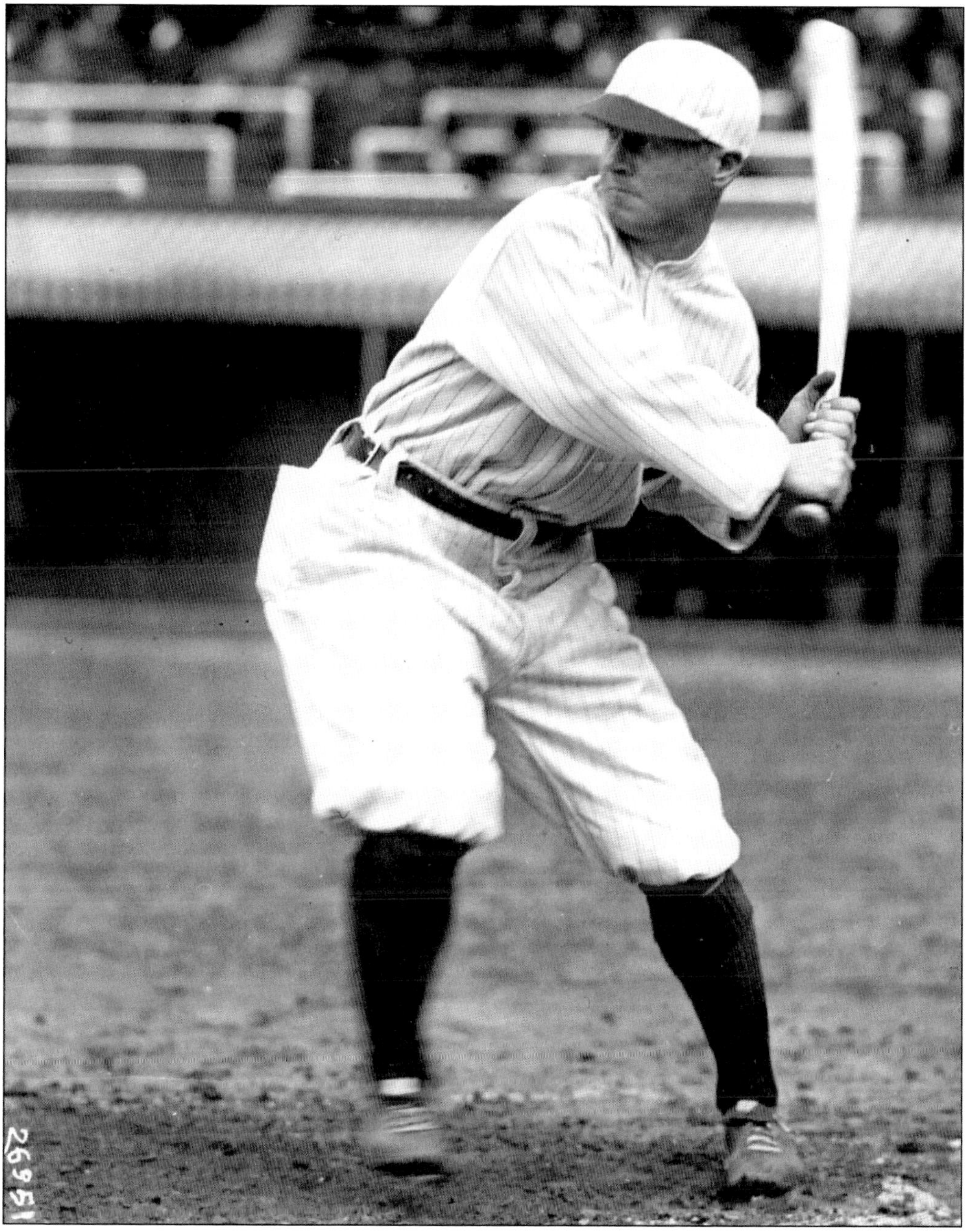

This image of Benny Kauff settles an argument that only photography could solve. The Giants outfielder, who had a bright but brief career, was so strong that his bat bowed mid-swing, a phenomenon that many thought was an illusion. Kauff used his strength to put together a number of fine seasons. In his best year for the Giants, he hit .308 with 30 stolen bases and 89 runs scored.

Casey Stengel

Career 1912–1925 New York 1921–1923

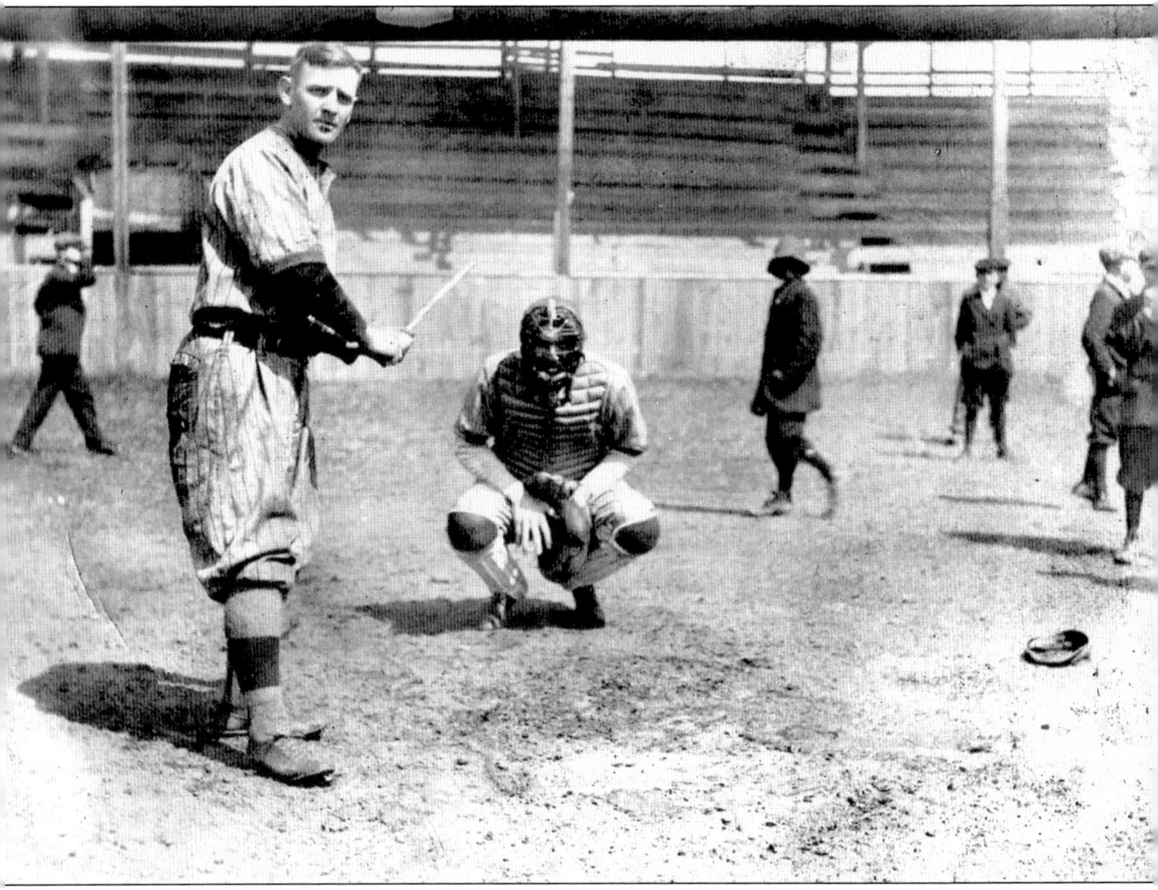

Yes, Casey Stengel was a player. Most baseball fans remember him as the highly successful manager of the New York Yankees in the 1950s and early 1960s. He was an outfielder and a pretty good hitter, and once led the National League in on-base percentage with a .404 mark. Stengel ended his 14 years in the National League with a very respectable .284 average. By the time he put on a Giants uniform, his best days as a hitter were over. In the photograph above, the catcher seems to be calling for the pumpkin ball, which Casey will hit with his little stick.

Pop Lloyd

Career 1906–1932 New York 1911–1915, 1919, 1926–1930, 1931

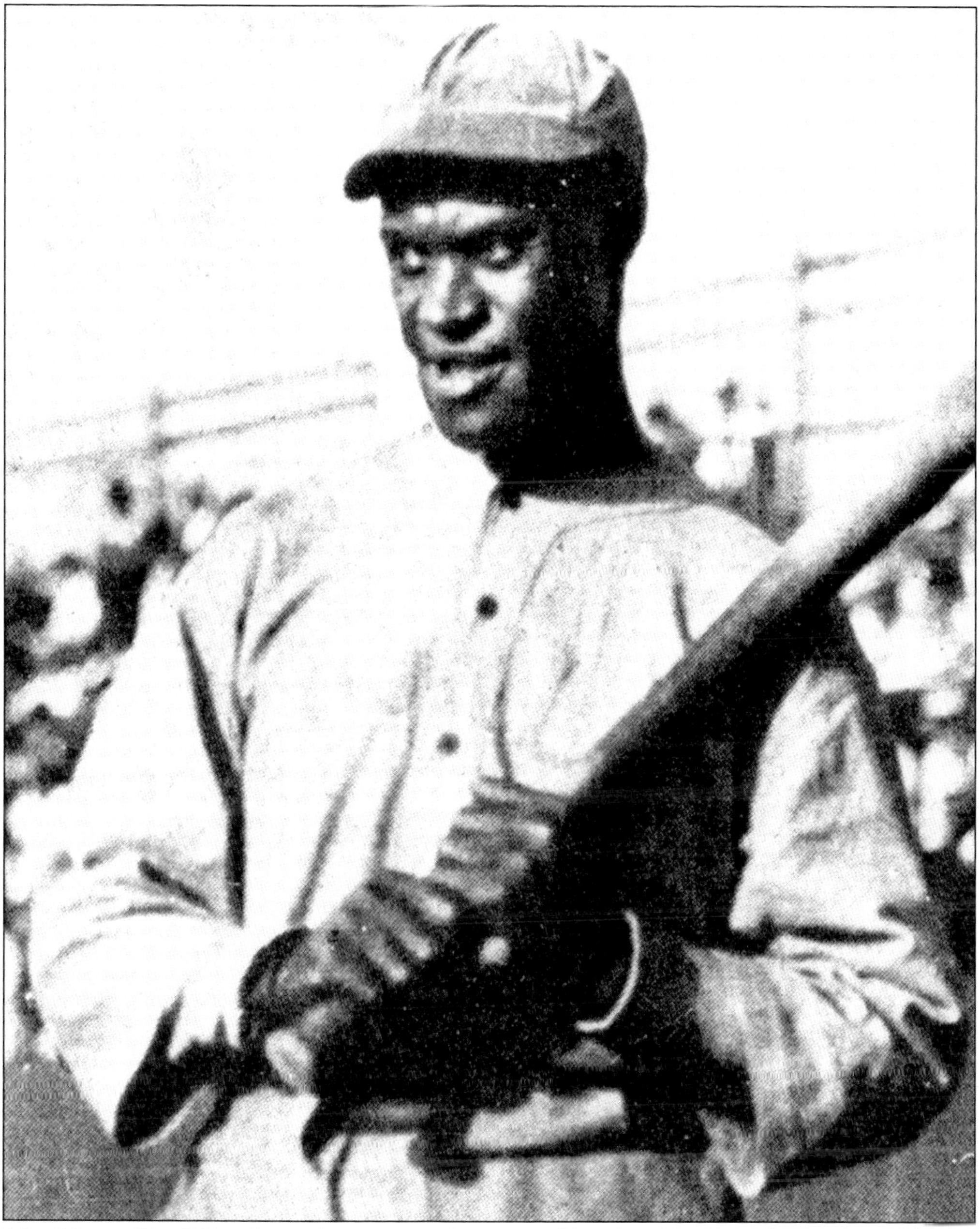

John Henry "Pop" Lloyd was the greatest shortstop of his day, black or white. He could have starred for any major-league club if not for his skin color. He spent a good part of his career in New York, first playing for the New York Lincoln Giants in 1911. Lloyd also was a headliner for the New York Lincoln Stars in 1915 and the New York Bachrach Giants in 1919. He later signed a contract with the Brooklyn Royal Giants across the river, serving as player-manager from 1918 to 1920.

Frankie Frisch

Career 1919–1937 New York 1919–1926

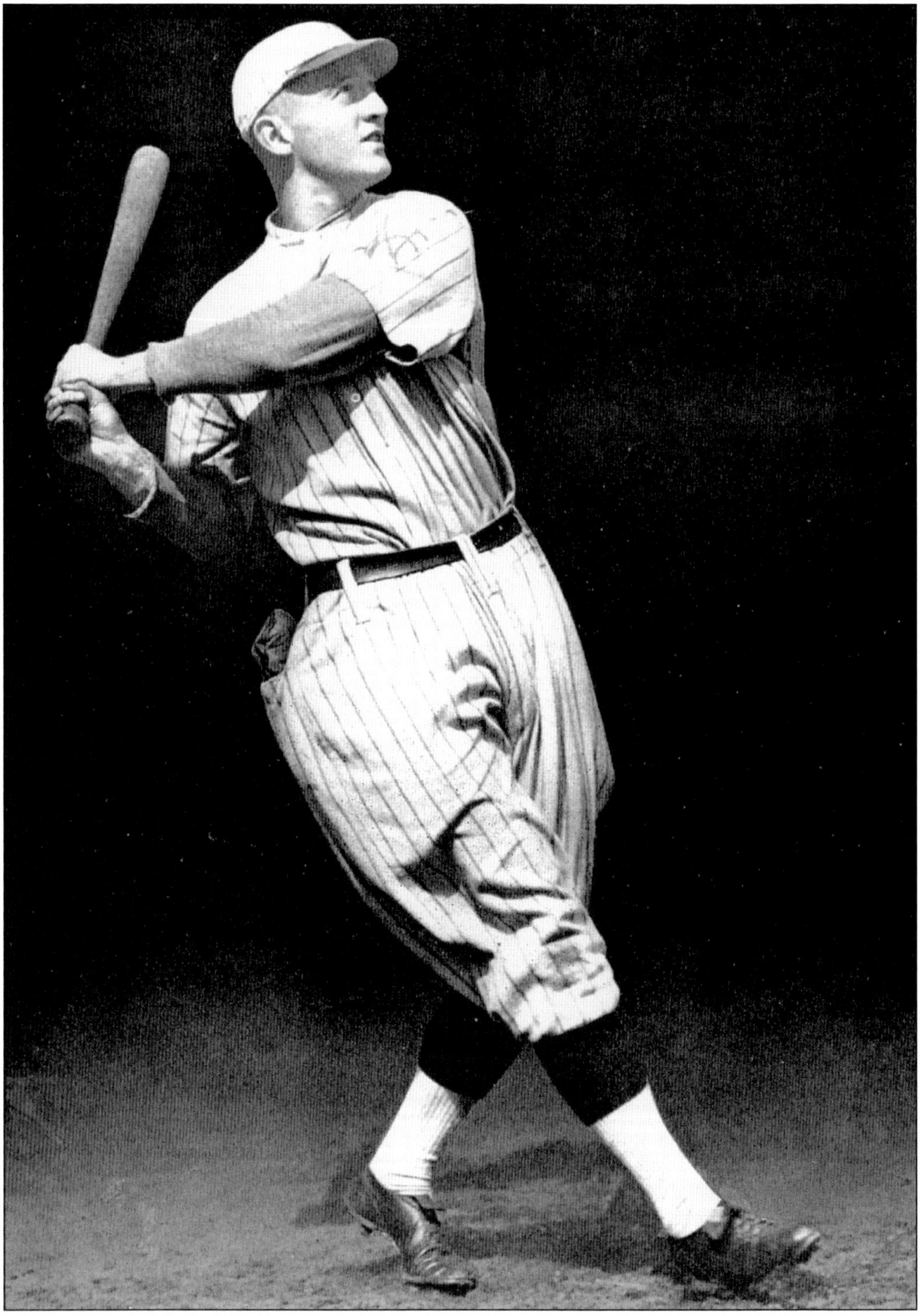

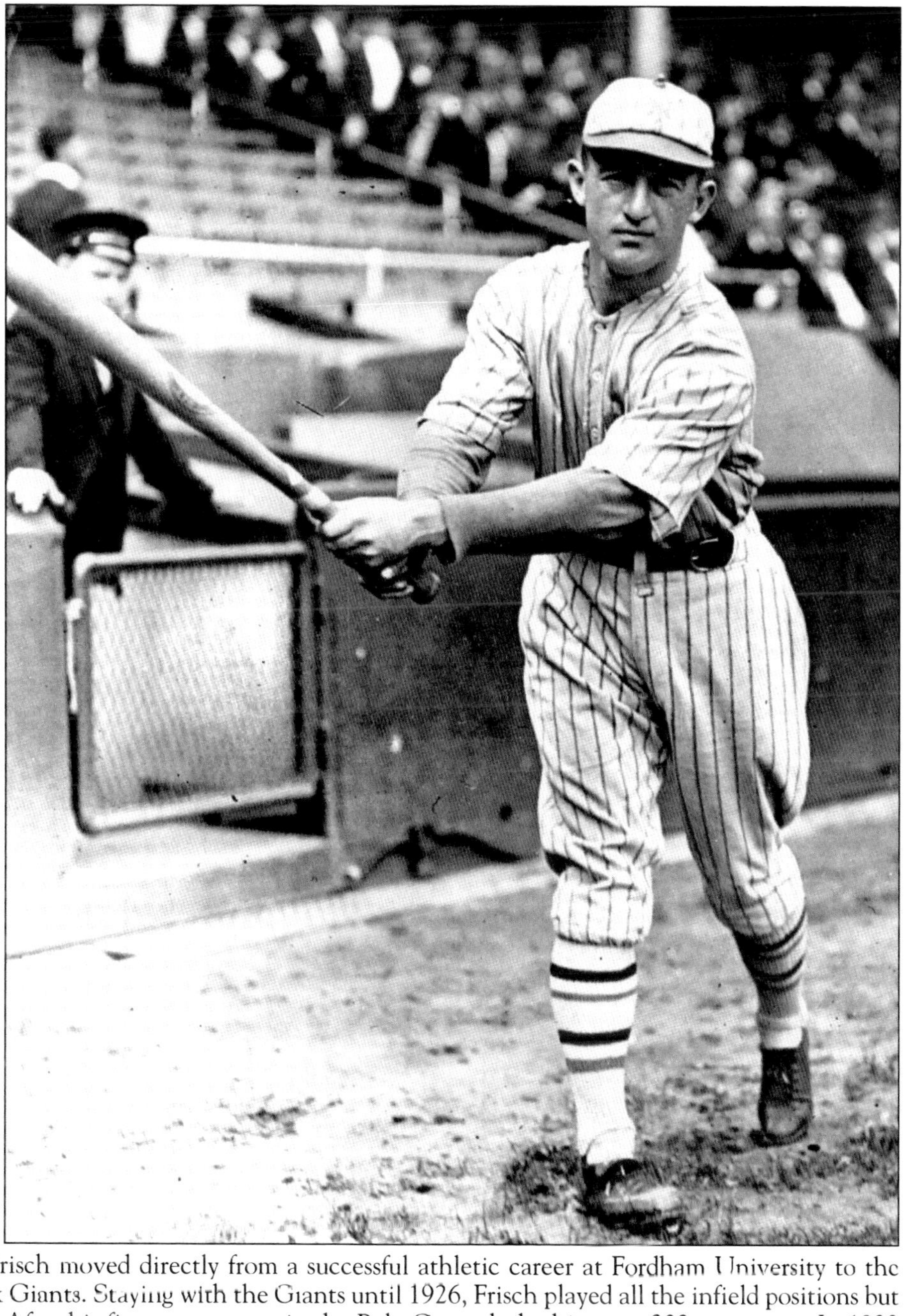

Frankie Frisch moved directly from a successful athletic career at Fordham University to the New York Giants. Staying with the Giants until 1926, Frisch played all the infield positions but first base. After his first two seasons in the Polo Grounds, he hit over .300 every year. In 1923 Frisch led the National League in hits with 223. In the following campaign, he led the league in runs scored with 121. Frisch was extremely swift on the base paths, winning the league's stolen-base crown three times and scoring 100 runs or more in 7 of his 19 seasons. His penchant for scoring runs helped the New Yorkers to win four straight National League flags from 1921 to 1924. Frisch batted no less than .300 in those four World Series, and batted .400 or higher twice. He was traded to the Cardinals for Rogers Hornsby in the winter of 1926, leaving Frisch with the task of replacing Hornsby in the hearts of Cardinals fans.

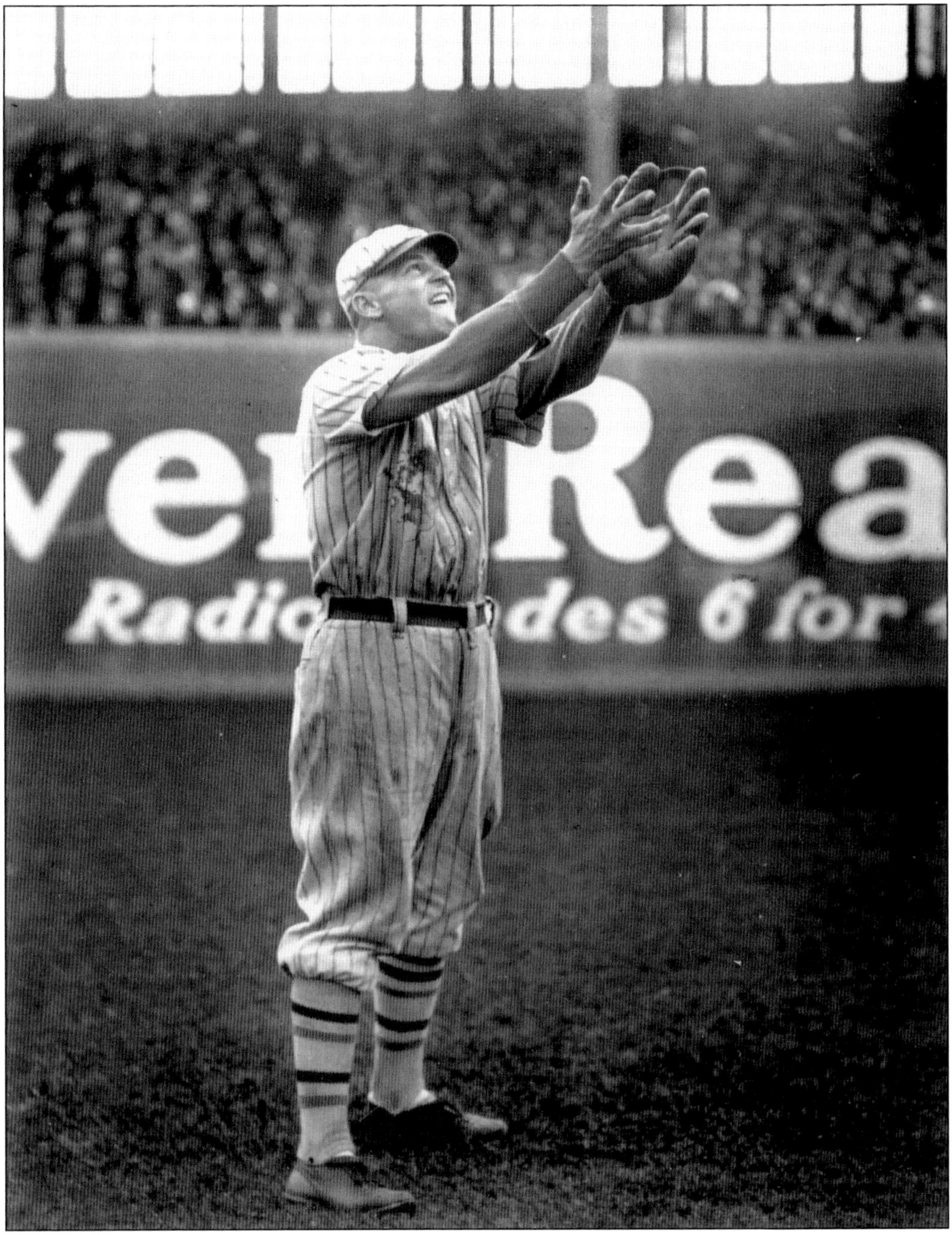

Arriving in the major leagues with the New York Giants in 1917, Ross Youngs proceeded to rattle off eight straight seasons of hitting above .300. Along the way, he led the league in doubles with 31 in 1919 and in runs scored with 121 in 1923. His best year statistically was 1924, when he recorded a slugging percentage of .521 while scoring 112 runs. He was John McGraw's favorite outfielder of all those who had appeared on his rosters because Youngs achieved excellence both offensively and defensively. His career was cut short by Bright's disease, which ended his life at the age of 30. Youngs finished up with a lifetime average of .322, and was admitted to the Hall of Fame in 1972.

Ross Youngs

Career 1917–1926 all in New York

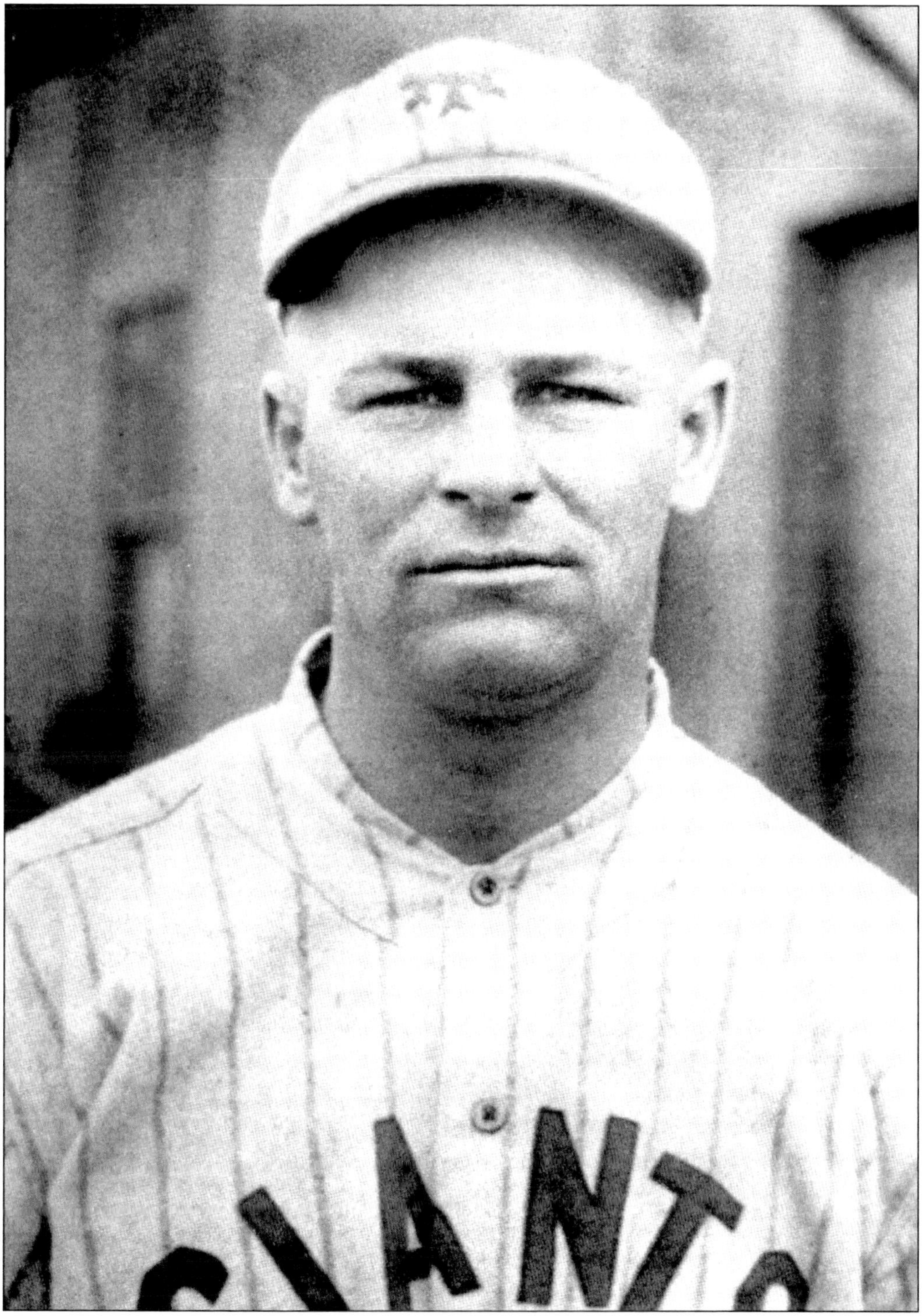

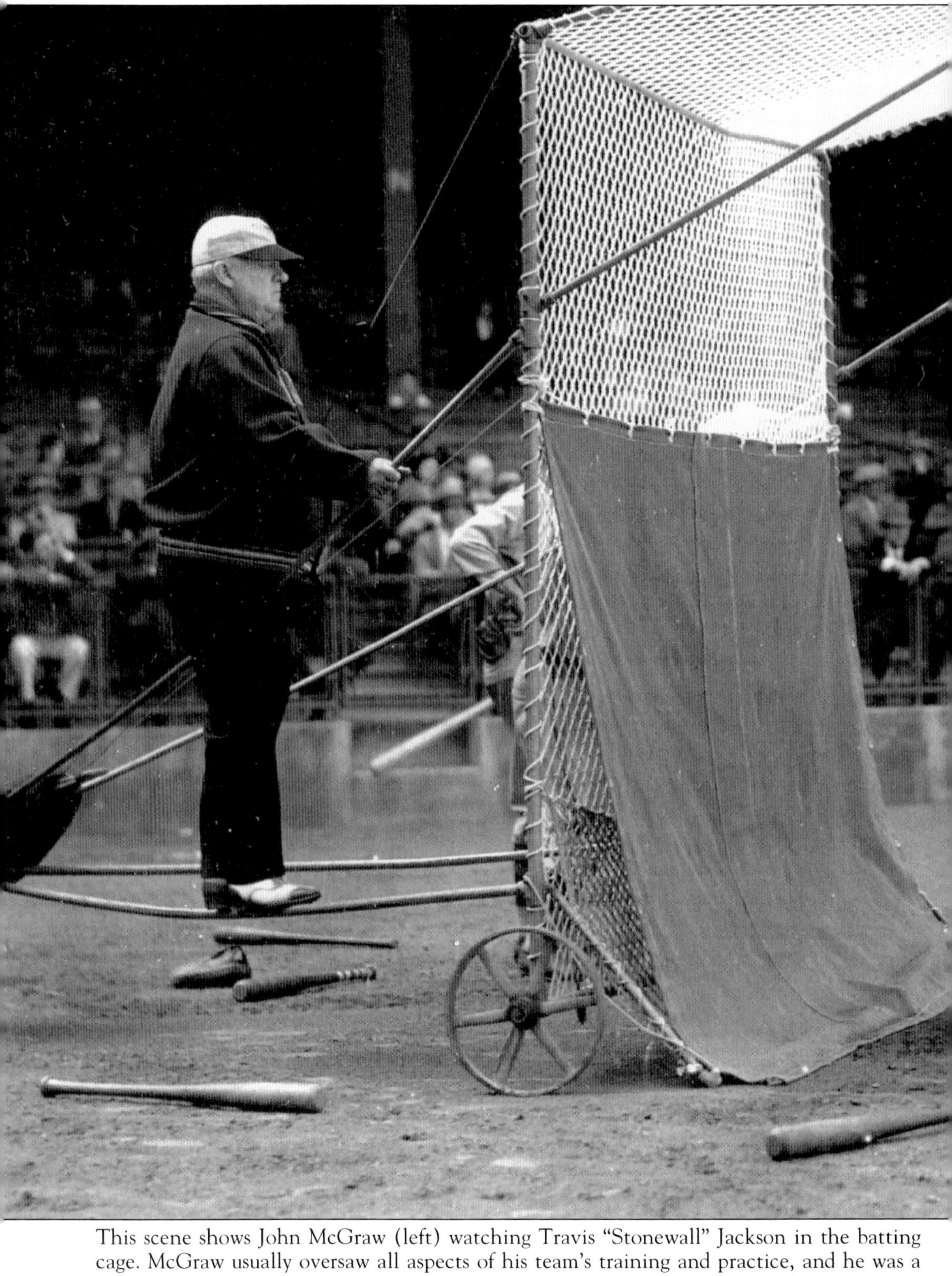

This scene shows John McGraw (left) watching Travis "Stonewall" Jackson in the batting cage. McGraw usually oversaw all aspects of his team's training and practice, and he was a

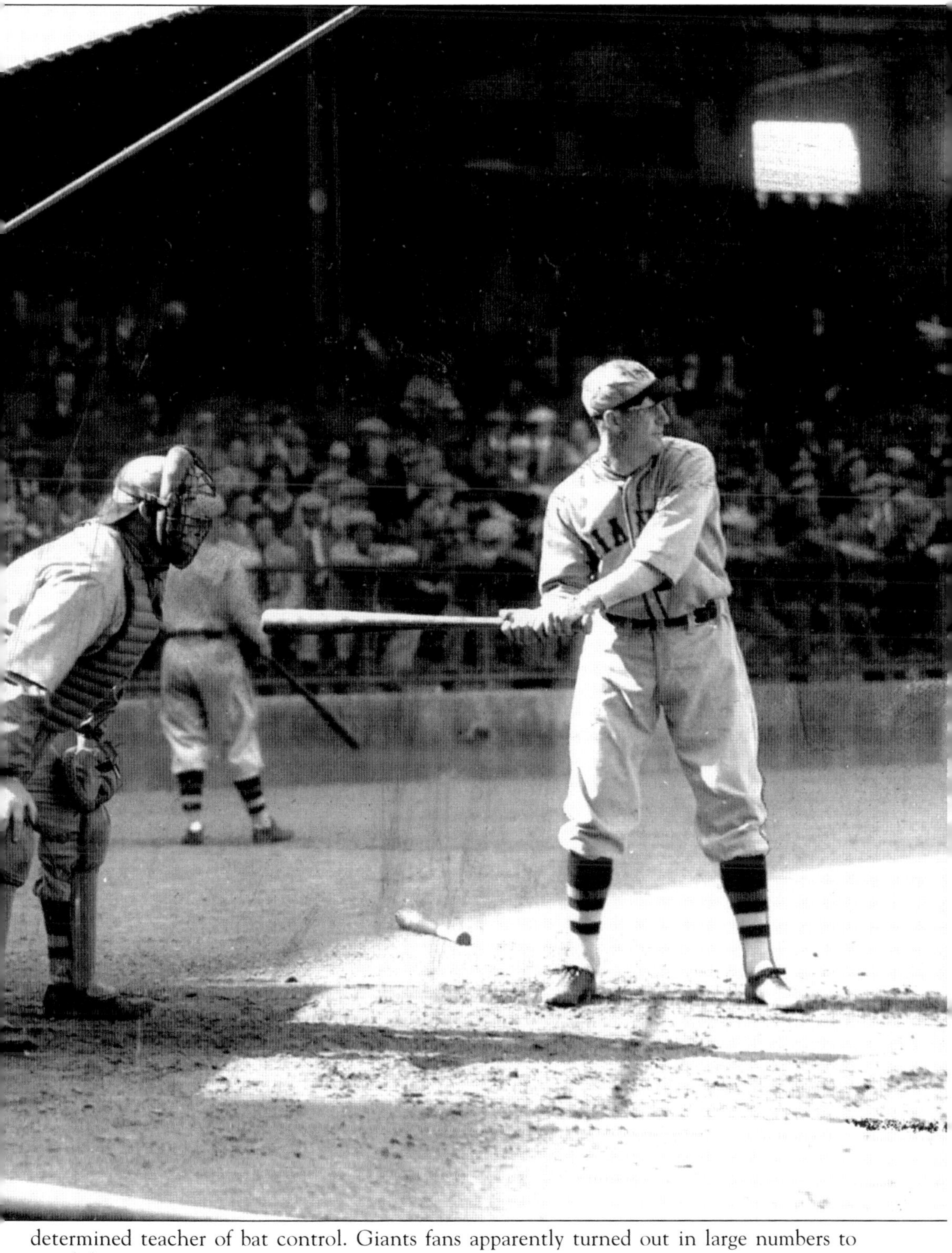

determined teacher of bat control. Giants fans apparently turned out in large numbers to watch batting practice.

EDD ROUSCH

CAREER 1913–1931 NEW YORK 1927–1929

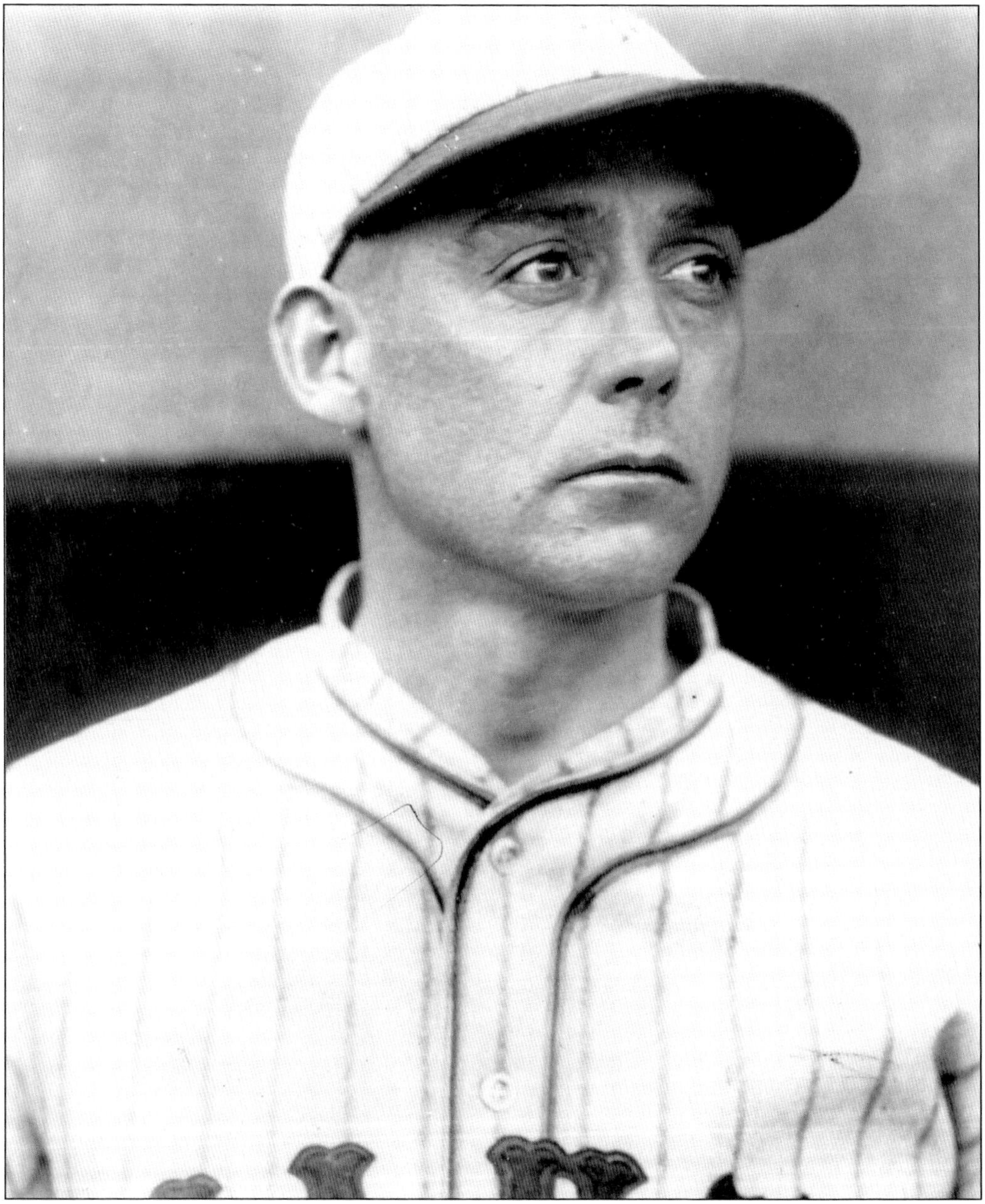

Edd Rousch played in New York both at the beginning of his career and near the end of it. Rousch did not begin playing full seasons until he arrived in Cincinnati in 1917. His bottle bat was famous in its own right; weighing in at about 47 ounces, it was the heaviest bat in all of baseball. Rousch was a dynamic hitter, topping .300 in 11 seasons and holding a .323 average for his lifetime. He won the National League batting title twice, with marks of .341 in 1917 and .321 in 1919. The latter year was the season in which Rousch led the Reds to the pennant and to a victory in the notorious 1919 World Series.

WALLY SCHANG

CAREER 1913–1931 NEW YORK 1921–1925

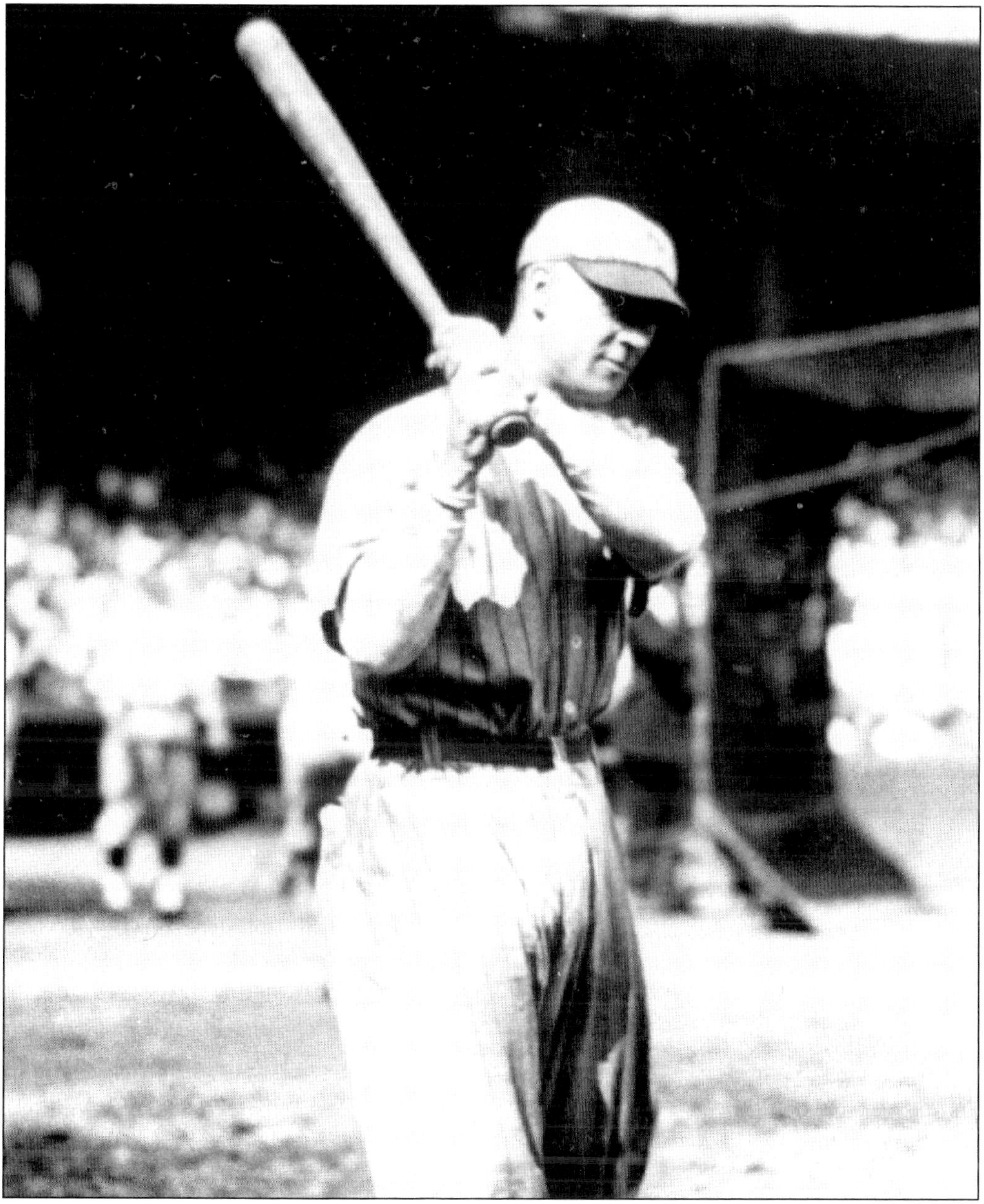

When the Yankees won their first three pennants in 1921, 1922, and 1923, Wally Schang was their starting catcher. He hit over .300 in six seasons, two of them during those World Series years. Schang played 19 games in three Series for the Yanks, though his finest postseason was with Boston in 1916. Schang had some speed, which was unusual for a catcher, and he was one of only a few backstops to steal more than 100 bases in his career. He racked up 769 lifetime runs scored. Schang started his baseball life with the Philadelphia Athletics and finished with the Detroit Tigers, but his seasons in New York were among his best.

PING BODIE

CAREER 1911–1921 NEW YORK 1918–1921

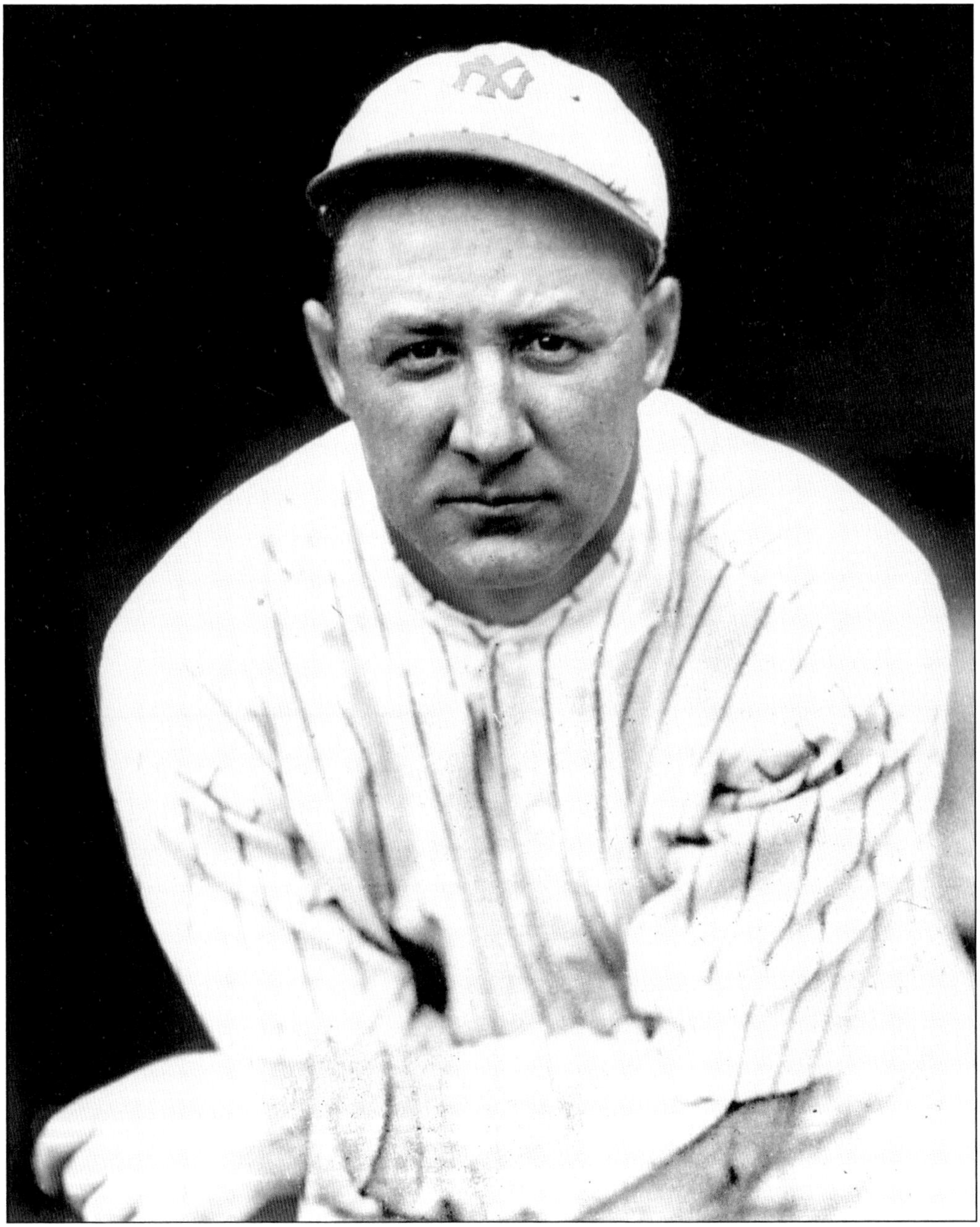

The player pictured above was born Stefano Pezzulo, but he renamed himself Bodie after a California town he lived in. A friendly and amusing teammate, Ping Bodie was assigned to be a roommate for the newly arrived Babe Ruth. Bodie was expected to keep an eye on the young slugger, but when asked about his new pal, he quipped, "I don't room with Ruth, I room with his suitcase!" Bodie was a major character on the team, but he was soon overshadowed by the monstrous personality and gargantuan talent of George Herman Ruth.

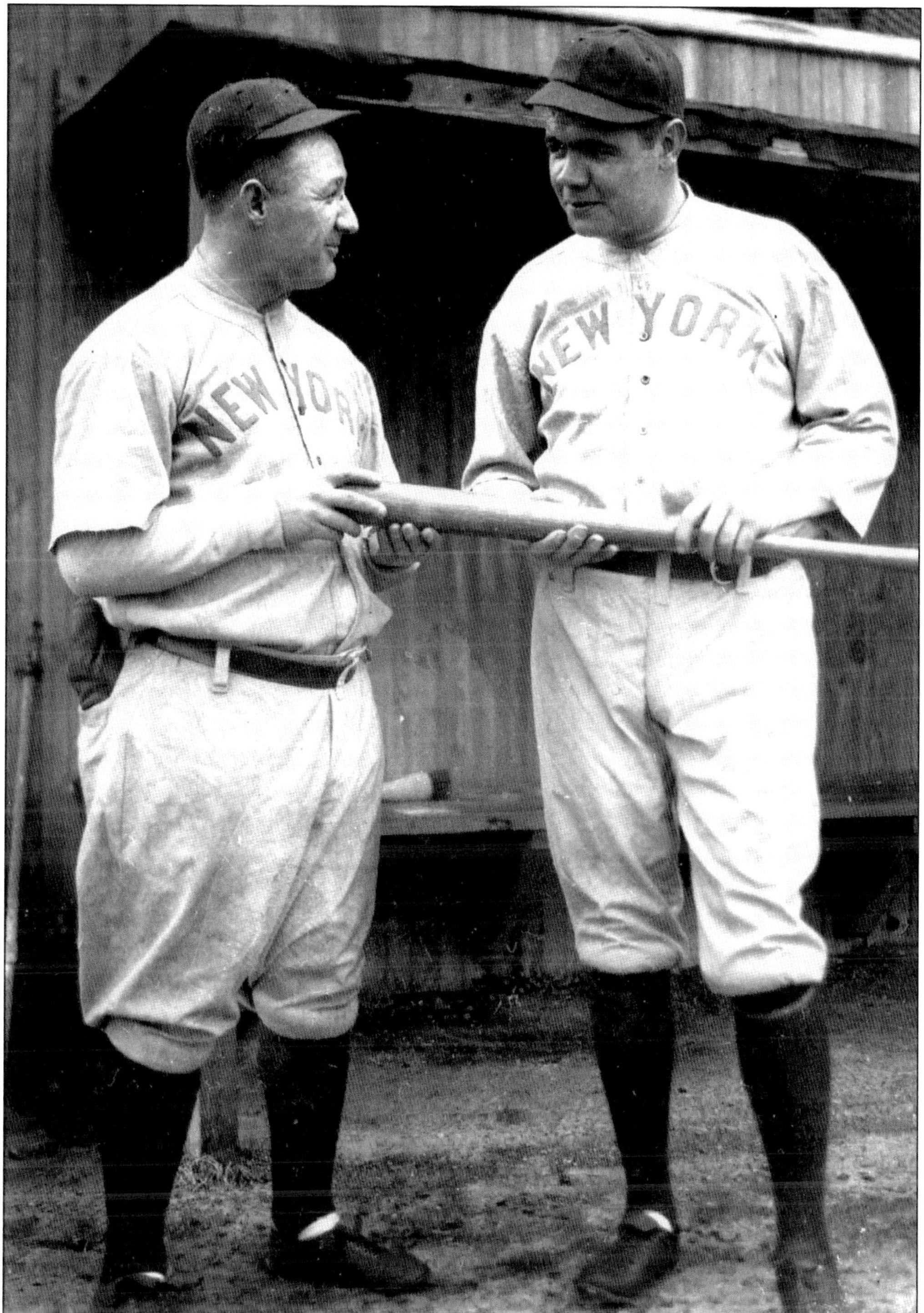

This 1920 photograph shows Bodie (at left) receiving information about the Babe's lumber. Ruth would soon hit more home runs in one season than Bodie did in his entire career, which ended in 1921. Bodie wrapped up his playing days with 43 homers and a .275 career batting average.

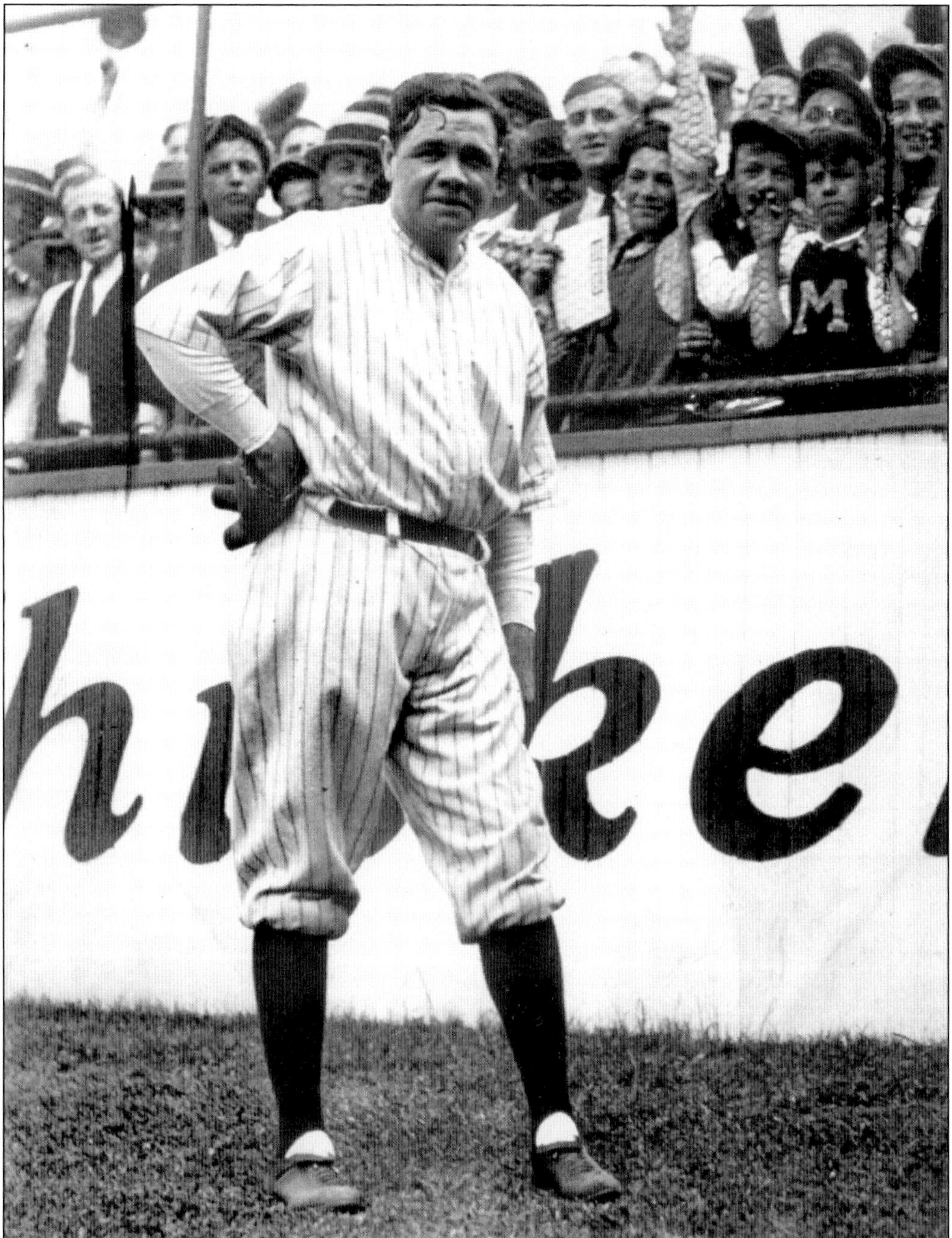

George Herman Ruth has to be the most recognizable baseball player in history—perhaps even the most recognizable American. The Babe's broad visage stood out in any crowd, and his antics put the spotlight on him wherever he went. But no matter how bold the bravado or how extreme the hyperbole, Ruth could live up to it, and America loved him for it. The photograph above shows him visiting with fans in the outfield of Yankee Stadium midseason in 1925.

Three

1921–1950

Babe Ruth

Career 1914–1935 New York 1920–1934

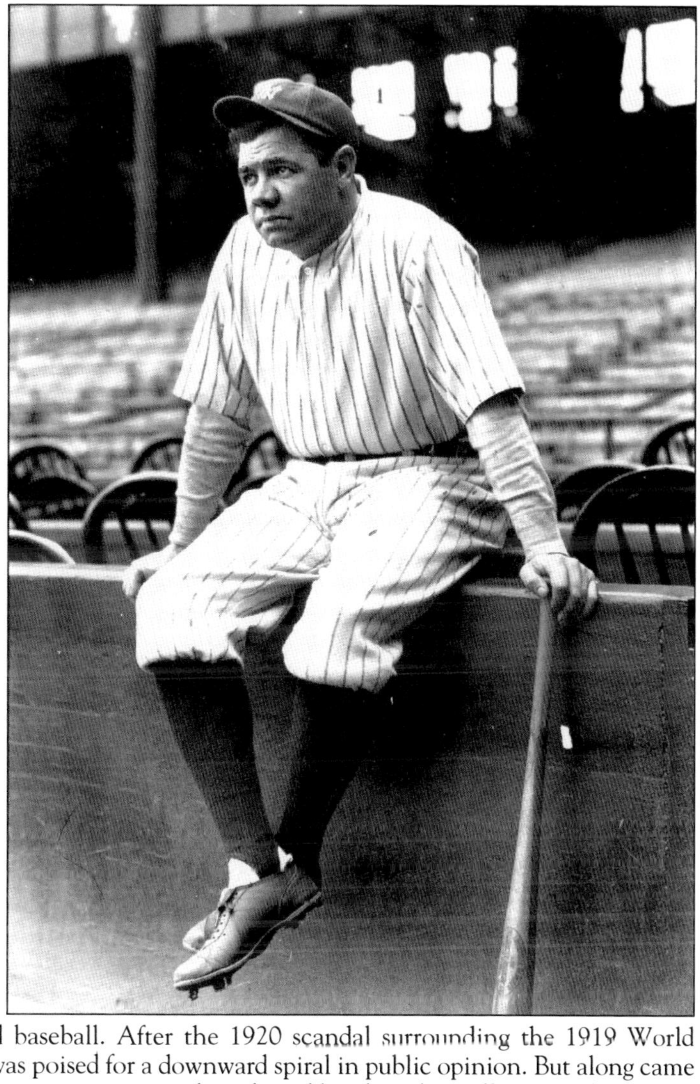

Ruth's hitting exploits saved baseball. After the 1920 scandal surrounding the 1919 World Series, the national pastime was poised for a downward spiral in public opinion. But along came Ruth to the rescue, blasting home runs in record totals and breaking box office records in every American League city. The Black Sox became a fading memory in the face of Ruth's powerful displays, and the headlines touted his latest exploits almost every day.

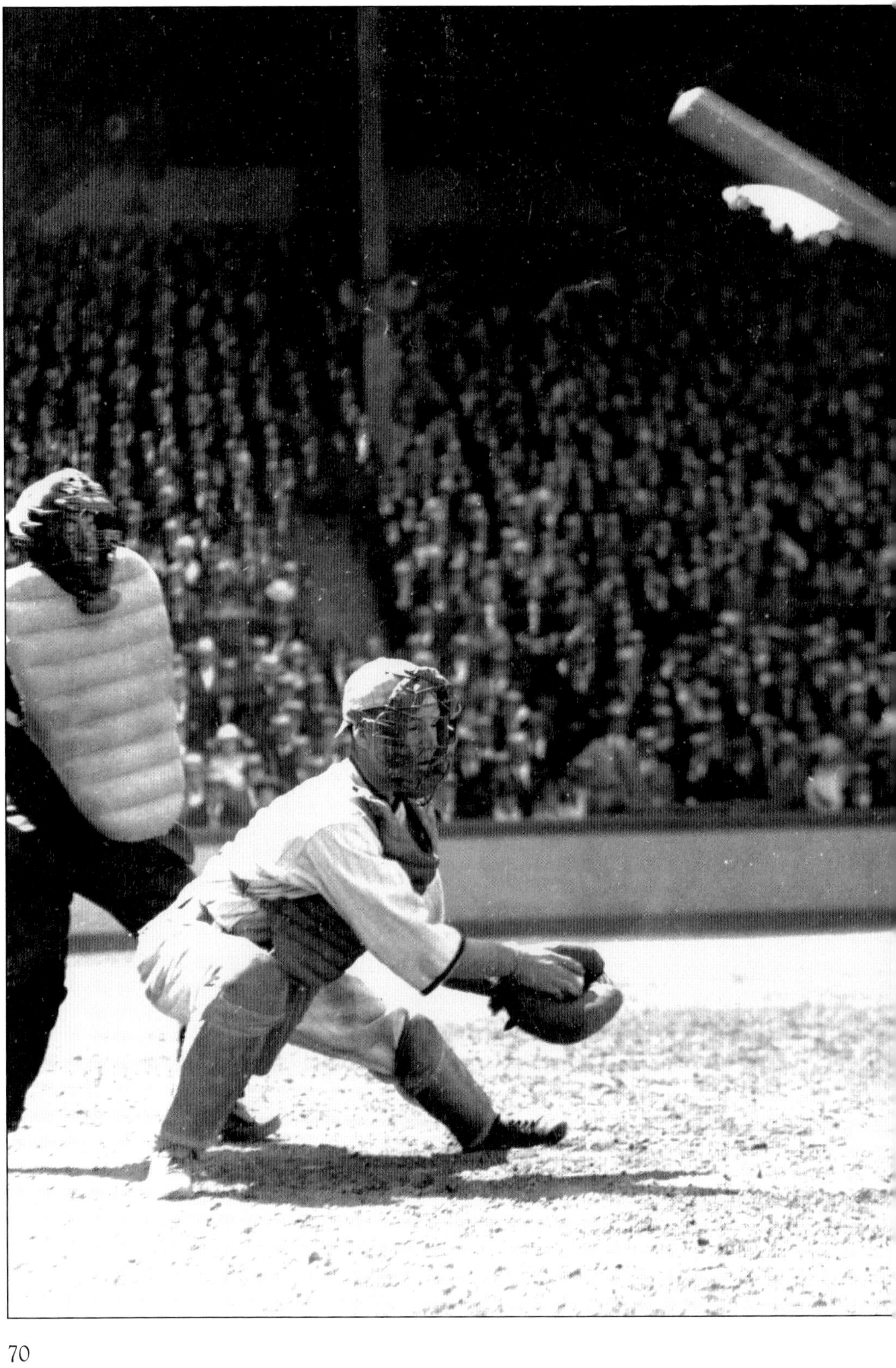

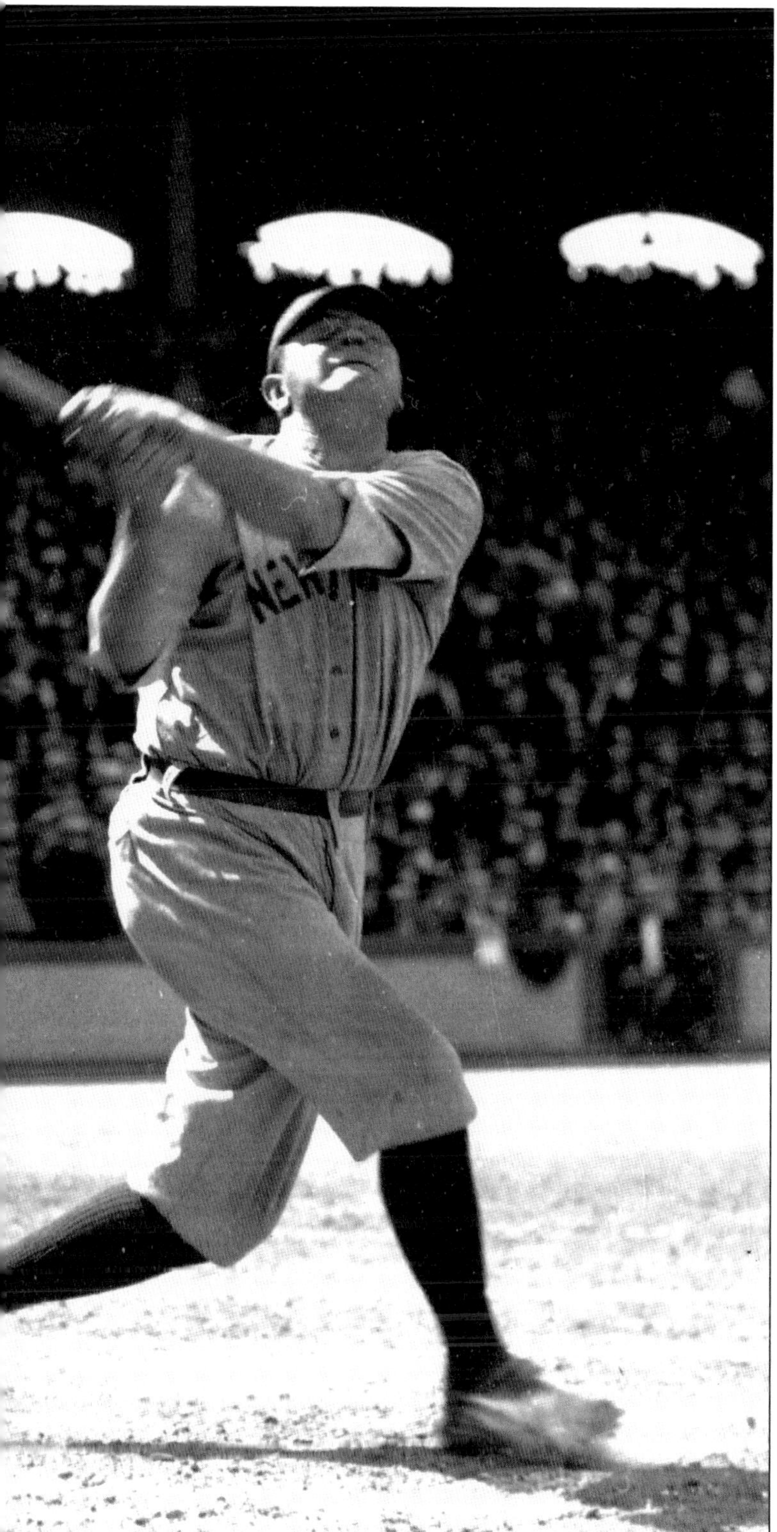

This spread shows Ruth taking one of his mighty cuts during a contest at Chicago's Comiskey Park. Ray Schalk is the White Sox catcher.

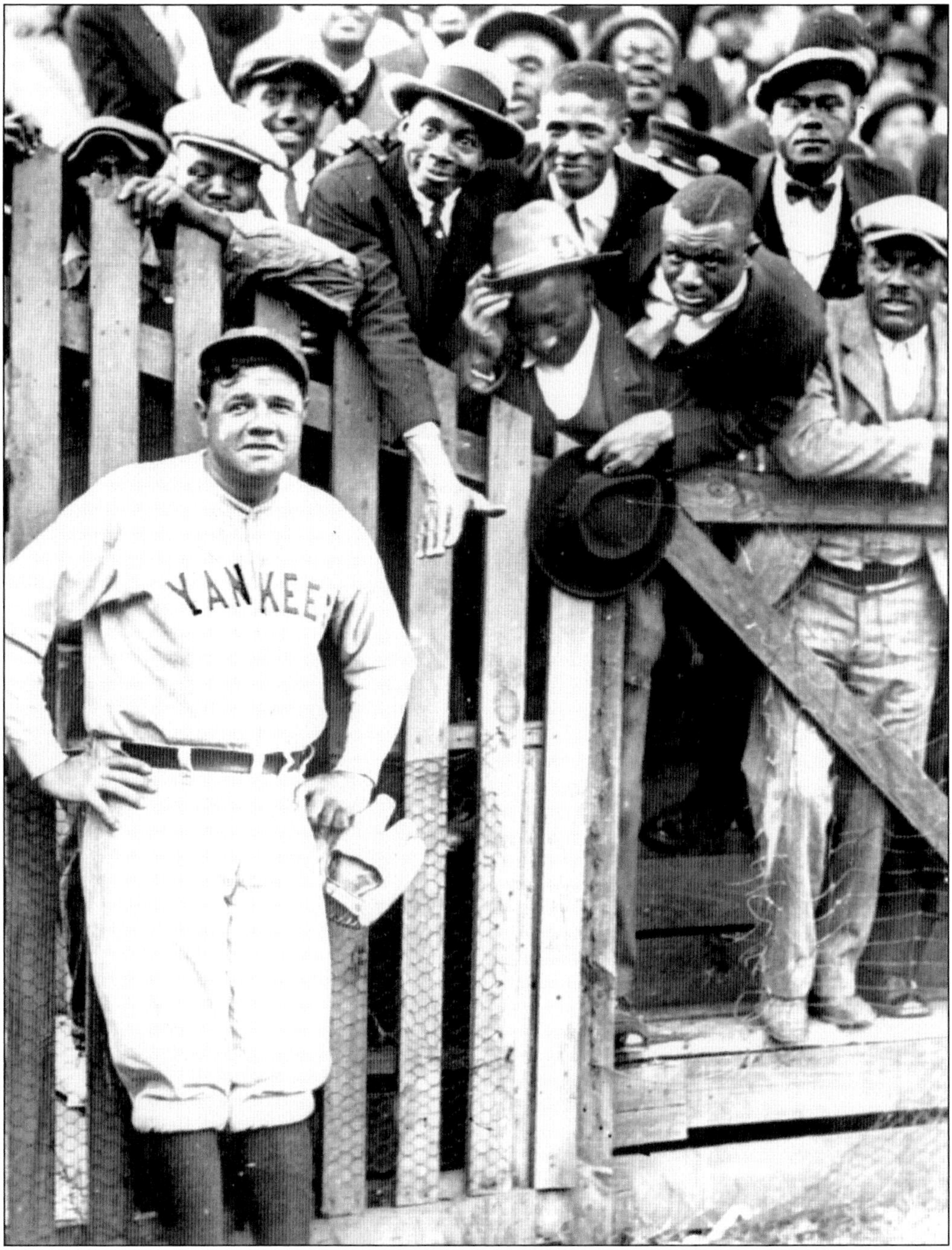

Above is a fabulous photograph of a barnstorming Ruth visiting with young African American fans. The Babe did not discriminate: he loved adulation, whomever it came from.

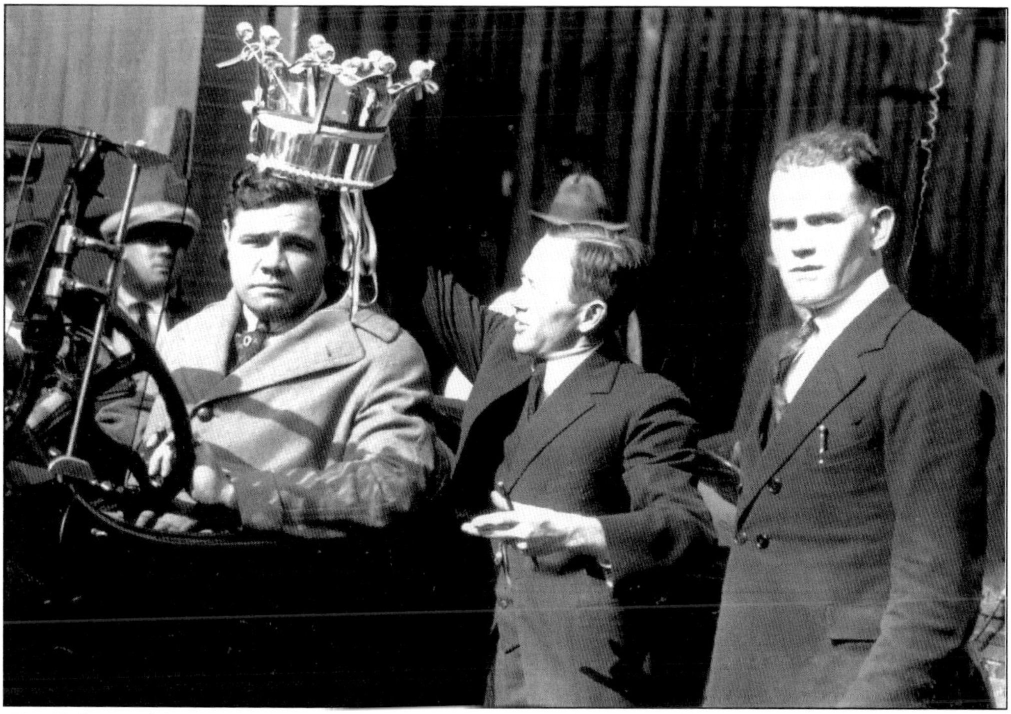

The Sultan of Swat is crowned by manager Miller Huggins right after the end of the incredible 1927 season. Huggins seems to be having fun, but Ruth does not want to be in the victory parade. A bodyguard stands on the right.

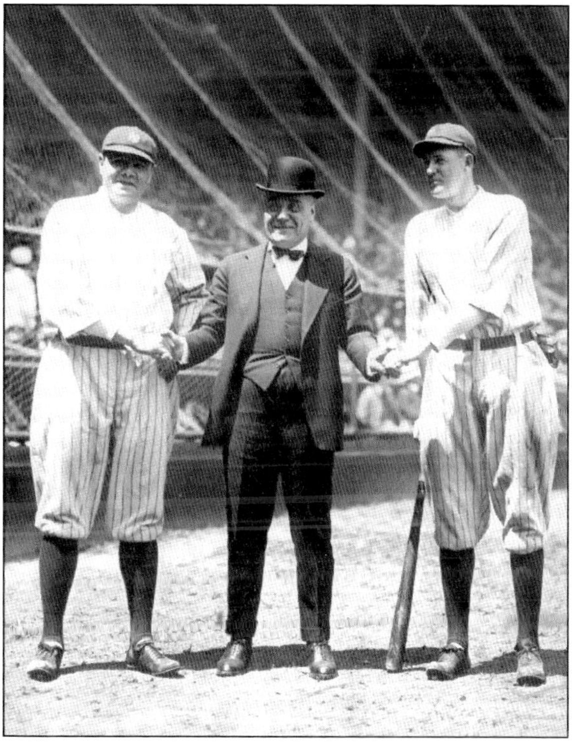

The Babe (left) and Bob Meusel flank Yankees owner Jacob Ruppert. In 1925, it was Meusel who won the only batting title not captured by Ruth in his early years in New York.

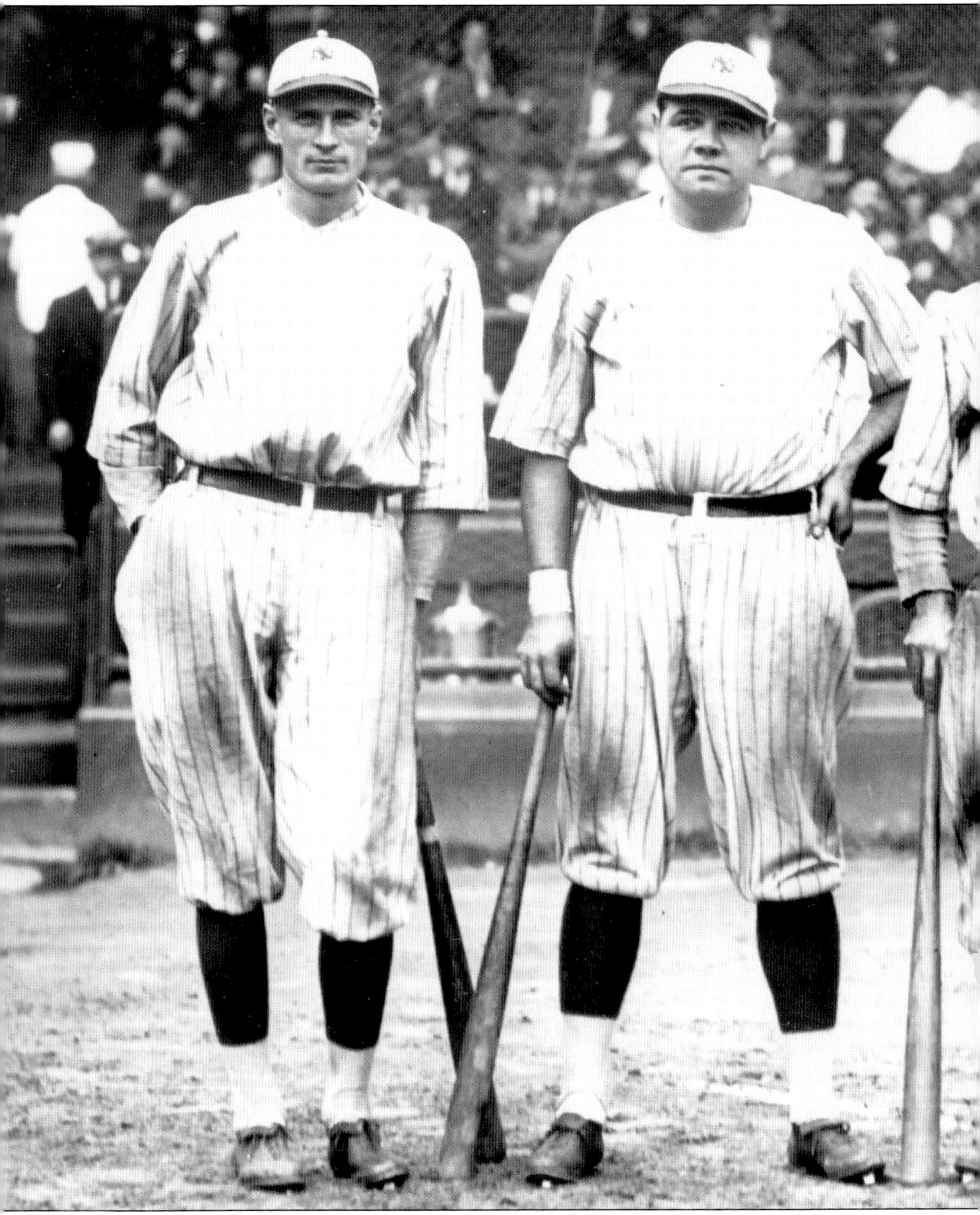

This lineup was called Murderers' Row in 1921. After only one season in New York, Ruth had changed the game and struck fear into the hearts of pitchers around the American League. With the string of sluggers the Yankees put together, manager Miller Huggins could count on dominating the opposition. Seen from left to right are Wally Pipp, the Babe, Roger Peckinpaugh,

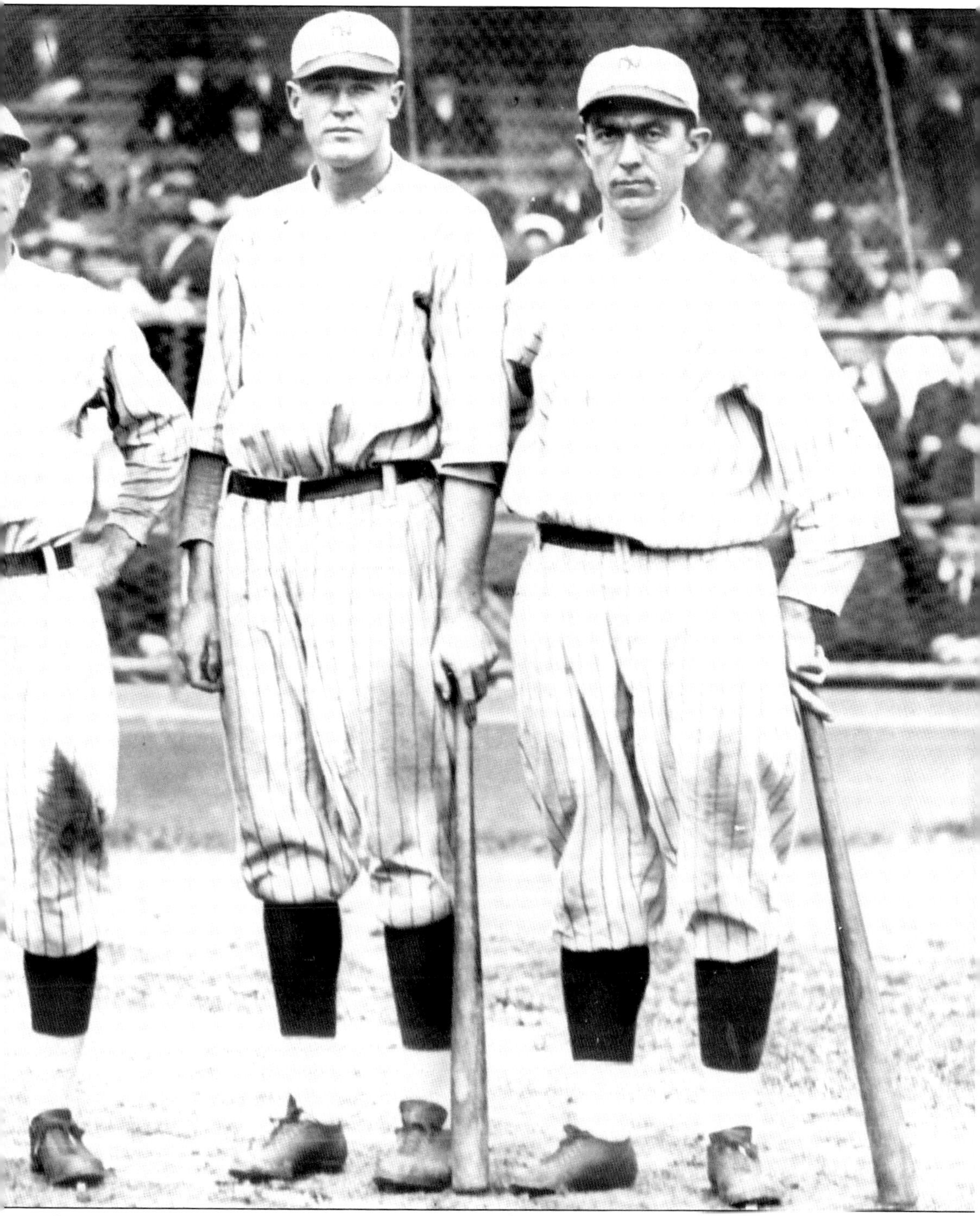

Bob Meusel, and Frank "Home Run" Baker. The fabulous five was often photographed, but this image is easy to date because the Yankees wore white hats in only one year of their existence: 1921. The quintet slammed 108 home runs that year, with Ruth chalking up a mind-boggling 59 of them.

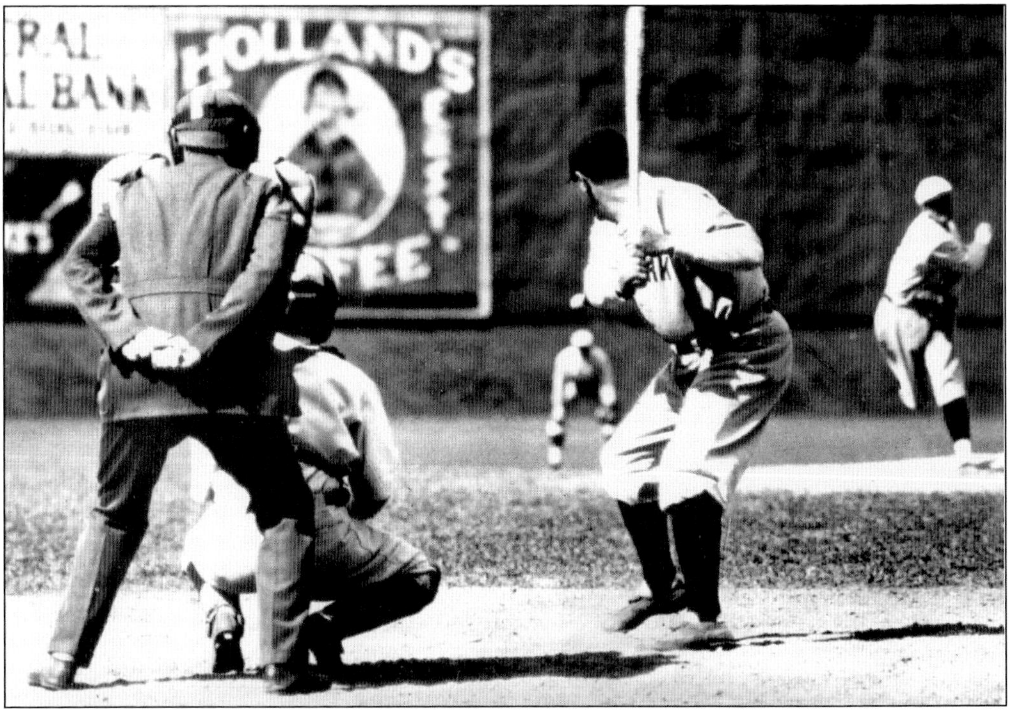
HOLLAND'S

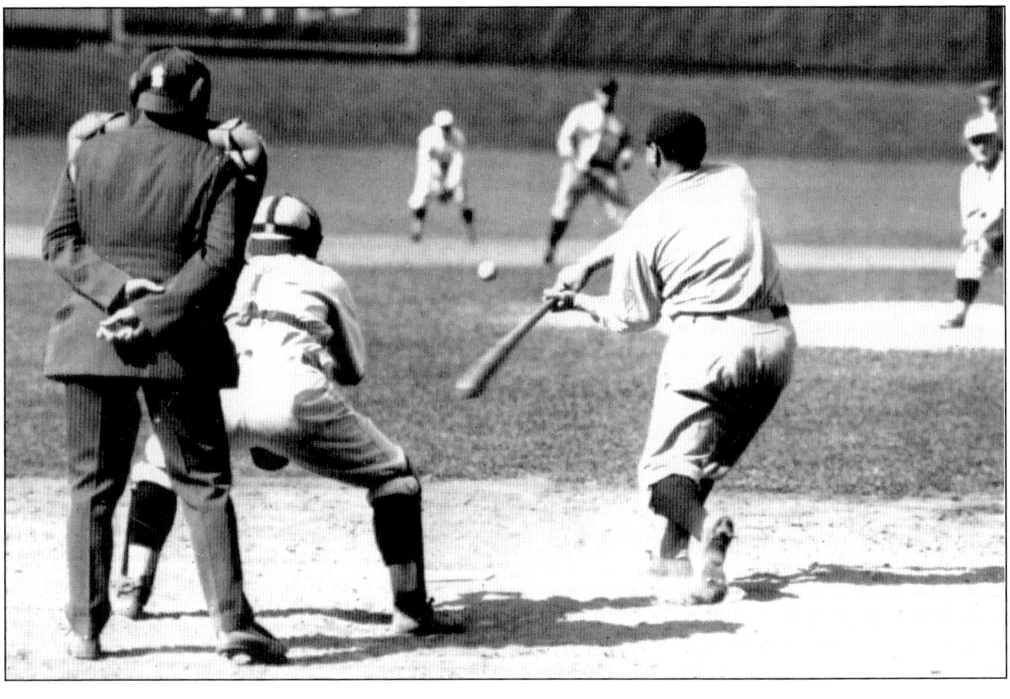

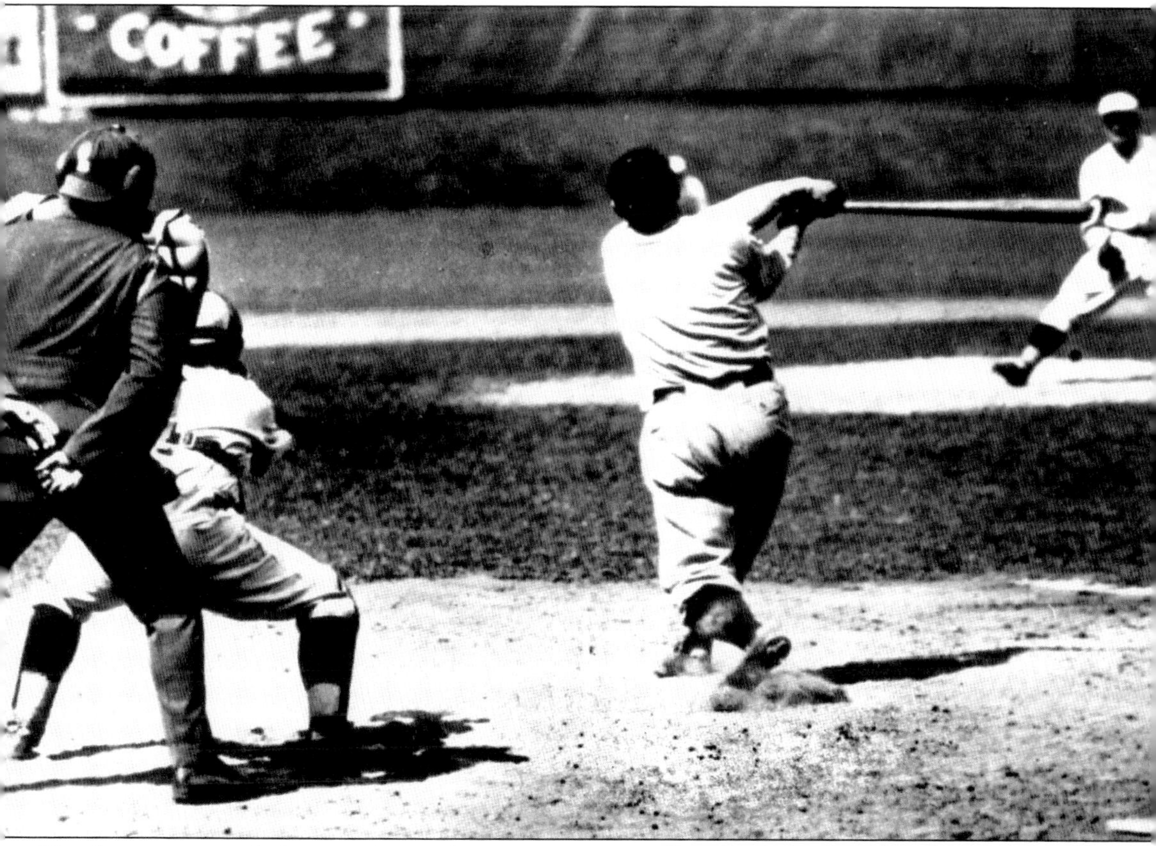

The three sequential photographs on these two pages are about torque. They illustrate clearly how Ruth put everything he had into every swing. No player before him had ever done this; years earlier, Ruth's style actually would have been discouraged as unproductive technique. But Ruth combined a keen eye with a body that could create a startling bat speed. Not only could Ruth screw himself into the ground after a mighty cut, but his vision allowed him to make contact so often that he statistically destroyed pitchers in the American League for 21 years. From the time of his last season in Boston, when Ruth had become an outfielder on the days when he was not pitching, until 1933, his next-to-last season in New York, Ruth led the league in one category or another. For most of his years in a Yankee uniform, the Babe led the world in runs scored, home runs, RBIs, on-base percentage, and slugging percentage. Before Ruth, a successful hitter used his bat strategically, knocking line drives over infielders, moving runners along, or occasionally socking a fat pitch deep into the outfield. Sometimes such swats would go out of the park, but in the dead-ball era, this was rare. For example, Frank Baker earned the nickname "Home Run" because of his game-winning homers on consecutive days during the 1911 World Series. But Home Run Baker never hit more than 12 in a year, though he led the league four times in round trips. Imagine the shock to fans when Ruth bashed 29 out of the park in 1919, although he was not even an everyday outfielder. And when he became a full-time right fielder in 1920, the home run total ballooned to 54, and he drove in 137 runs at the same time. His numbers for bases on balls also exploded, as he received 148 free passes at a time when the century mark had seldom been topped before. There is no need to run through the Babe's incredible lifetime statistics, but what these numbers make clear is that the Babe was a phenomenon like none other baseball had ever seen. After he had demonstrated how he could flatten a baseball, kids, trainers, and managers began looking for others who might be able to duplicate Babe's feats.

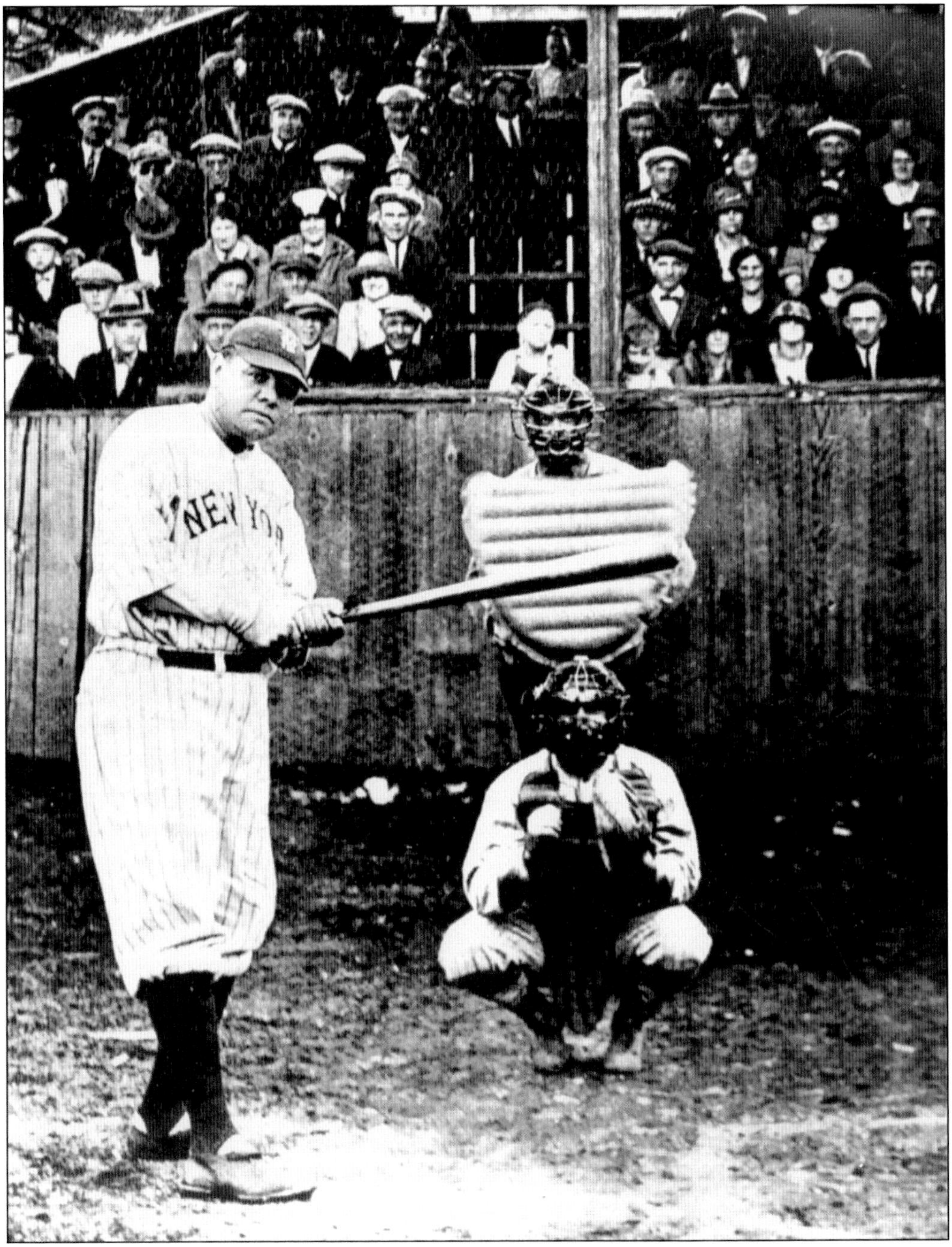

The Babe really got around. When not starring in Yankee Stadium during the summer, he would be barnstorming across America, greeting fans at events nationwide, and appearing in the movies—both shorts and feature-length films. Here, Ruth takes his batting stance in a baseball film from the early 1920s. Ruth did not have to share many headlines in New York from the time he arrived in 1920 until the season of 1925, when the young Lou Gehrig came into the spotlight.

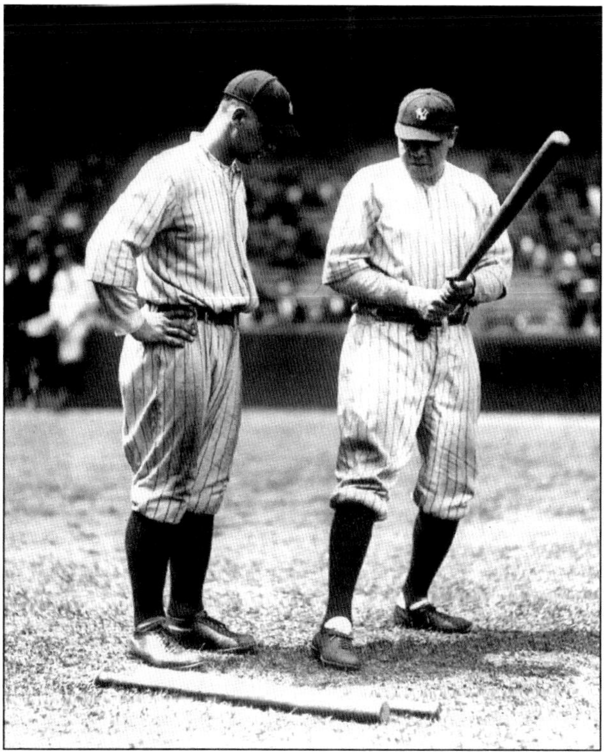

Gehrig and Ruth get together for photographs in two different sessions. Their relationship was more or less contentious during their many years together with the Yankees, but fanatics and photographers always wanted to see the dynamic duo together, no matter how things were going between them.

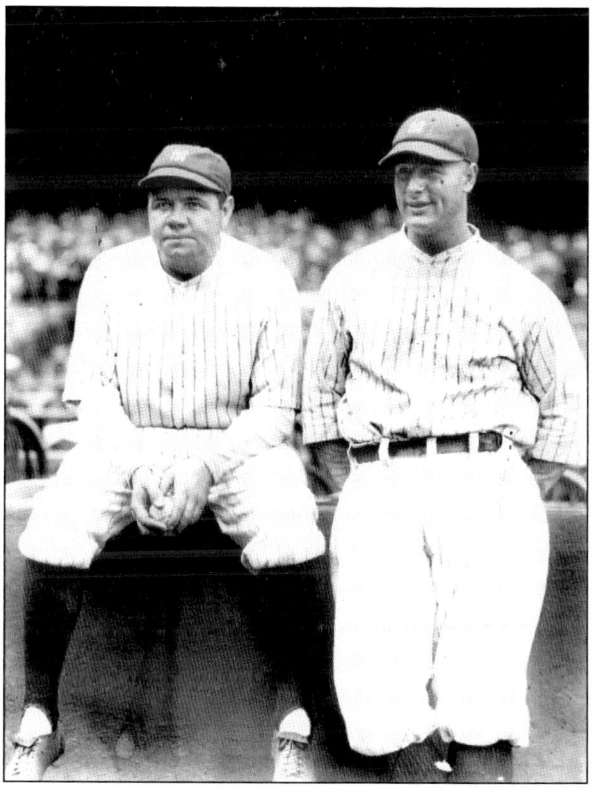

Lou Gehrig

Career 1923–1939 all in New York

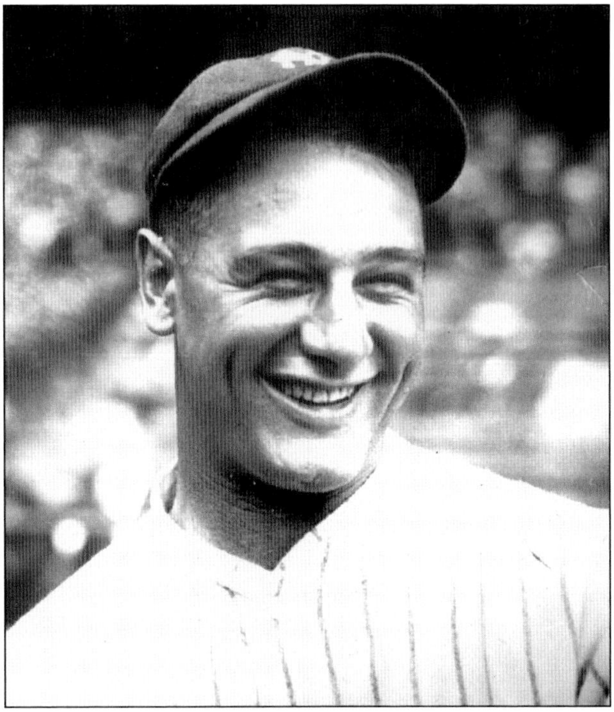

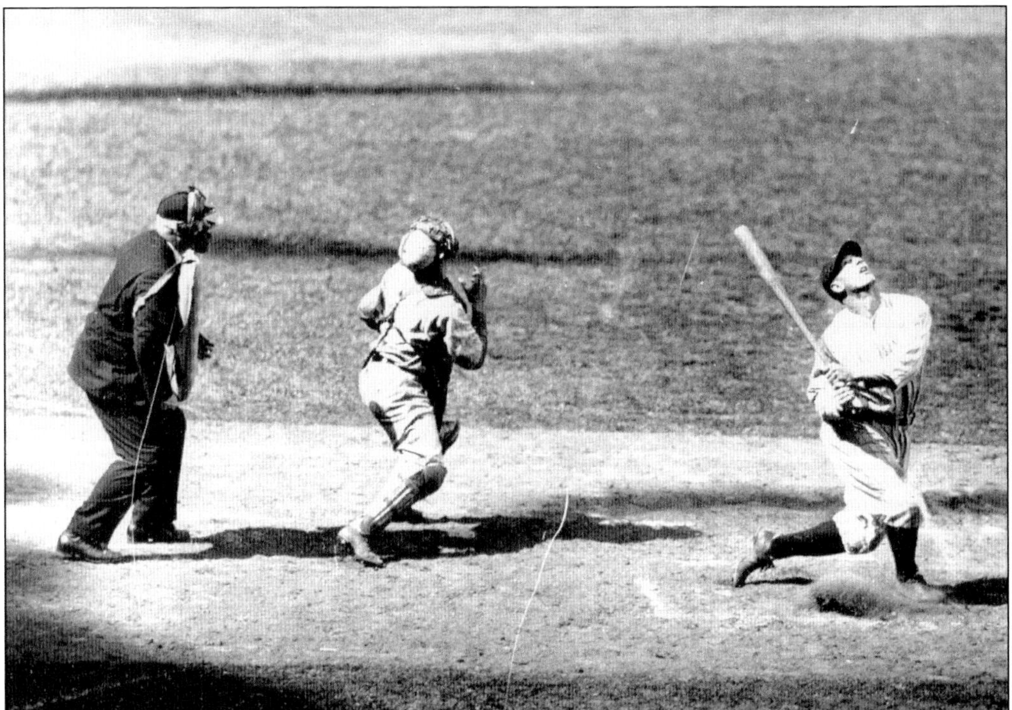

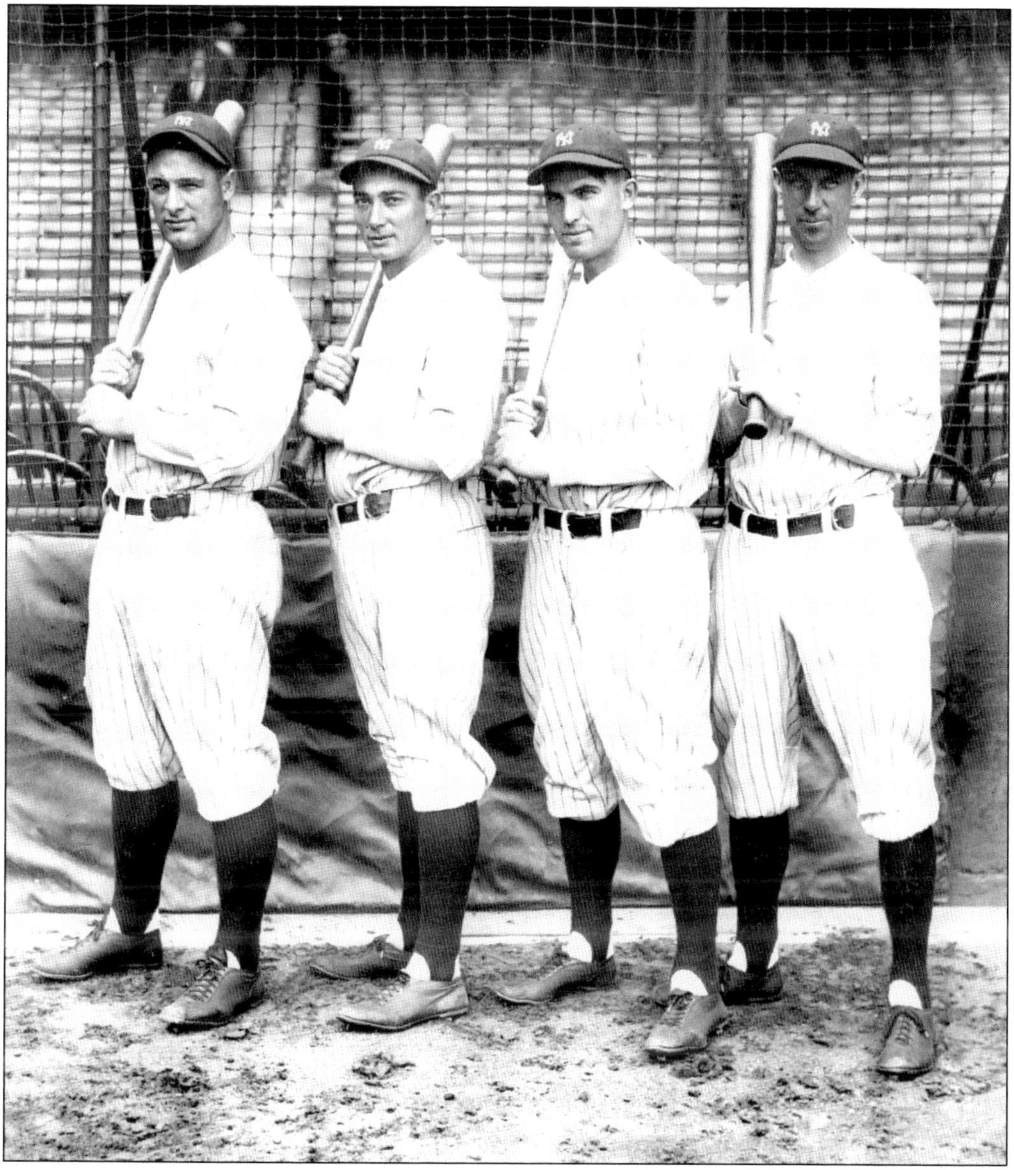

Under normal circumstances, Lou Gehrig would have been the king of his team, the supreme hero of his city. But he was always in Babe Ruth's shadow. Gehrig put up massive numbers almost every year, but for most of his career, he looked like the second man in line. Many managers would have preferred Gehrig's silent work ethic to Ruth's boisterous style. Gehrig never made off-field headlines—he just worked hard, did his job between the lines, and lived quietly. In the bottom photograph on the opposite page, Gehrig's powerful follow-through is evident. It looks like he hit a pop-up, but he was so strong that the ball may have been on its way over the fence. Above is a shot of the 1927 Yankees infield, the best in baseball at that time. From left to right are first baseman Lou Gehrig, second baseman Tony Lazzeri, shortstop Mark Koenig, and third baseman Joe Dugan. Each one of these athletes could punish a baseball, but Gehrig stood head and shoulders above the others. The statistics that he generated from 1926 to 1938 would have topped all others in slugging categories were it not for his teammate and unofficial nemesis, Babe Ruth.

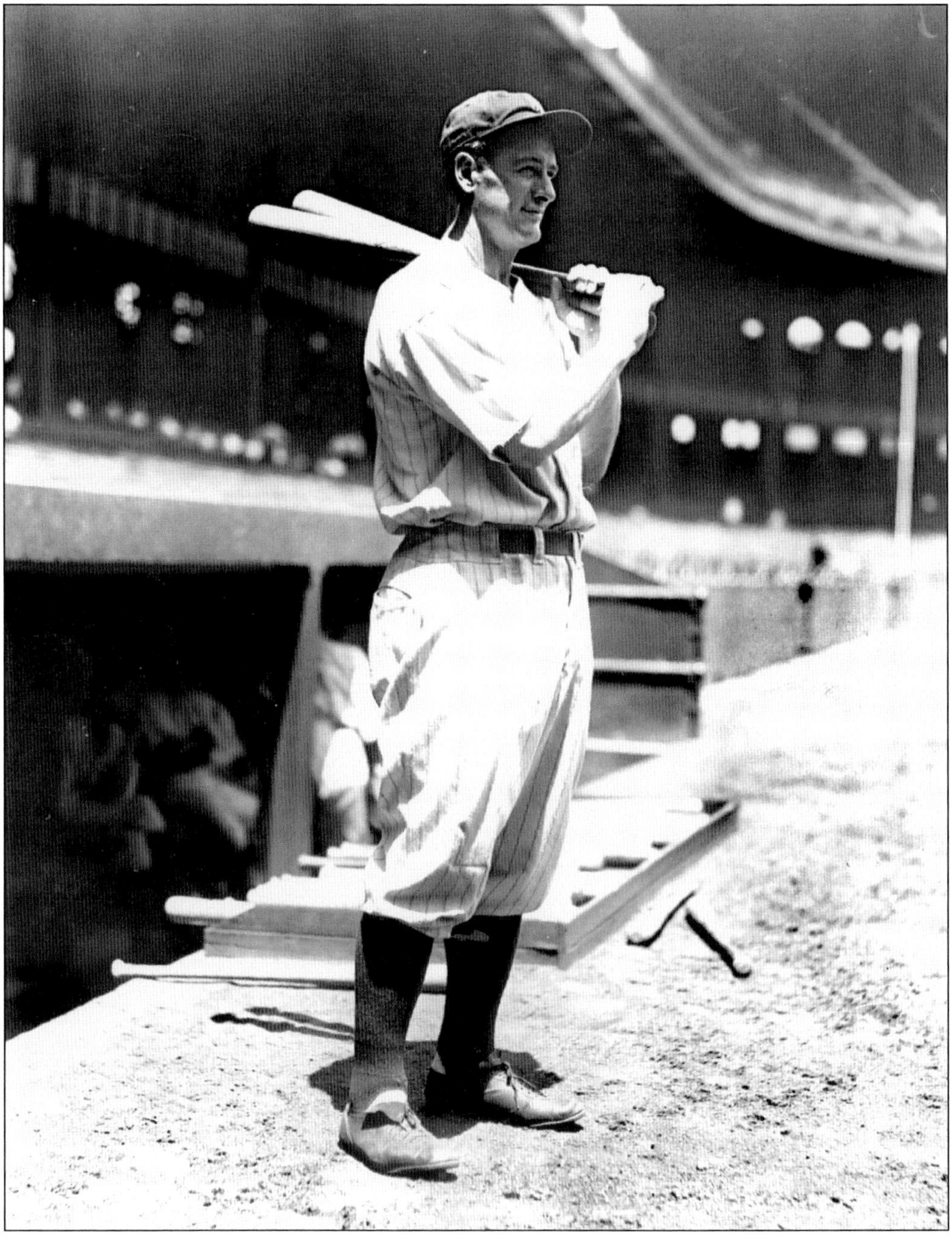

Gehrig was shy in social situations, but he was not hesitant to attack a baseball. Ruth received most of the attention from fans and reporters, but Gehrig over-reached him in the record books a number of times. He holds the all-time single-season RBI mark in the American League with 184, and though his home run total was nowhere near Ruth's, he holds the record for the most grand slams with 23. Gehrig was a run-producing machine, driving in 150 runs or more in seven different years and scoring more than 130 runs five times. In those years, he led the American League five times in RBIs and four times in runs.

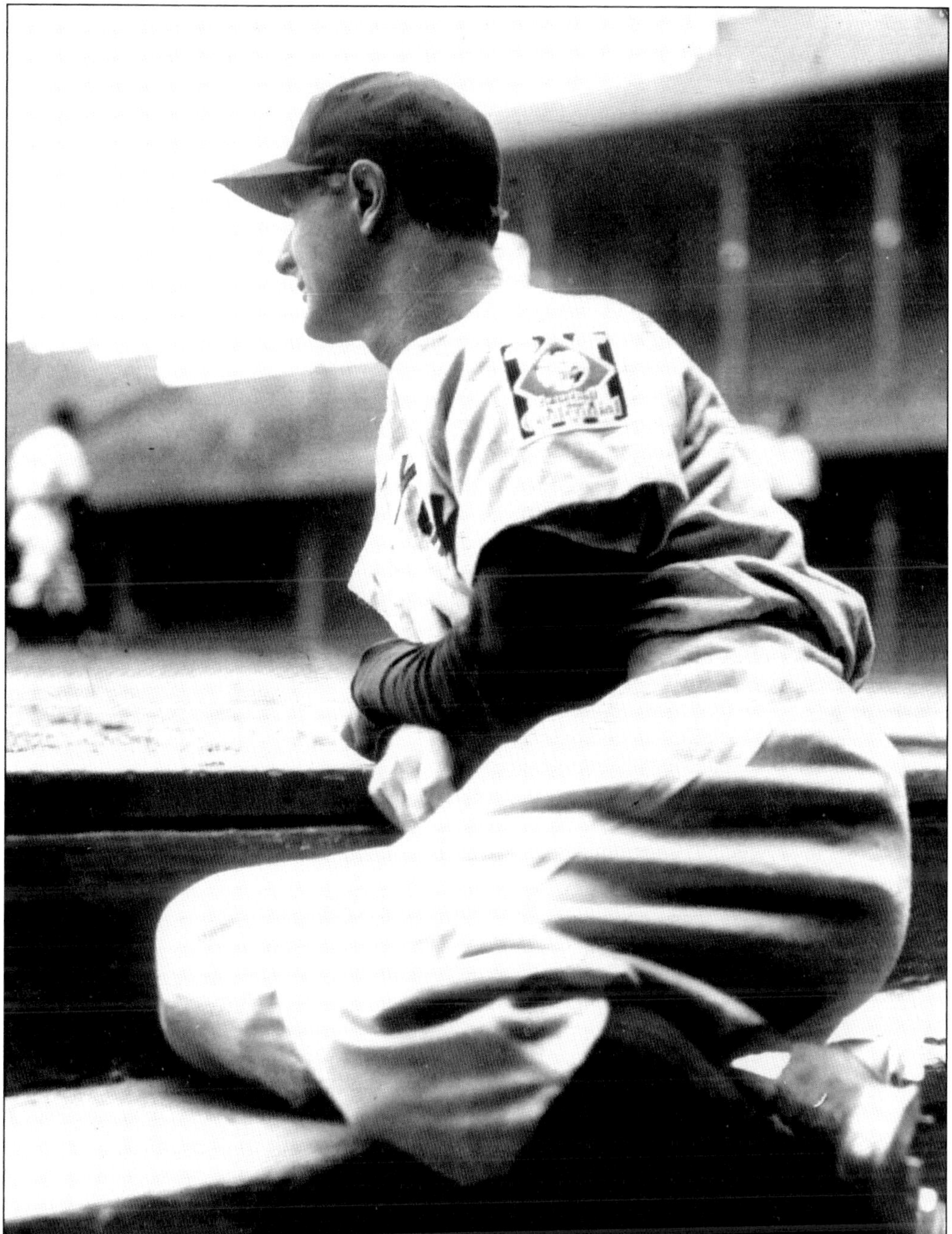

Lou Gehrig did more than hit home runs, usually topping Ruth in doubles and triples. In 1927, Gehrig led the league in doubles with 52, while the Babe only recorded 29. The next year Gehrig again ruled, with 47 doubles versus Ruth's 29. Gehrig's lifetime totals show 534 doubles and 163 triples, as compared to the Babe's 506 doubles and 136 triples, which Ruth produced with 398 more at-bats. The only triple crown Gehrig won was in 1934, when he banged out 49 homers, knocked in 165 runs, and batted .363. Ruth also won but a single triple crown.

Home Run Baker

Career 1908–1922 New York 1916–1922

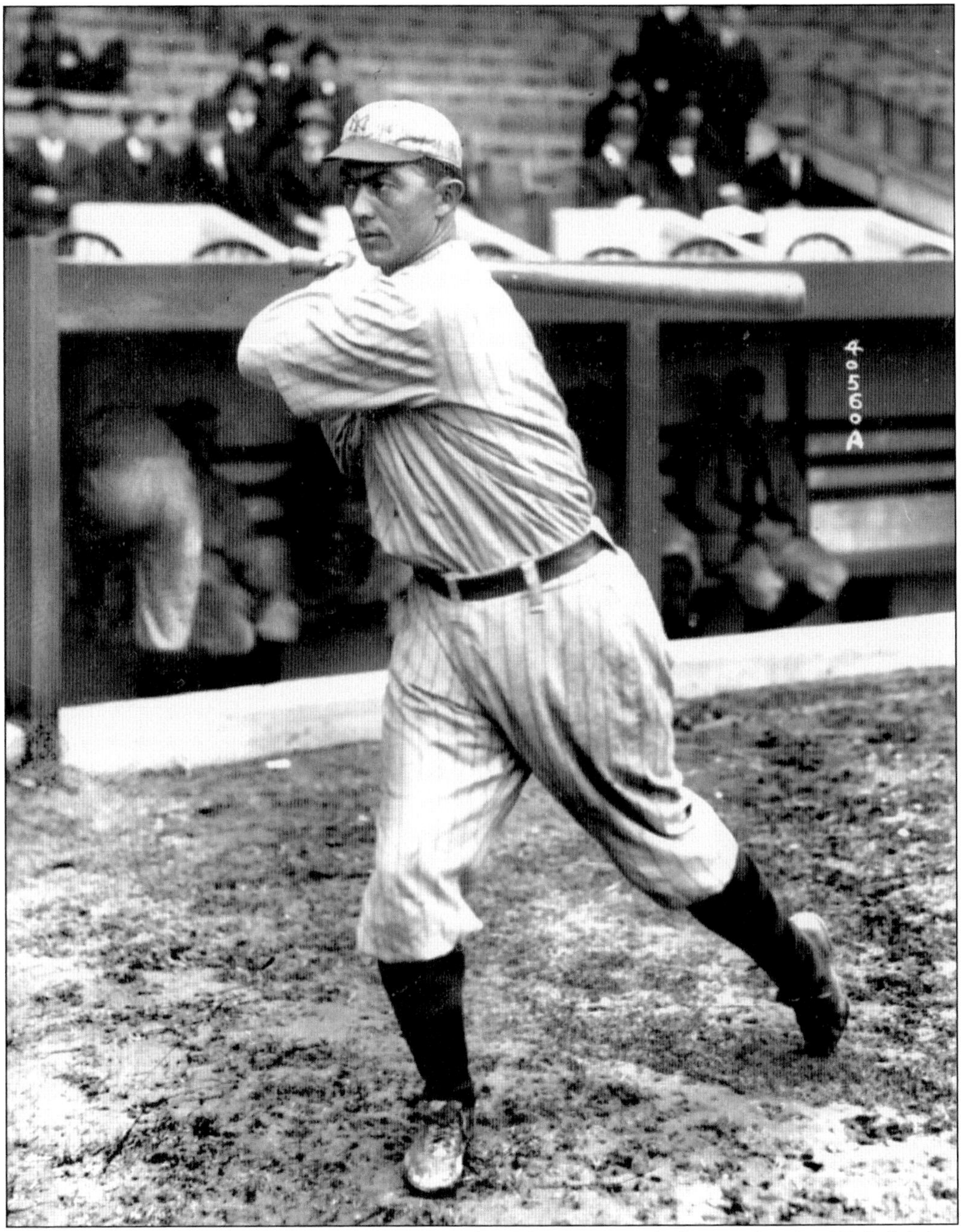

Frank "Home Run" Baker gained fame as a third baseman and slugger for the Philadelphia Athletics in the first seven years of his major-league career. Baker joined the Yankees in 1916, but he never again led the league in home runs after he left Philly. His .307 lifetime mark helped him earn election into the Baseball Hall of Fame. Baker's career lasted just long enough for him to share a roster spot with the real home run king, Babe Ruth.

MARK KOENIG

CAREER 1925–1936   NEW YORK 1925–1930, 1935–1936

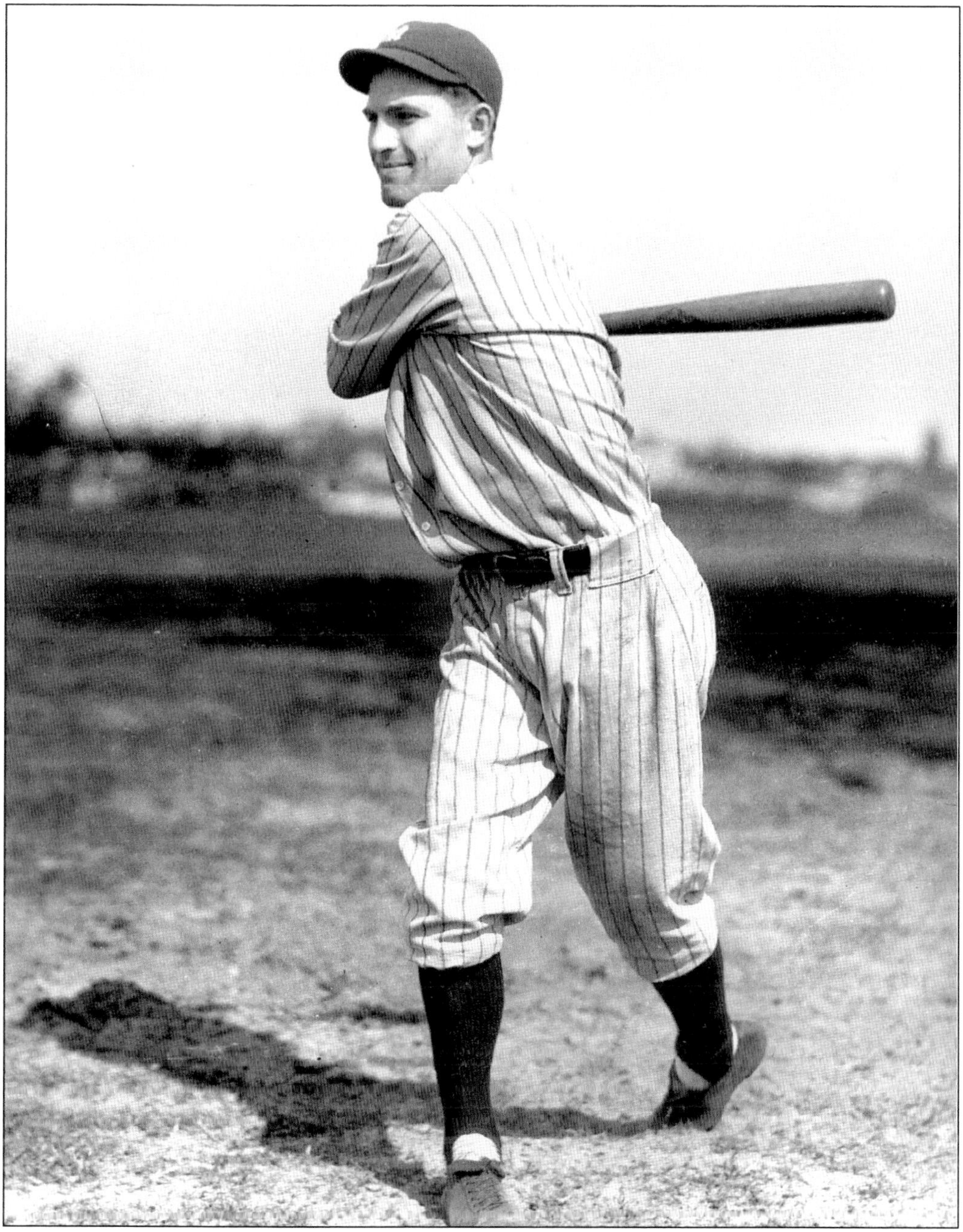

In 1925, Mark Koenig was added to the Yankees roster, and by the following year he was starting at shortstop. He was paid for his dependable glove, but Koenig could make things happen in the batter's box, as well. In 1928, he hit .319, his second-highest mark ever. He was a leading run scorer for the team, crossing home 93 times in 1926, 99 times in 1927, and 89 times in 1928. Koenig closed out his career in the National League with the Giants.

JOE DUGAN

CAREER 1917–1931 NEW YORK 1922–1928

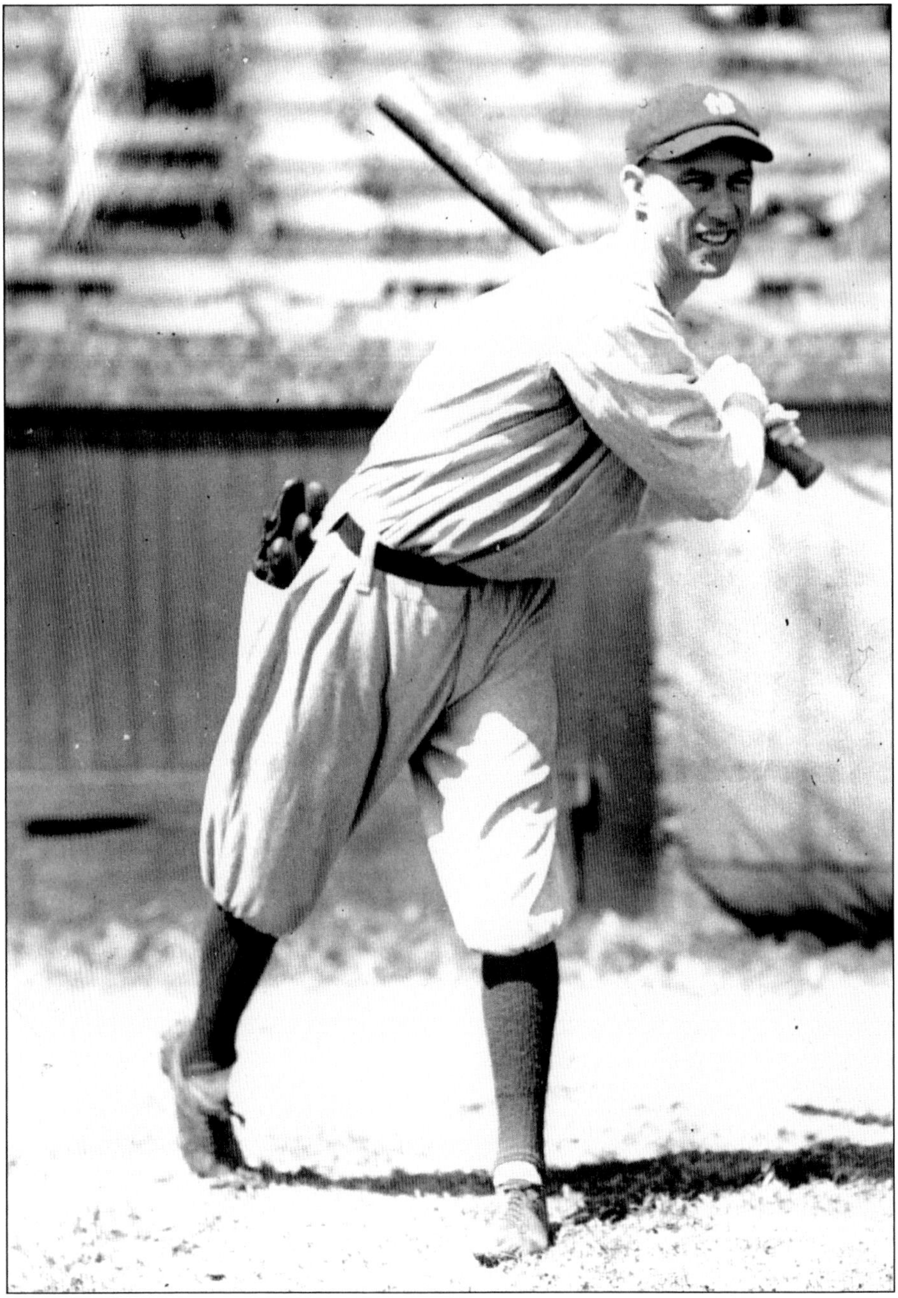

Joe Dugan held down third base for the Yankees as they won pennants in the years 1922, 1923, 1926, 1927, and 1928. He batted in the high .200s or low .300s each year in New York. Dugan hit 30 doubles in 1923 and 31 in 1924, and he played in nearly every game for the Yanks in those years. Dugan's good timing landed him in 25 World Series games, where he batted .267 with one homer and eight RBIs.

AARON WARD

CAREER 1917–1928 NEW YORK 1917–1926

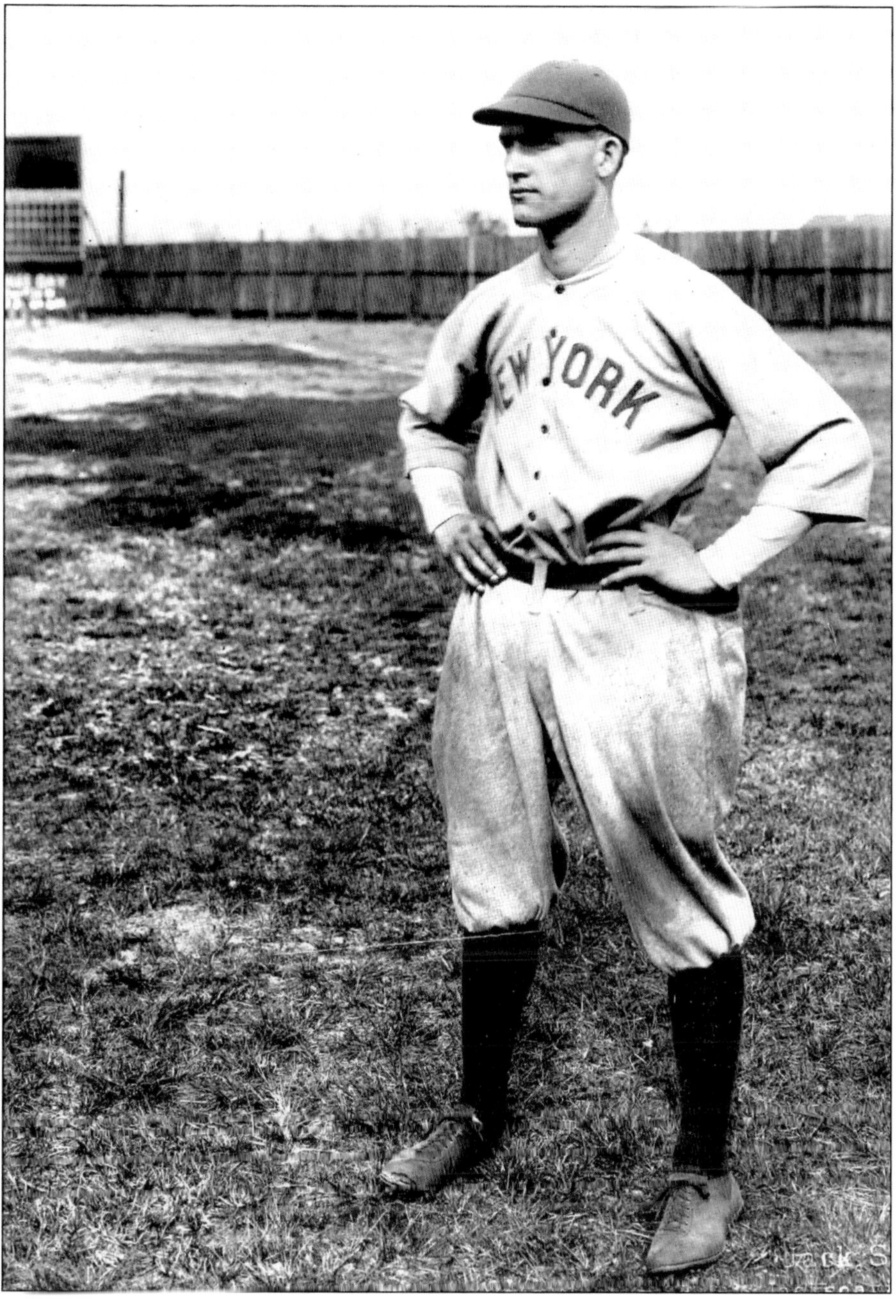

Aaron Ward came to the New York Americans before they became league dominators, but he lasted long enough in a Yankees uniform to see action in three World Series. He batted .286 over 19 games, with 3 home runs and 9 runs batted in. Hired mainly for his glove work, Ward was a good enough hitter to hold on to his job at second base for six full seasons, until the arrival of Tony Lazzeri.

Lefty O'Doul

Career 1919–1934 New York 1919–1922, 1928, 1933–1934

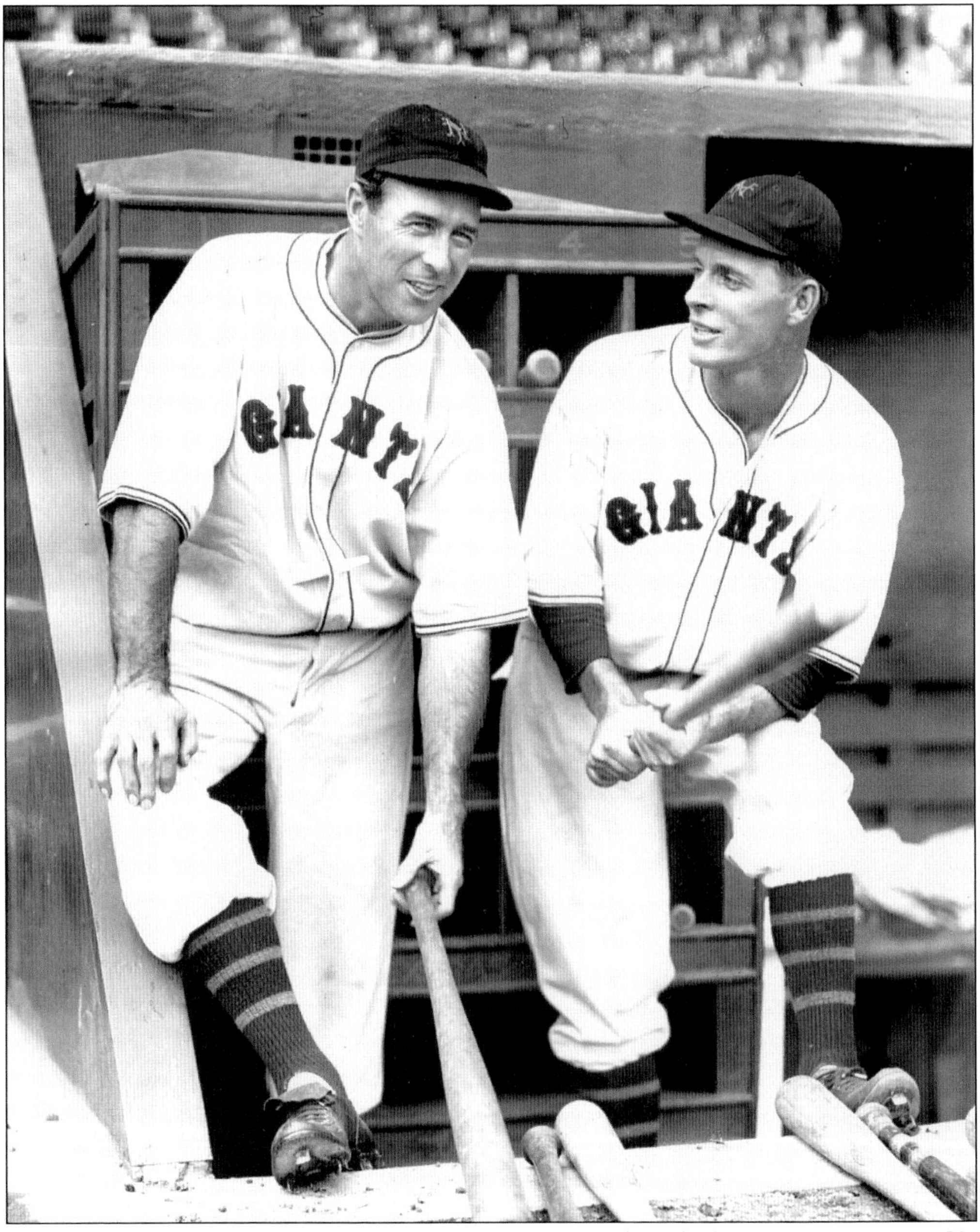

Francis "Lefty" O'Doul (on left), seen here with George Watkins, had a very strange career. He preferred the Pacific Coast League to the majors, and he was over 30 years old when he played his first full National League season. O'Doul came up with the Yankees in 1919, but he never played more than 19 games with them in a season, and later he ended his career as a New York Giant. O'Doul had his dream season with Philadelphia in 1920, when he hit an eye-popping .398, with 254 hits and a .465 on-base percentage.

FREDDIE LINDSTROM

CAREER 1924–1936 NEW YORK 1924–1932

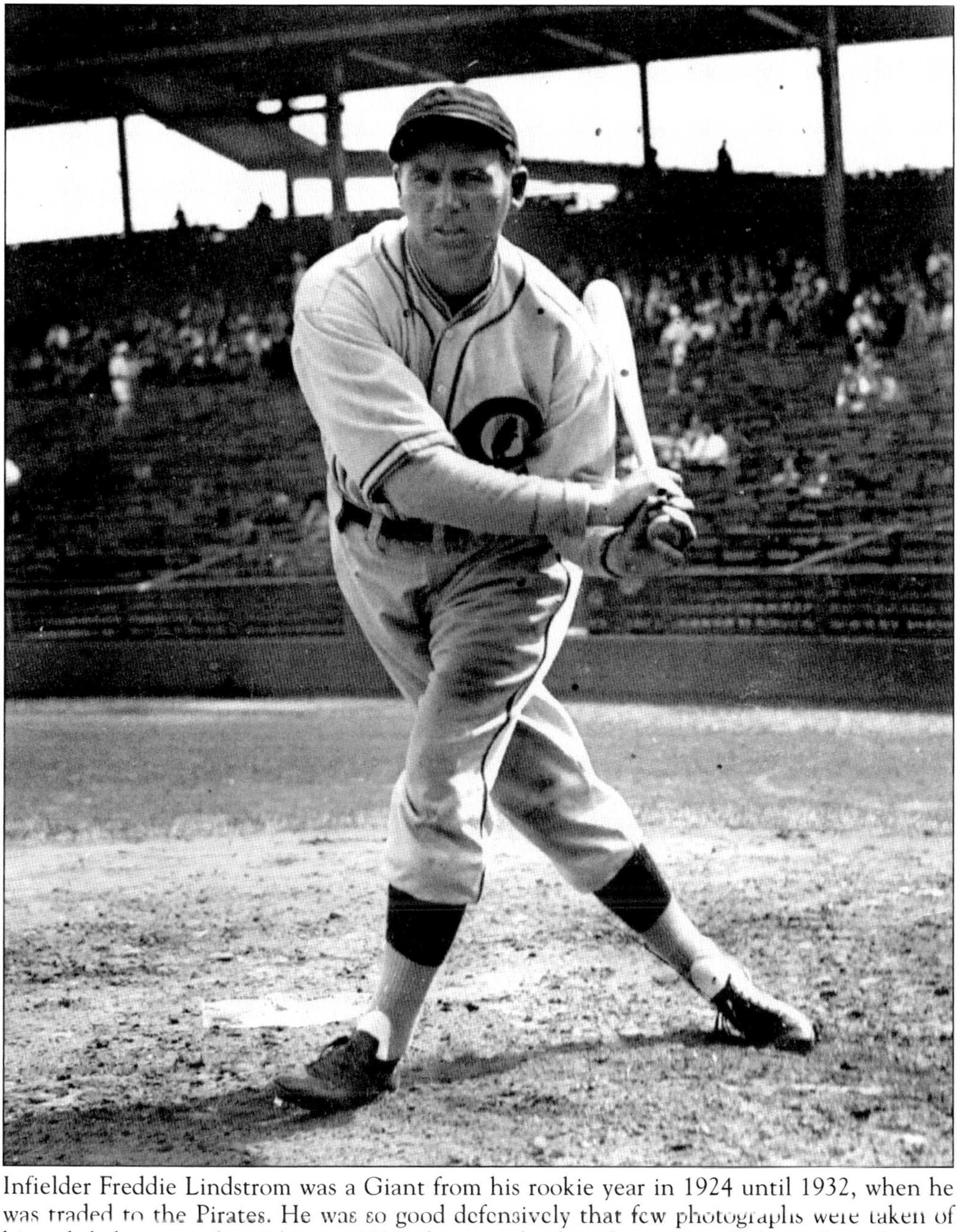

Infielder Freddie Lindstrom was a Giant from his rookie year in 1924 until 1932, when he was traded to the Pirates. He was so good defensively that few photographs were taken of him while he was at bat. This is a 1935 photograph of Lindstrom in a Cubs uniform. He was a .300 hitter six times in 10 years with the Giants, and he led the entire league in hits with 231 in 1928. His most potent year at bat was 1930; although he did not lead the league in any category, Lindstrom had 231 hits, 22 home runs, and 127 runs scored, and he batted .379 with a .575 slugging percentage.

Travis Jackson

Career 1922–1936 all in New York

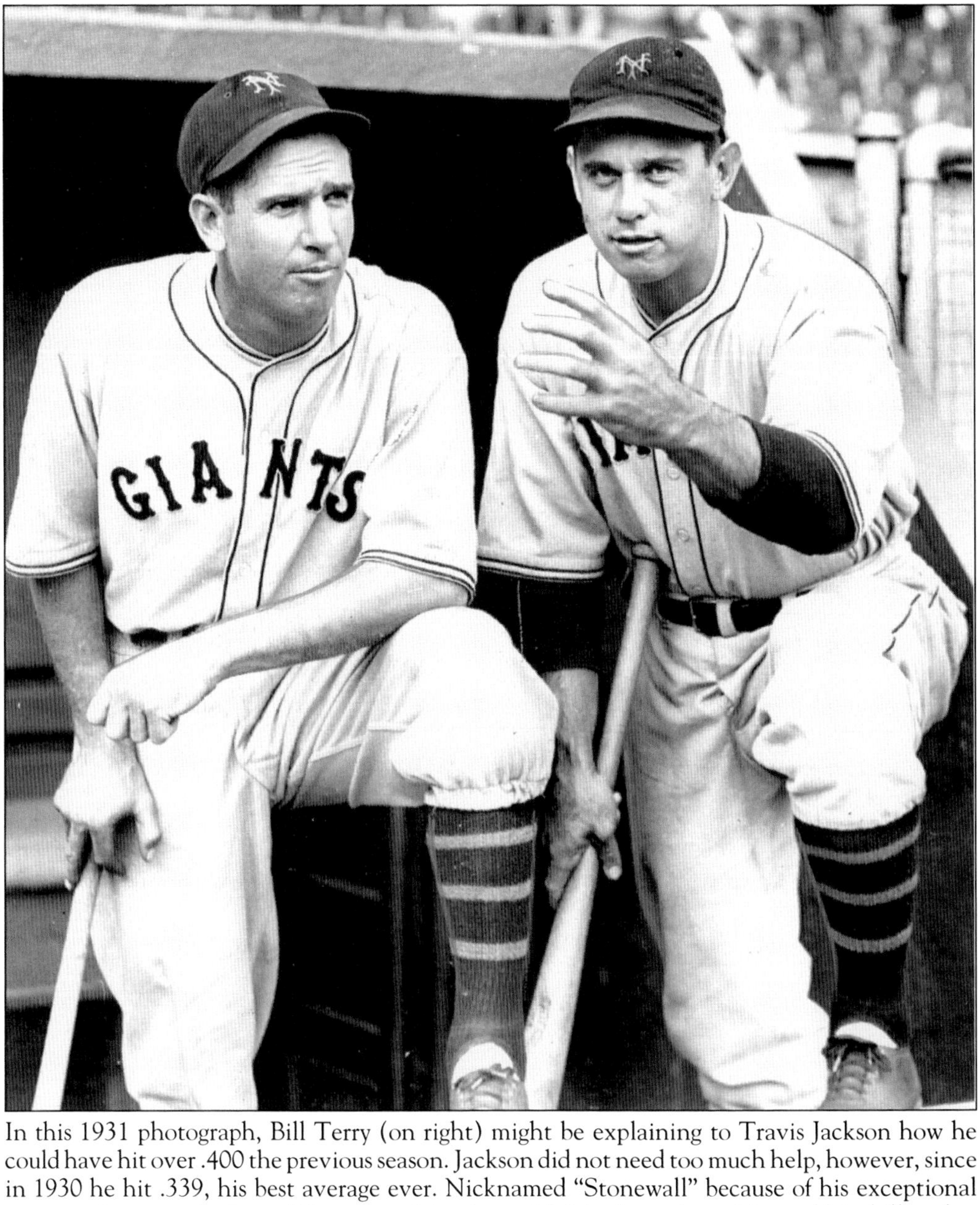

In this 1931 photograph, Bill Terry (on right) might be explaining to Travis Jackson how he could have hit over .400 the previous season. Jackson did not need too much help, however, since in 1930 he hit .339, his best average ever. Nicknamed "Stonewall" because of his exceptional range at shortstop, Jackson did not earn his salary with his glove alone. He used his skills at bat control and the short porches in the Polo Grounds to hit 135 home runs over the years for the Giants. In his top year, 1929, he popped 21 homers. Jackson's lifetime batting average was a very respectable .291, and he had 1,768 hits and 833 runs scored. These merely decent numbers make it clear that it was Jackson's glove that brought him most of his votes for the Hall of Fame. Jackson used that glove in four World Series for the Giants in two different decades, helping the New Yorkers to win the championship in 1933.

EARLE COMBS

CAREER 1924–1935 ALL IN NEW YORK

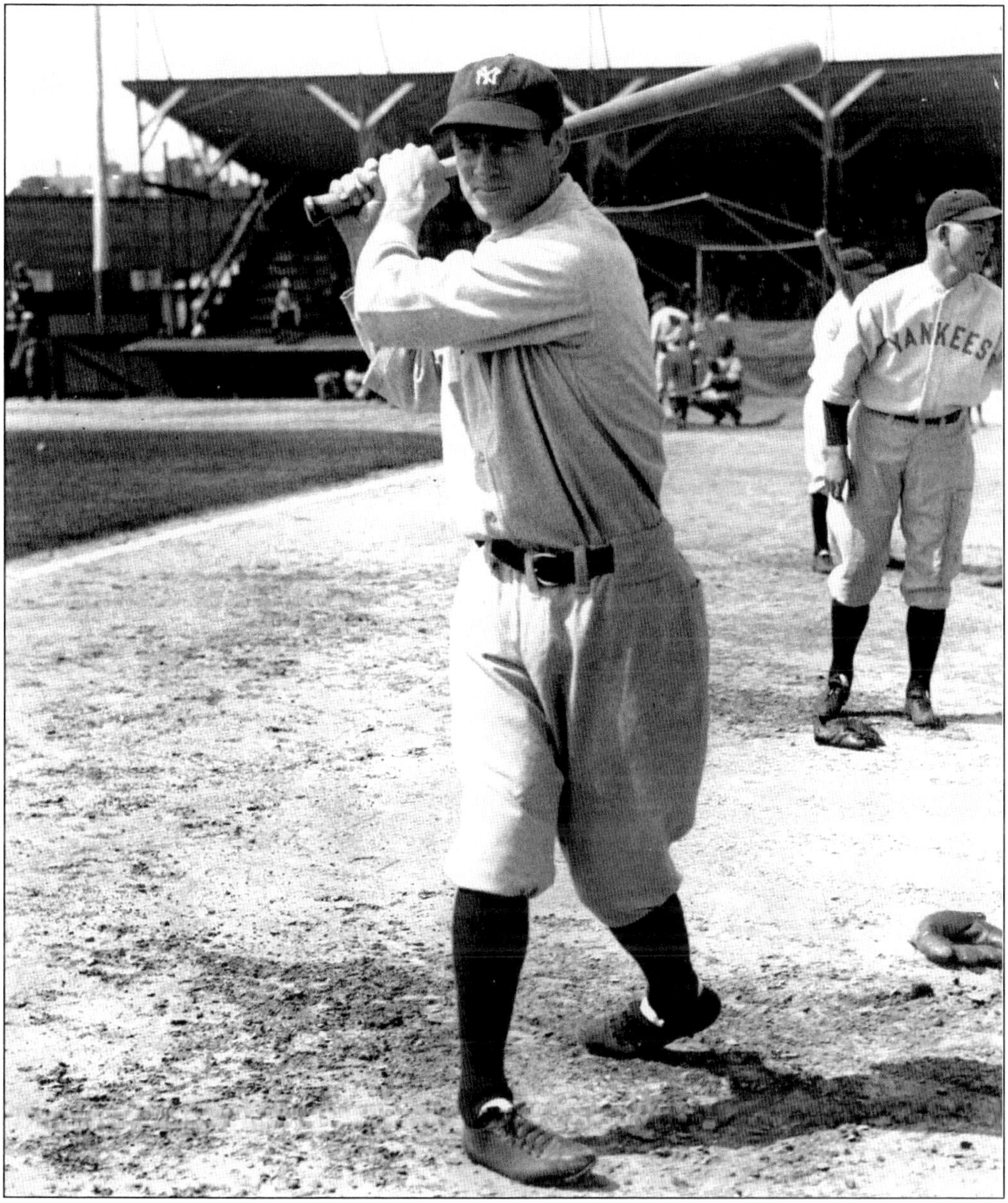

In 1927, Yankee center fielder Earle Combs used his bat to lead the league in hits with 231, and he called on his speed to lead in triples with 23. Combs had 154 triples during his 12-year career and led the American League in triples three times, hitting more than 20 in each of those seasons. While sharing space in team pictures with Ruth, Gehrig, and other Yankees stars, Combs quietly went about hitting .300 every year from 1924 to 1934, without much acclaim. But his manager, Miller Huggins, took notice of Combs's steadiness at the plate and his secure coverage of center field in Yankee Stadium. In 1934, Combs suffered a career-ending injury when he ran into a wall while chasing down a fly ball in St. Louis.

Bill Terry

Playing Career 1923–1936 all in New York

Managerial Career 1932–1941 all in New York

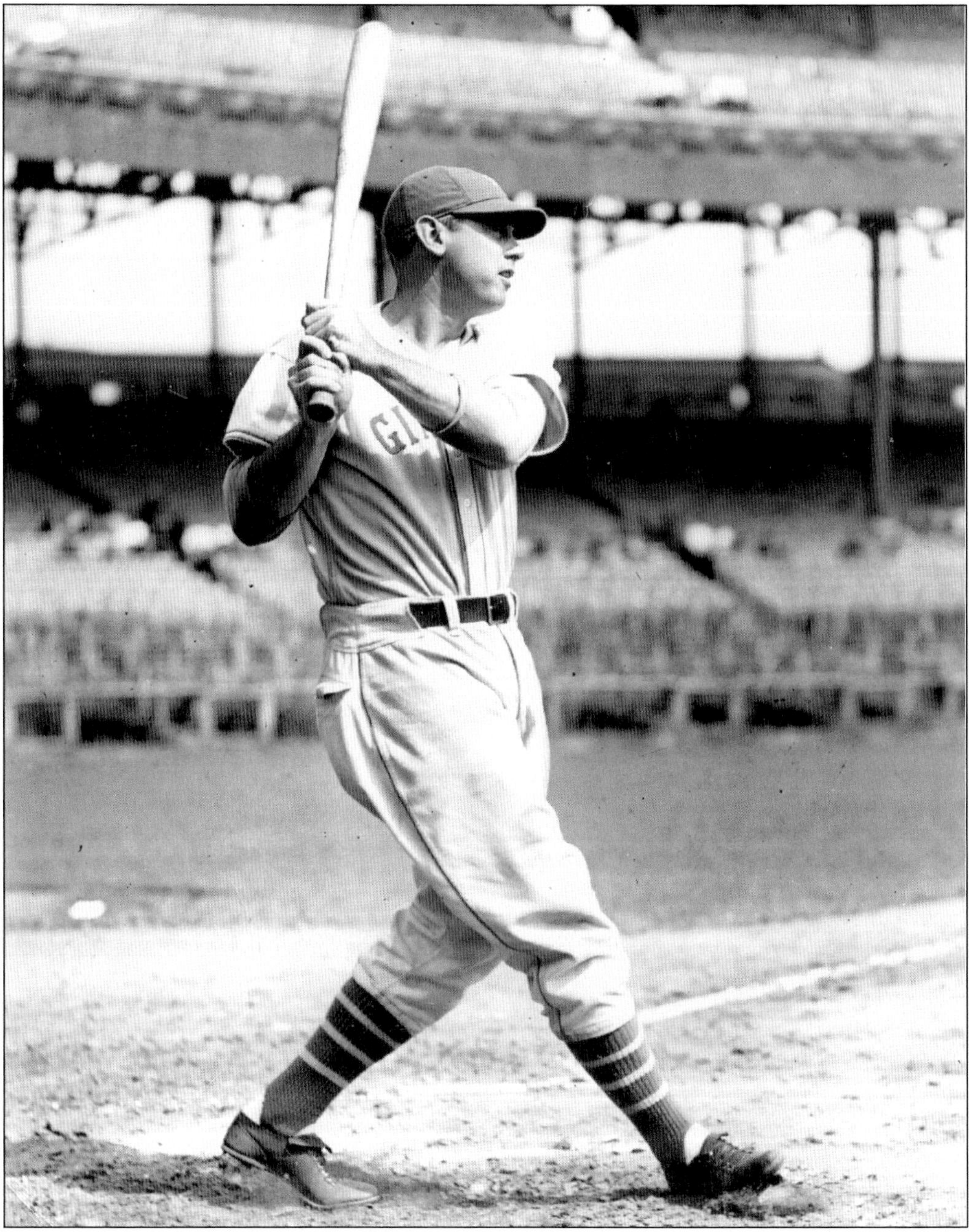

The lifetime batting average of Bill Terry was .341, which ties him for 11th-highest career average in the baseball annals. No more need be said to convince anyone of his hitting ability. Terry hit .401 in 1930 and had 254 hits, two statistics that led the National League. He also had some speed, topping the National League in 1931 with 20 triples.

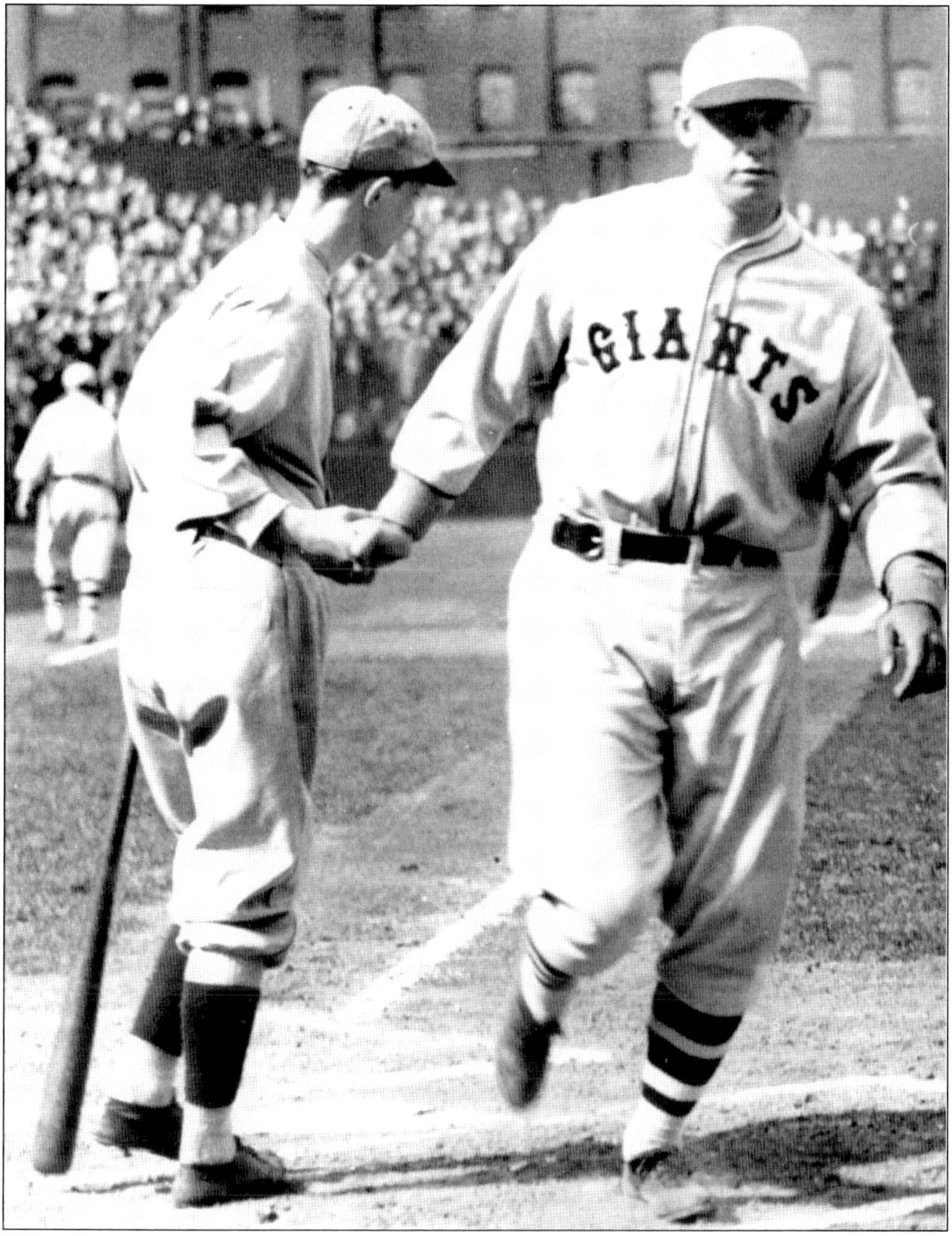

Bill Terry used the deep left- and right-field alleys in the horseshoe-shaped Polo Grounds to hit .350 or higher three times, usually scoring over 100 runs a year. Terry gained the trust of the Giants' front office and was tapped to become New York's manager in 1932, in the midst of his playing career. Terry's 10 years at the helm outlasted his days at first base; he managed for five years after his retirement from playing in 1936. He led the team to win three National League pennants, and his club was in contention almost every year. When John McGraw's health forced him to retire in 1932, Terry quickly got the team back on track, leading the Giants back in 1933 to win the National League pennant and then the World Series.

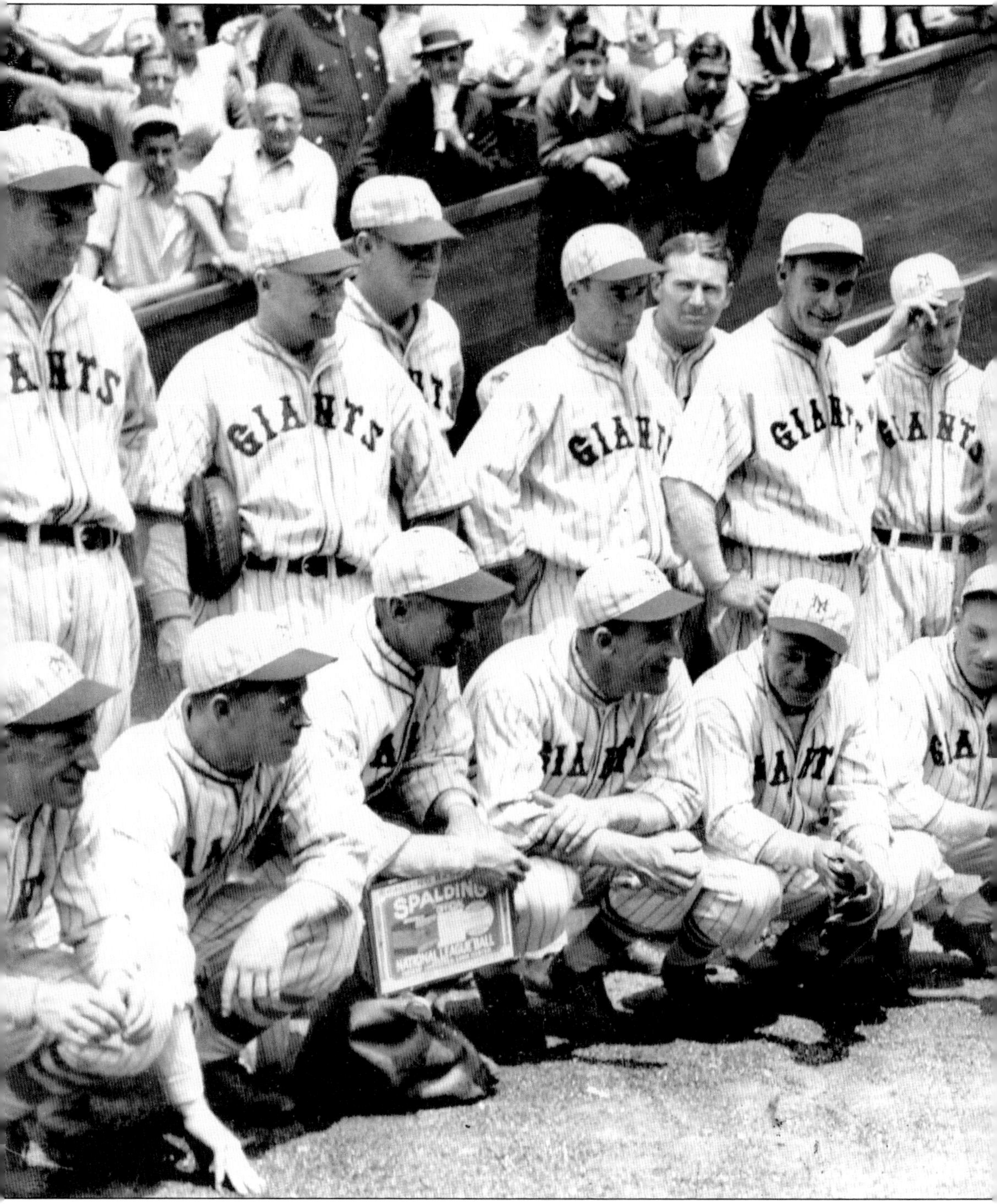

Things change quickly in baseball. The 1931 New York Giants had a good year, finishing in second place, 13 games behind the Cardinals, and leading the National League in batting with a very solid team average of .289. But 1932 was a different story. The players above, remnants of the 1931 team, are smiling and laughing in this 1932 spring training photograph, but they had no idea what the season had in store. From its strong runner-up showing in 1931, the team

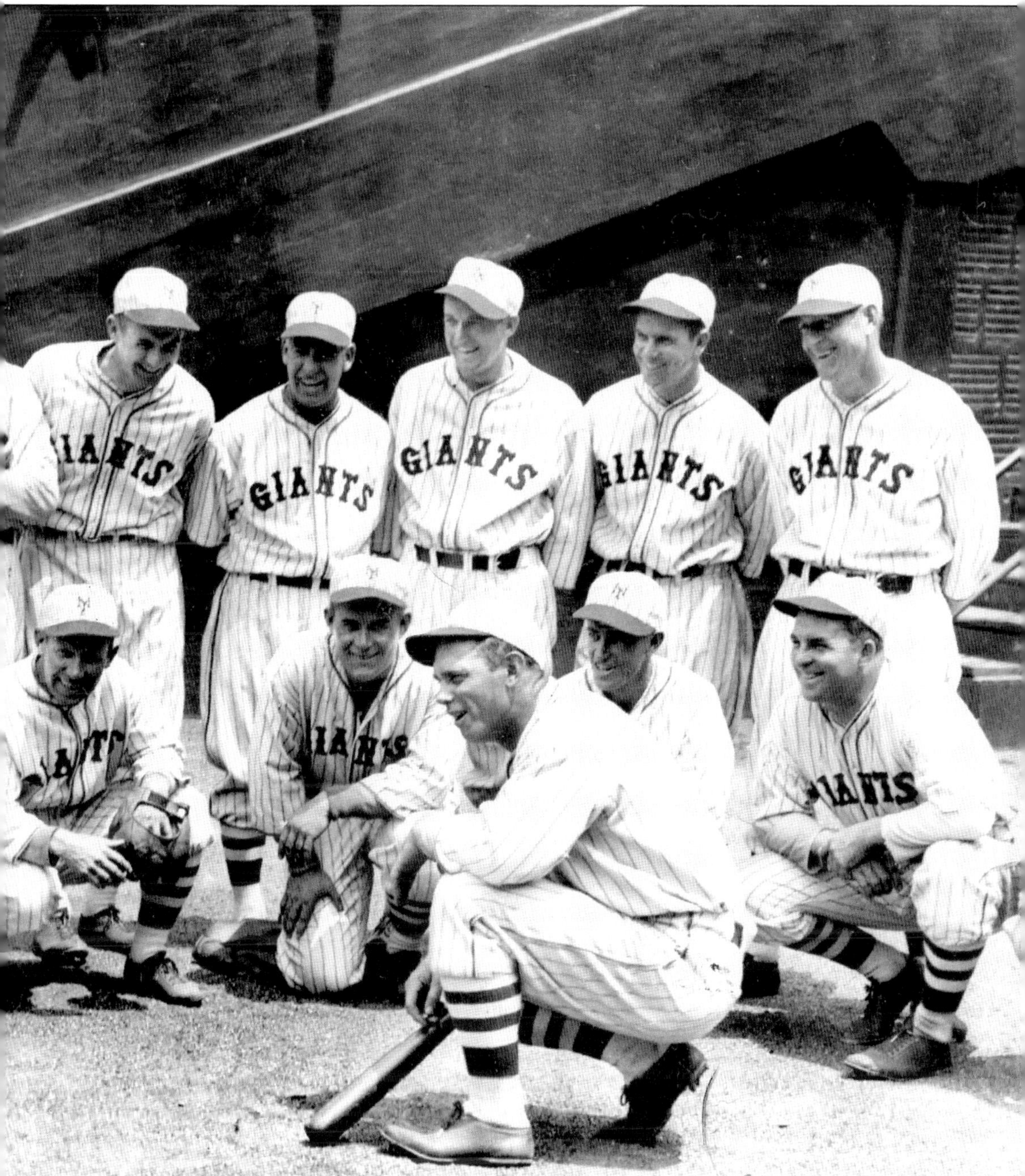

plummeted to seventh place—next to last. McGraw left the team midseason, and Bill Terry was named to replace him. Terry's charges were also teammates whom he had lived and worked with for years. By the following season, the lectures at spring training yielded better results, and the Giants' winning machine rolled on into the 1930s.

Bill Dickey

Career 1928–1946 all in New York

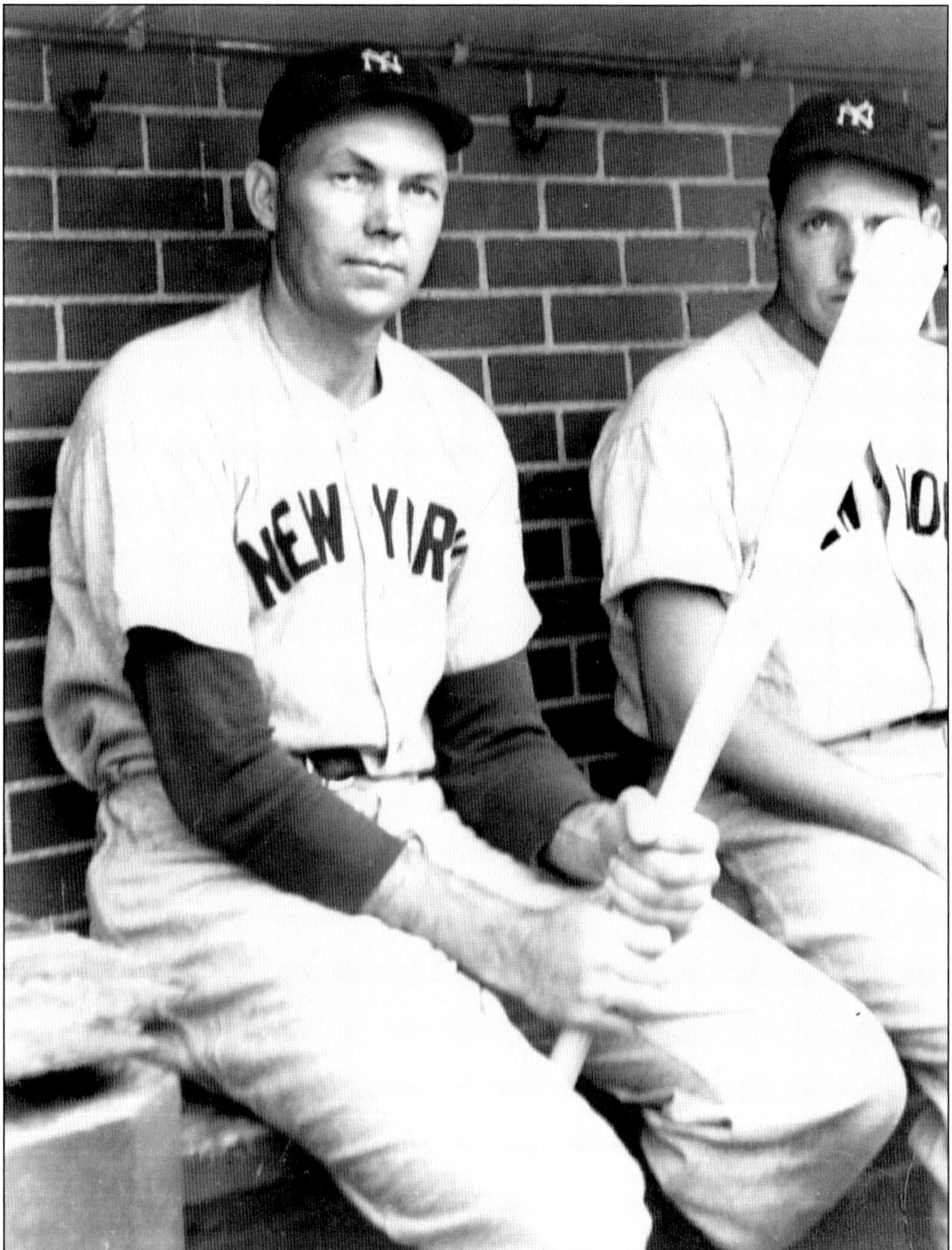

Bill Dickey, a native of Bastrop, Louisiana, played in 1,789 games with the Yankees; he caught 1,708 of them and pinch hit in the others. A Hall of Famer, Dickey had a lifetime average of .313, the second-highest average for major-league catchers.

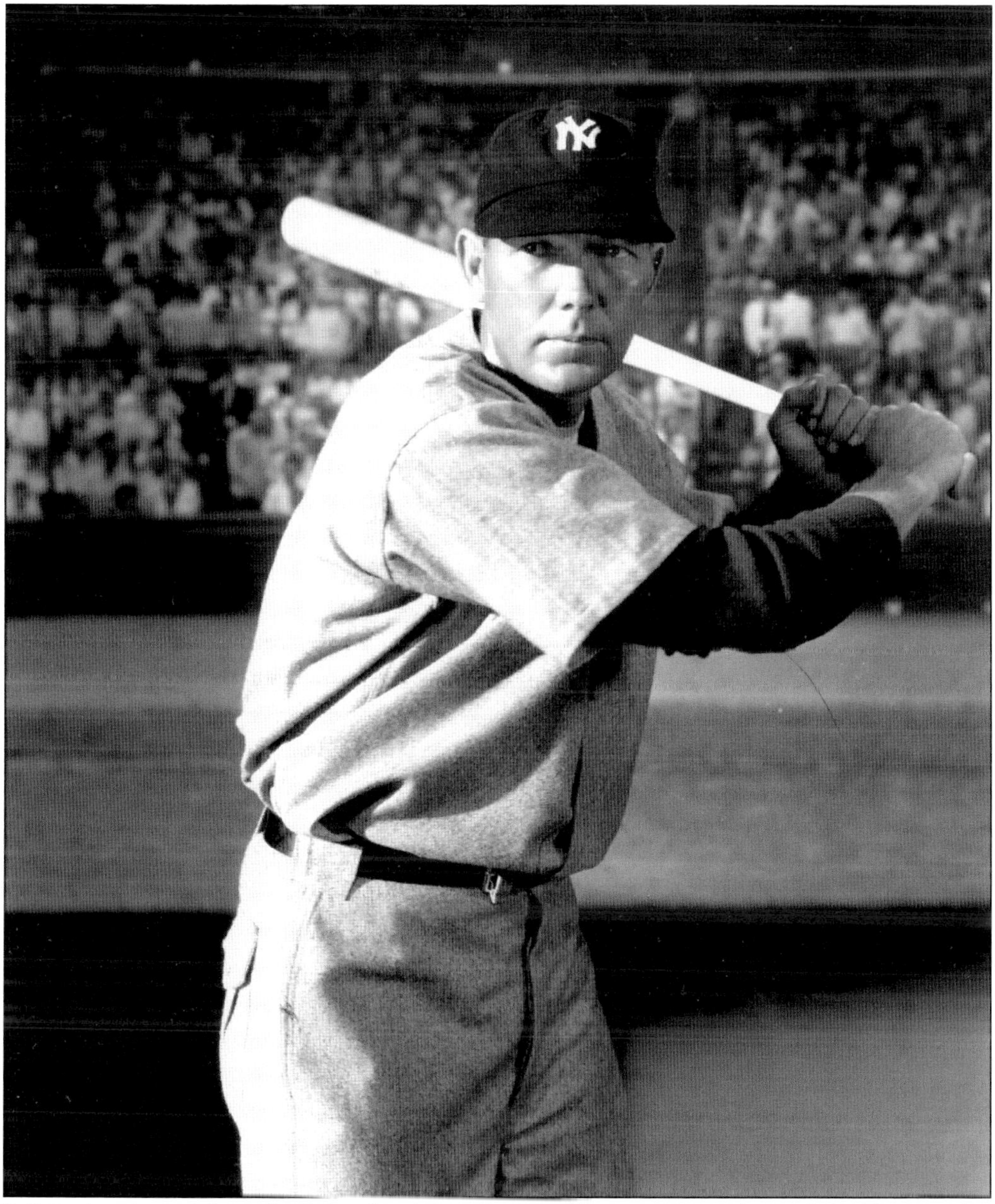

Bill Dickey batted from the left side of the plate, and hit mostly singles and doubles over his first eight years in Yankee Stadium. But something must have happened over the winter of 1935–1936. The following season, Dickey suddenly hit 22 home runs, 10 more than he ever hit before, and drove in 107. He continued slugging, connecting for 29 round-trippers in 1937, 27 in 1938, and 24 in 1939. In those same years, Dickey drove in 133, 115, and 105 runs respectively. Dickey's World Series record alone is better than some players' lifetime accomplishments: He appeared in the fall classic in eight different years, during which he played in 38 games, hit 5 home runs, and knocked in 24 runs. In Game 2 of the 1936 World Series against the crosstown Giants, Dickey drove in five runs, including a two-run homer, to help the Yankees win a laugher, 18-4. He briefly managed the Yanks after putting away the catcher's gear, and he later coached for a decade under Casey Stengel.

BABE YOUNG

CAREER 1936–1948 NEW YORK 1936–1947

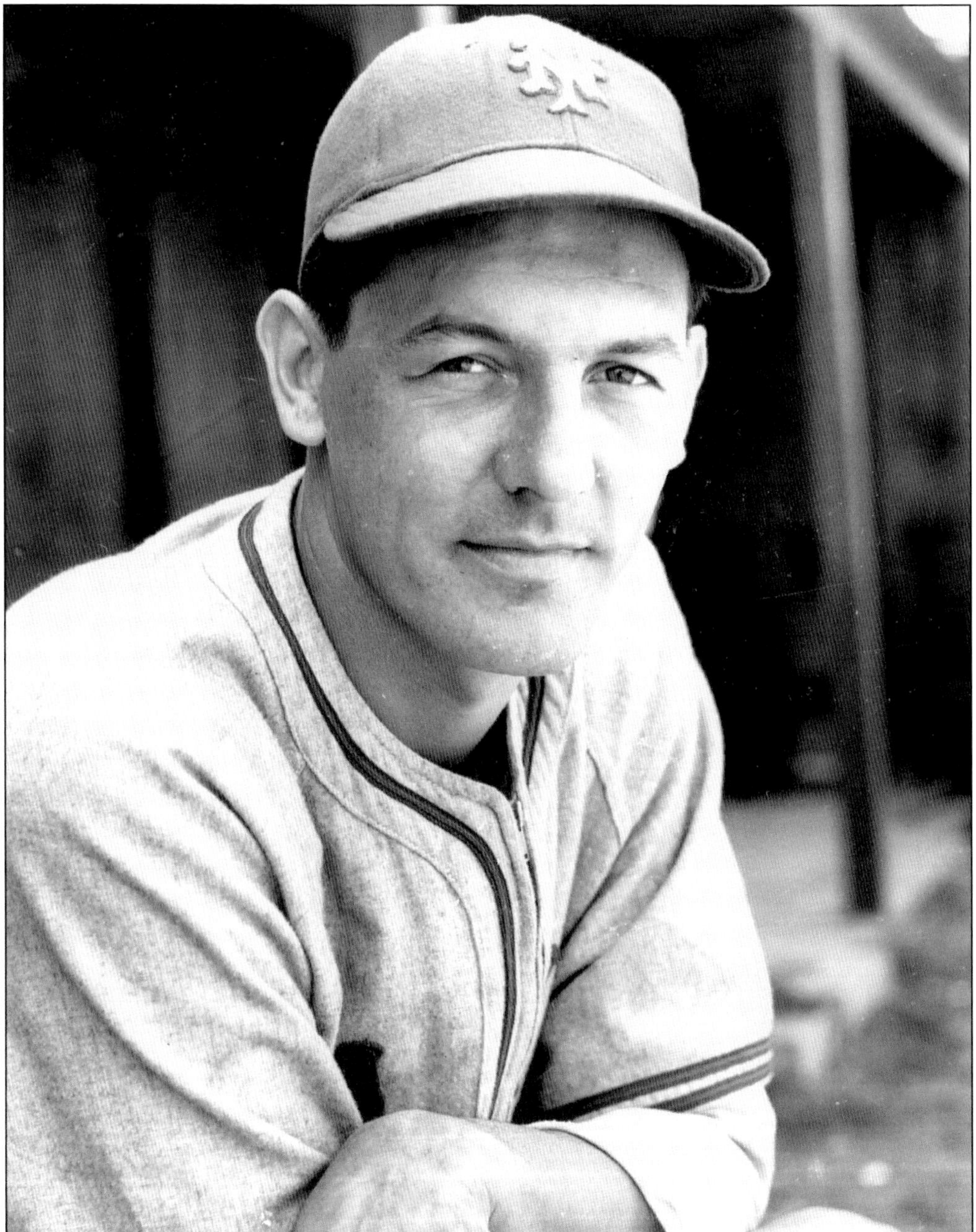

His seven seasons with the New York Giants were Norman "Babe" Young's first in the majors. Of those, he played two full years as a starter, and they were very good years. In 1940, at the age of 25, Young hit 17 home runs to go with his 101 runs batted in. The following year, he upped the totals to 25 homers and 104 RBIs. After serving in World War II, Young returned in 1946 to the Polo Grounds to lead the league in pinch hits. The following year was his last as a Giant.

Harry Danning

Career 1933–1942 All in New York

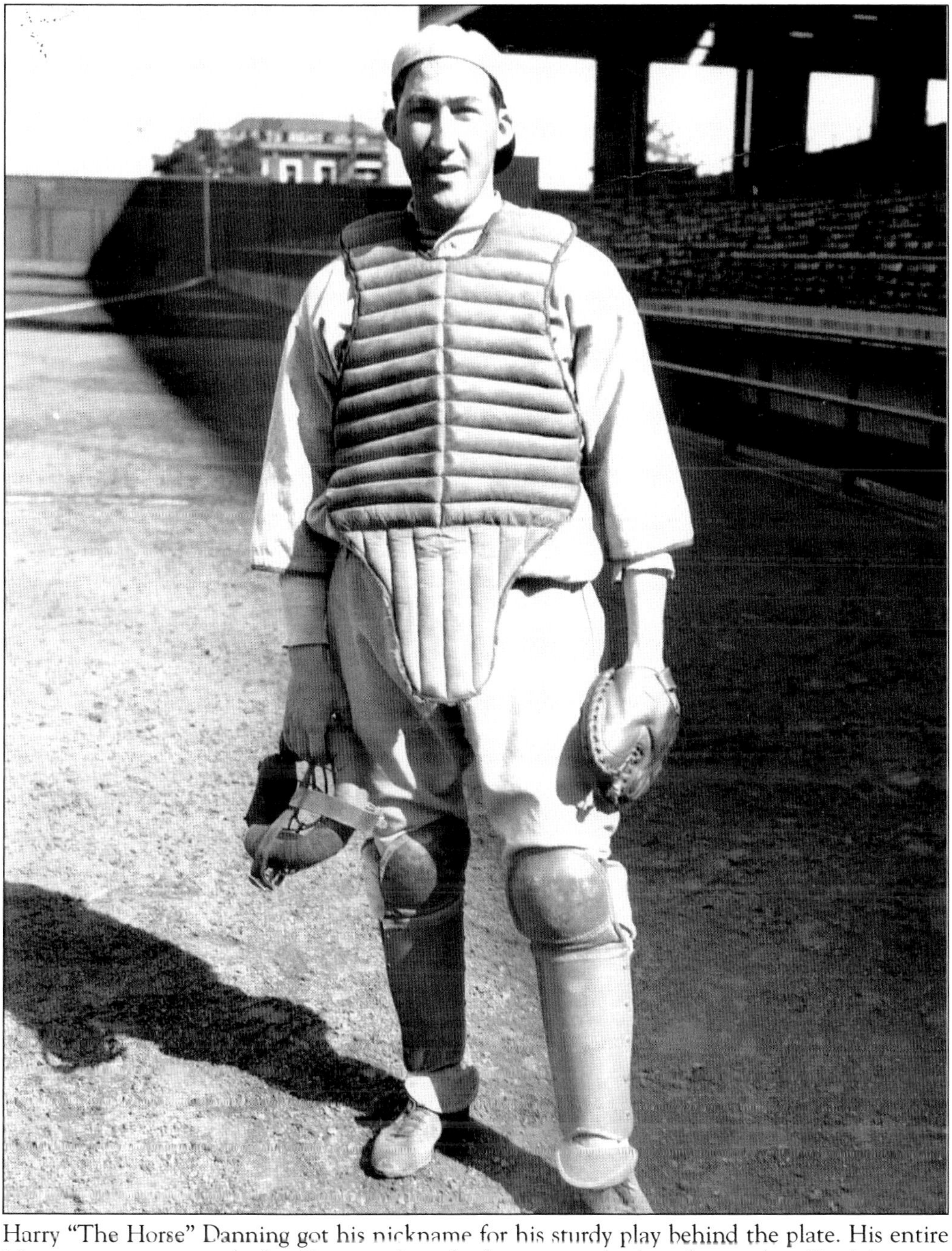

Harry "The Horse" Danning got his nickname for his sturdy play behind the plate. His entire 10-year career was with the Giants, where he began as a backup for catcher Gus Mancuso. Danning took over the starting duties in 1938. His best years with the bat were 1939, when he clubbed 16 homers, and 1940, when he hit 13. Danning batted .300 or better in three seasons, and participated in two World Series, in 1936 and 1937.

Ray Dandridge

Career 1933–1949 New York 1949

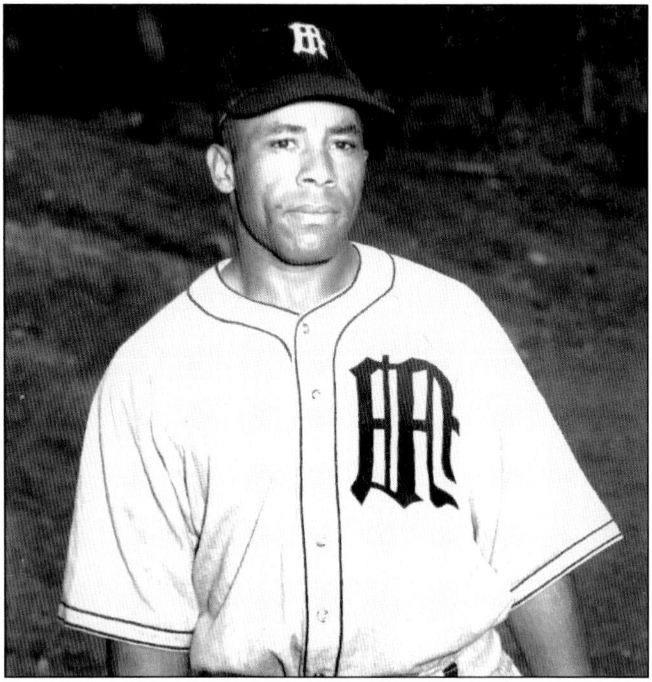

As the years rolled by, while the Giants and the Yankees were playing to large crowds and making big headlines, the Negro Leagues were operating in parallel. Ray Dandridge played for most of a decade across the Hudson, for the Newark Eagles. He batted .368 in 1935 while in Newark, and later signed with the New York Cubans. Dandridge appears in the center of the image below, between star pitcher Pat Scantleberry on the left, and an unidentified teammate.

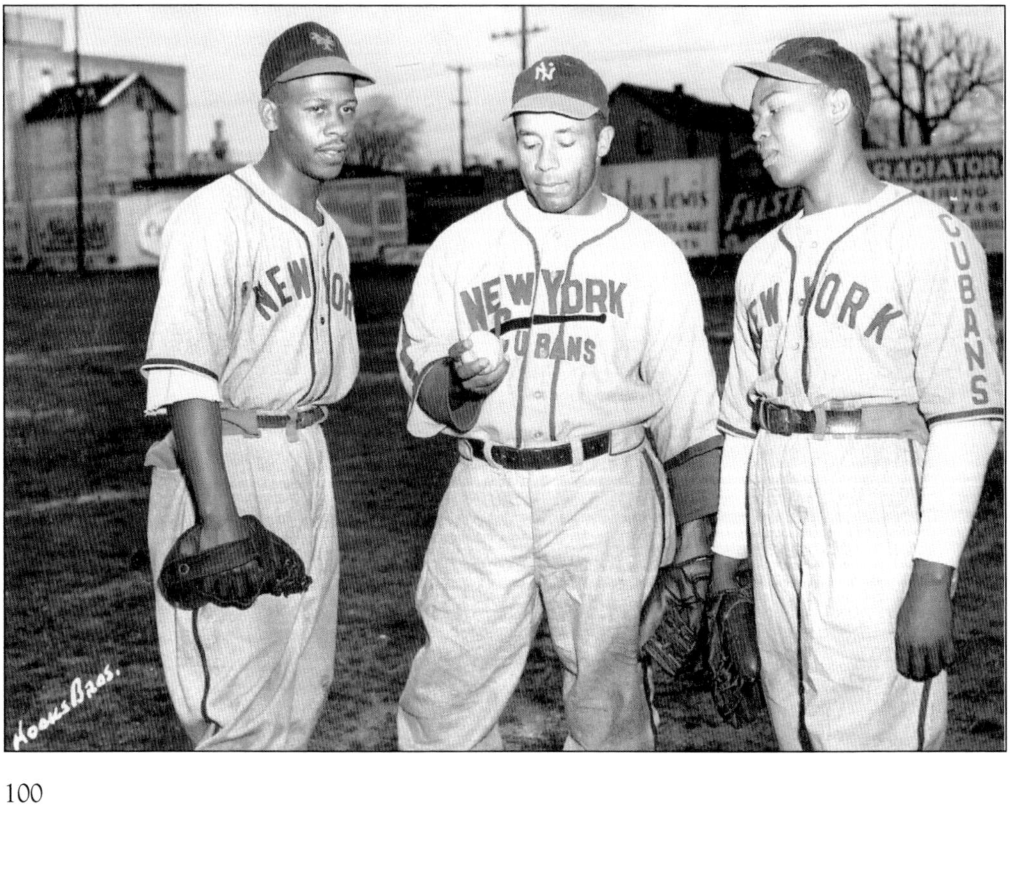

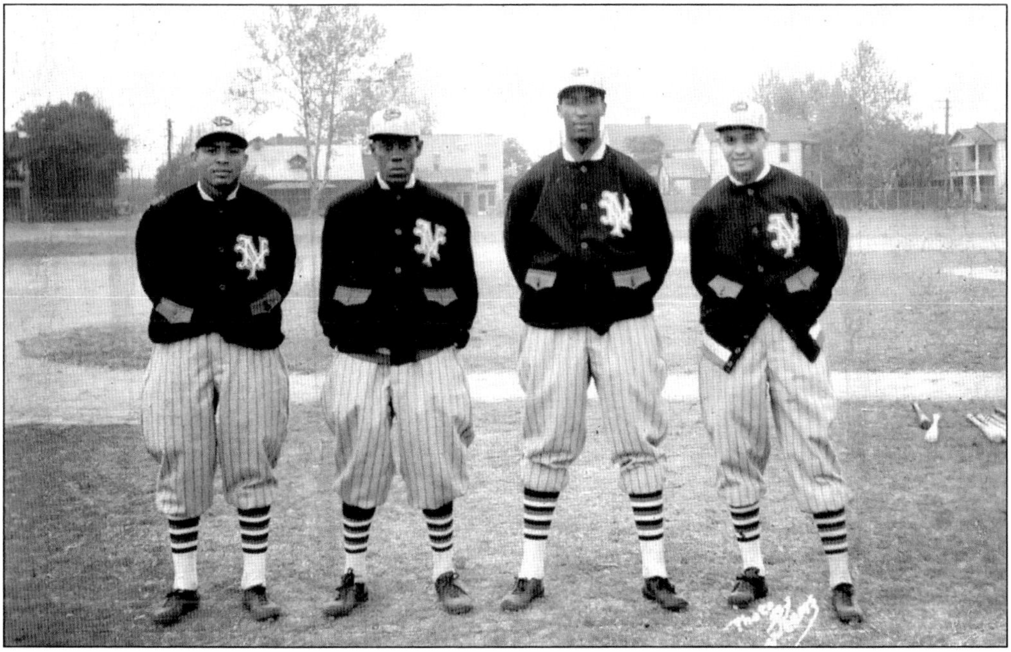

Above and below are some rare photographs of the 1935 New York Cubans. The team won the second half of the season in the Negro National League with a mark of 20-7. Helping bring home those wins were, from left to right in the picture above, outfielders Cando Lopez, Alejandro Oms, Martin Dihigo, and Lazaro Salazar. Dihigo was the greatest black player from the days of segregation, and he could pitch as well as hit for power. He is a member of four national baseball halls of fame. Shown below are the team's infielders. They are, from left to right, Anastasio Santaella (second base), Horacio Martinez (shortstop), Francisco Correa (shortstop), Javier Perez (second base), Fermin Valdes (first base), and Pedro Arango (third base).

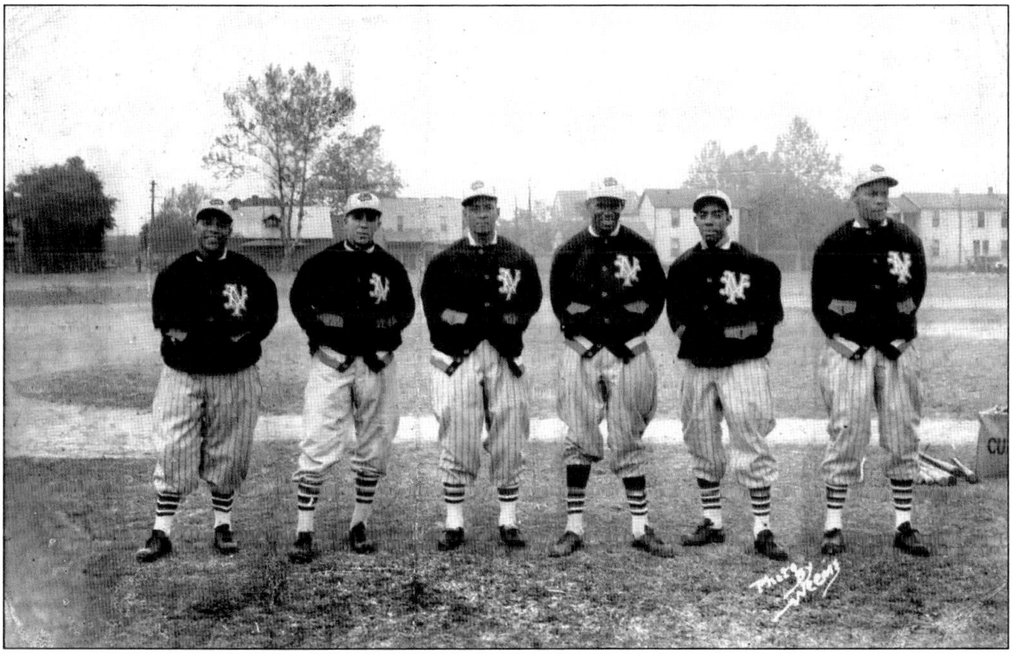

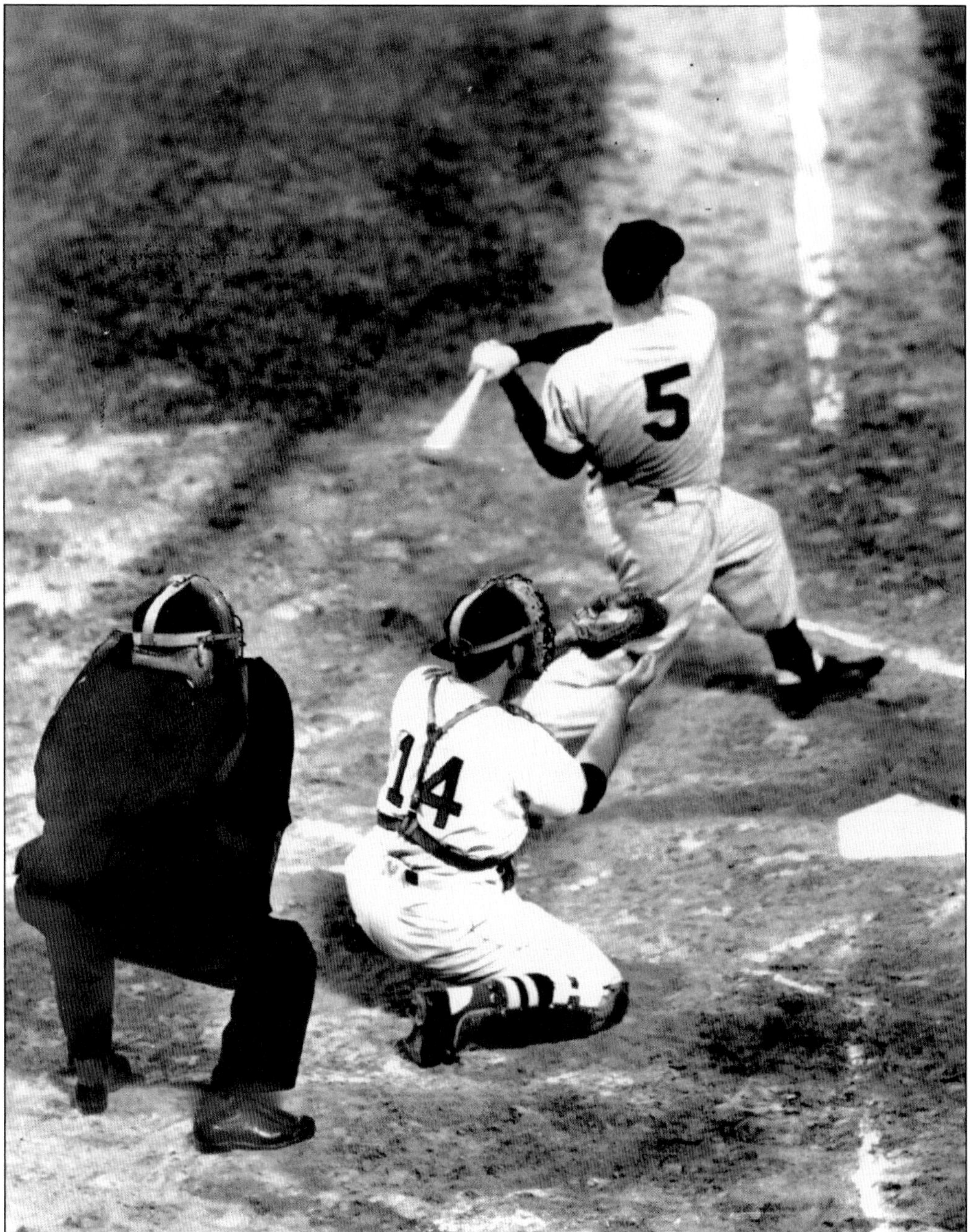

For 13 years, Joe DiMaggio dazzled crowds in Yankee Stadium with his graceful speed in the outfield—cutting off balls in the alley, picking balls off the wall in deep center, and making diving catches in clutch situations. DiMaggio's grace carried over into the batter's box, where the smooth-swinging power hitter made Yankee fans forget the loss of Lou Gehrig, who retired in DiMaggio's rookie year. DiMaggio had an unusual batting stance, with legs wide apart, and he generated his power from his upper body and wrists. This photograph, taken from slightly above the field, gives a clear idea of what DiMaggio's forceful follow-through looked like.

JOE DIMAGGIO

CAREER 1936–1951 ALL IN NEW YORK

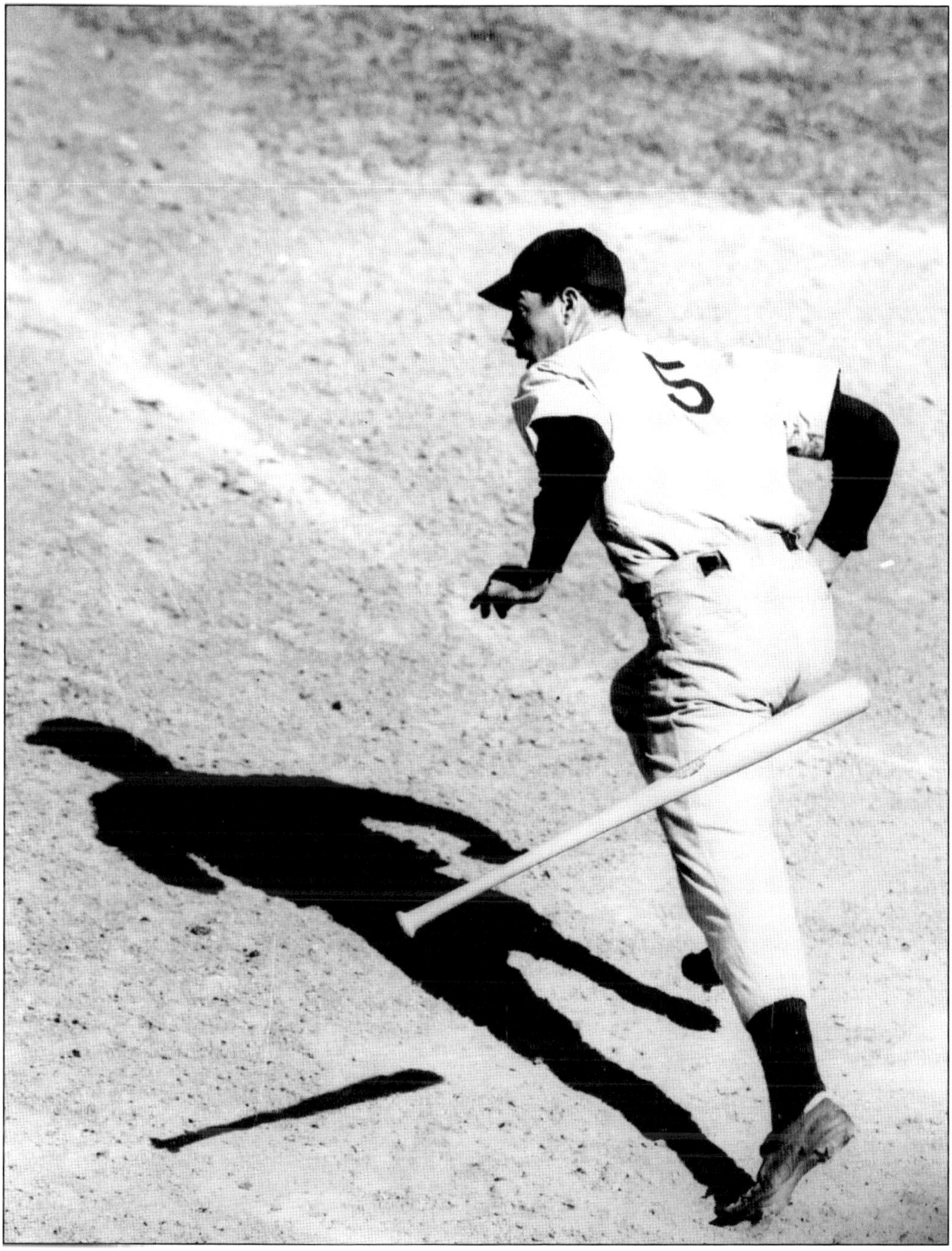

The image above, demonstrating a photographic "critical moment," shows DiMaggio leaving the box after rapping out another hit. Many still claim that Joltin' Joe was the finest all-around ballplayer of all time. He starred first in his hometown of San Francisco, playing for the minor-league Seals, where the five-tool talent demonstrated his complete command of the game.

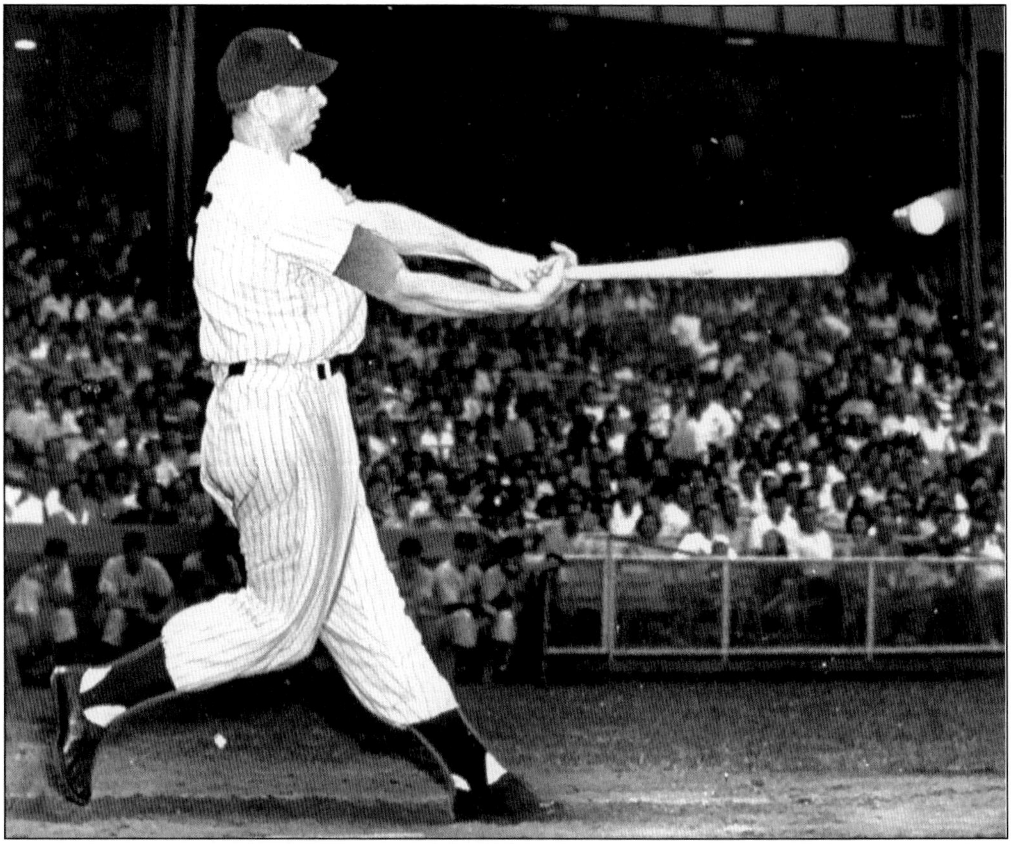

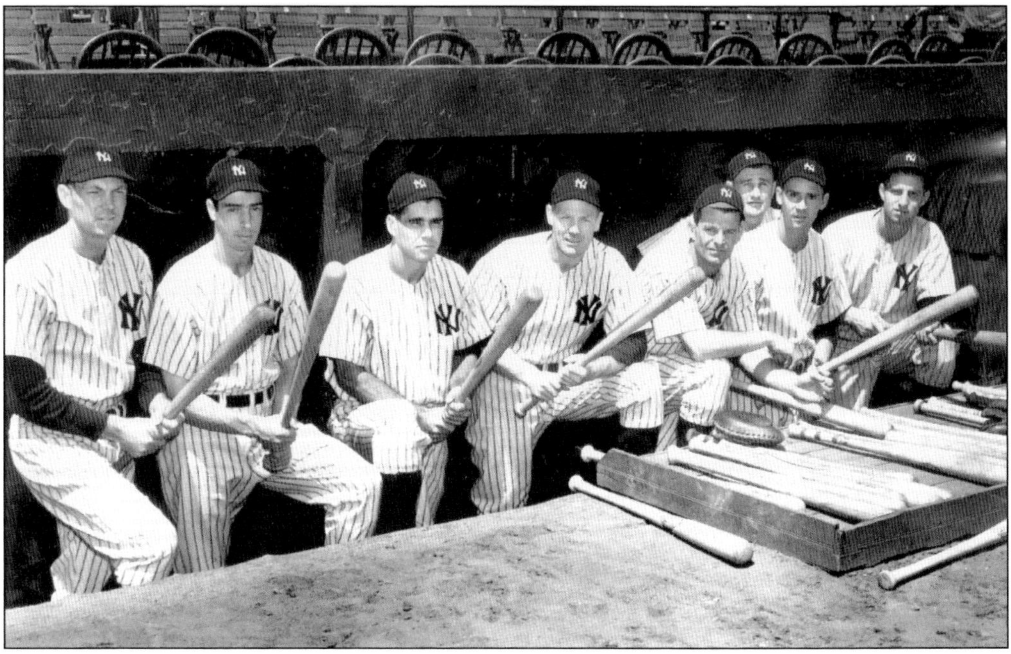

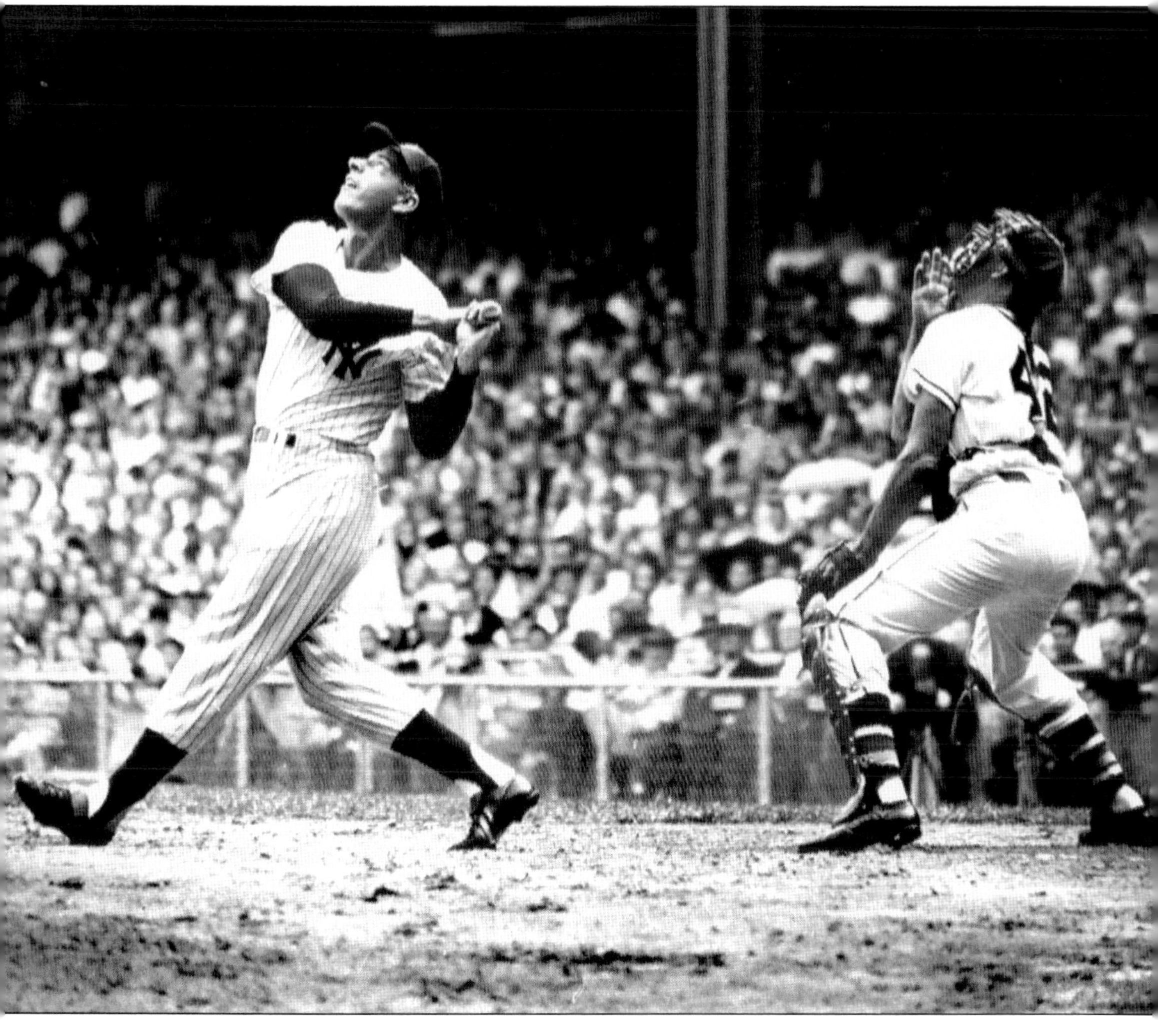

Joe DiMaggio displays his hitting style in the top photograph on the facing page and in the image above. Below, on the opposite page, the Yankees show off their 1940 version of Murderers' Row, featuring catcher Bill Dickey, center fielder Joe DiMaggio, right fielder Charlie Keller, third baseman Red Rolfe, left fielder George Selkirk, shortstop Frank Crosetti, and outfielder Tommy Henrich.

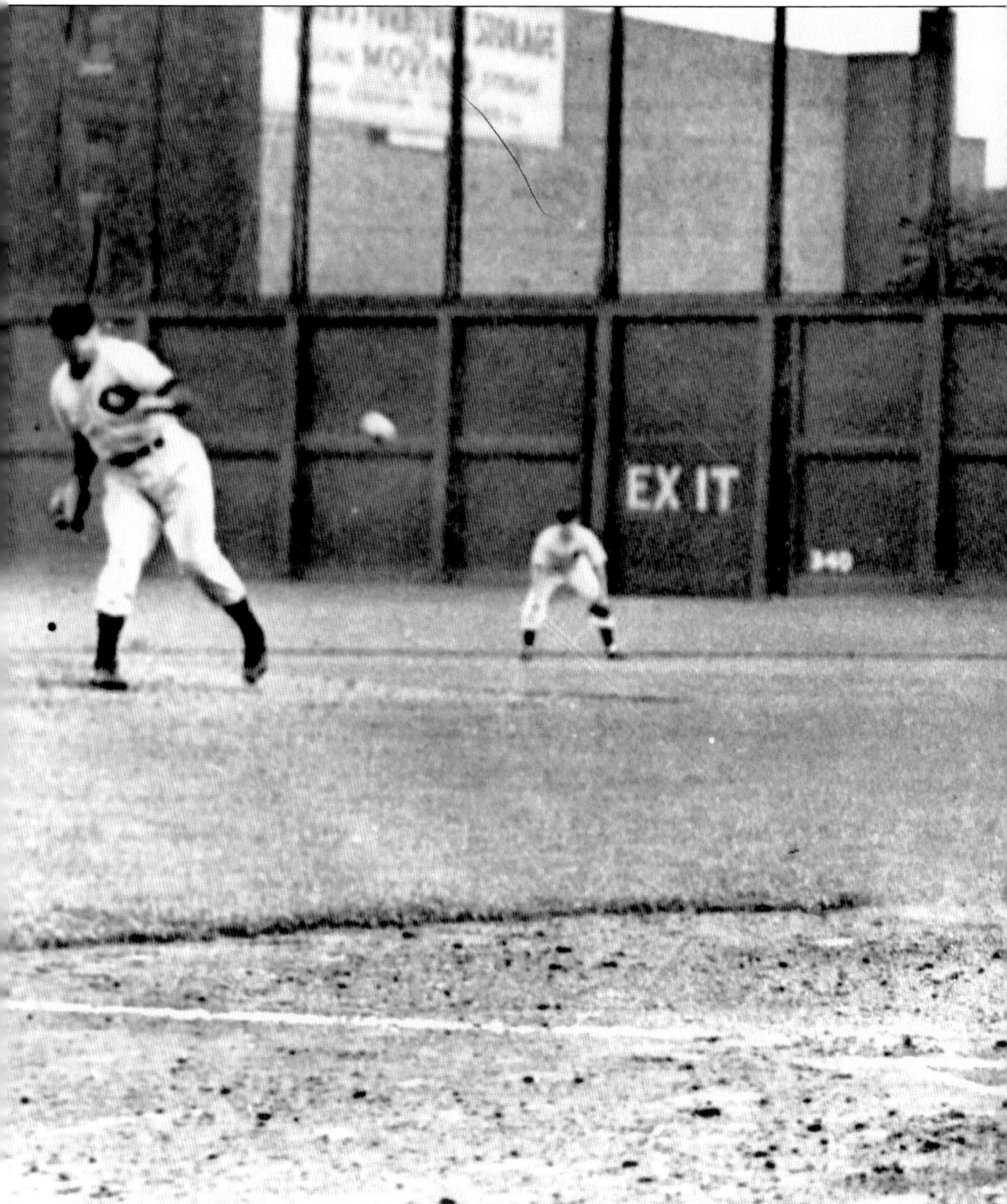

This fabulous photograph was taken in Cleveland on July 16, 1941. The pitcher, who had delivered the ball and seems to be ducking out of the way of the resulting line drive, was Joe Krakauskas. DiMaggio went three for four that day and, more importantly, extended his hitting streak to 56 games. The image shows the first of his three hits that day. DiMaggio was used to hitting streaks, having reached safely in 61 straight games while playing in the Pacific Coast

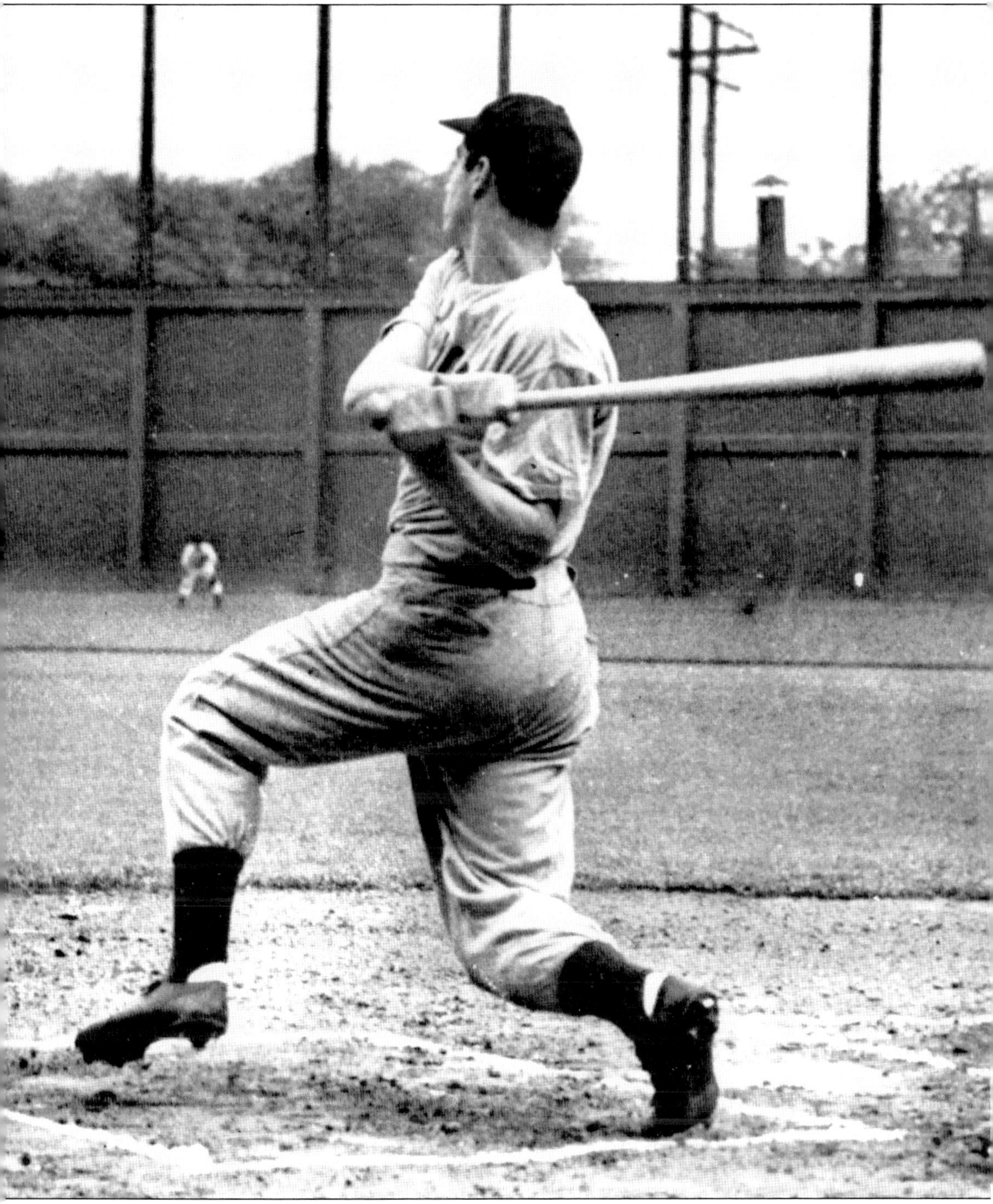

League. During the 56-game major-league streak, DiMaggio hit a sparkling .408. The Yankees won the 1941 pennant, and DiMaggio was presented with the award for Most Valuable Player at season's end. One of the few baseball records that many consider untouchable, DiMaggio's record hitting streak has weathered onslaughts by Pete Rose, who had hits in 44 straight games in 1978; Paul Molitor, who had 39 in 1987; and Luis Castillo, who had 35 in 2002.

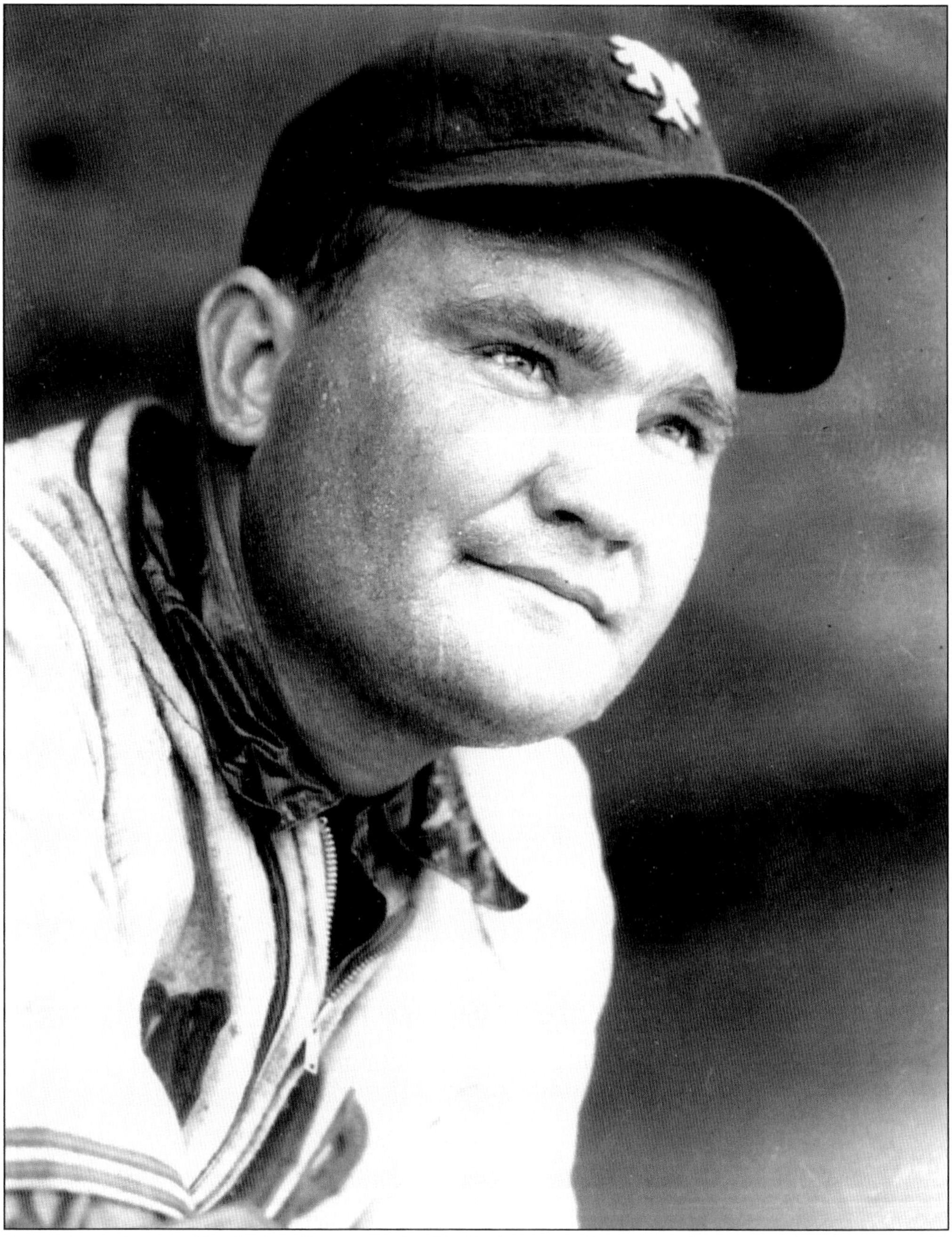

Great big Johnny Mize had a "Casey at the Bat" physique. He was a slugger in the classic mold, using his height and weight to provide the leverage needed to hit the ball very hard. Always a careful student of the pitchers he faced, the first baseman played his first six years with the St. Louis Cardinals. His initial season in a Giants uniform saw him lead the league in runs batted in with 110, and he was the RBI champ again two years later, when he knocked in 138. He also accumulated 359 home runs and a fat .562 slugging average over his career. He had an excellent eye and was very hard to strike out. This image shows Mize with the Giants, where he played from 1942 to 1949.

JOHNNY MIZE

CAREER 1936–1953 NEW YORK 1942–1953

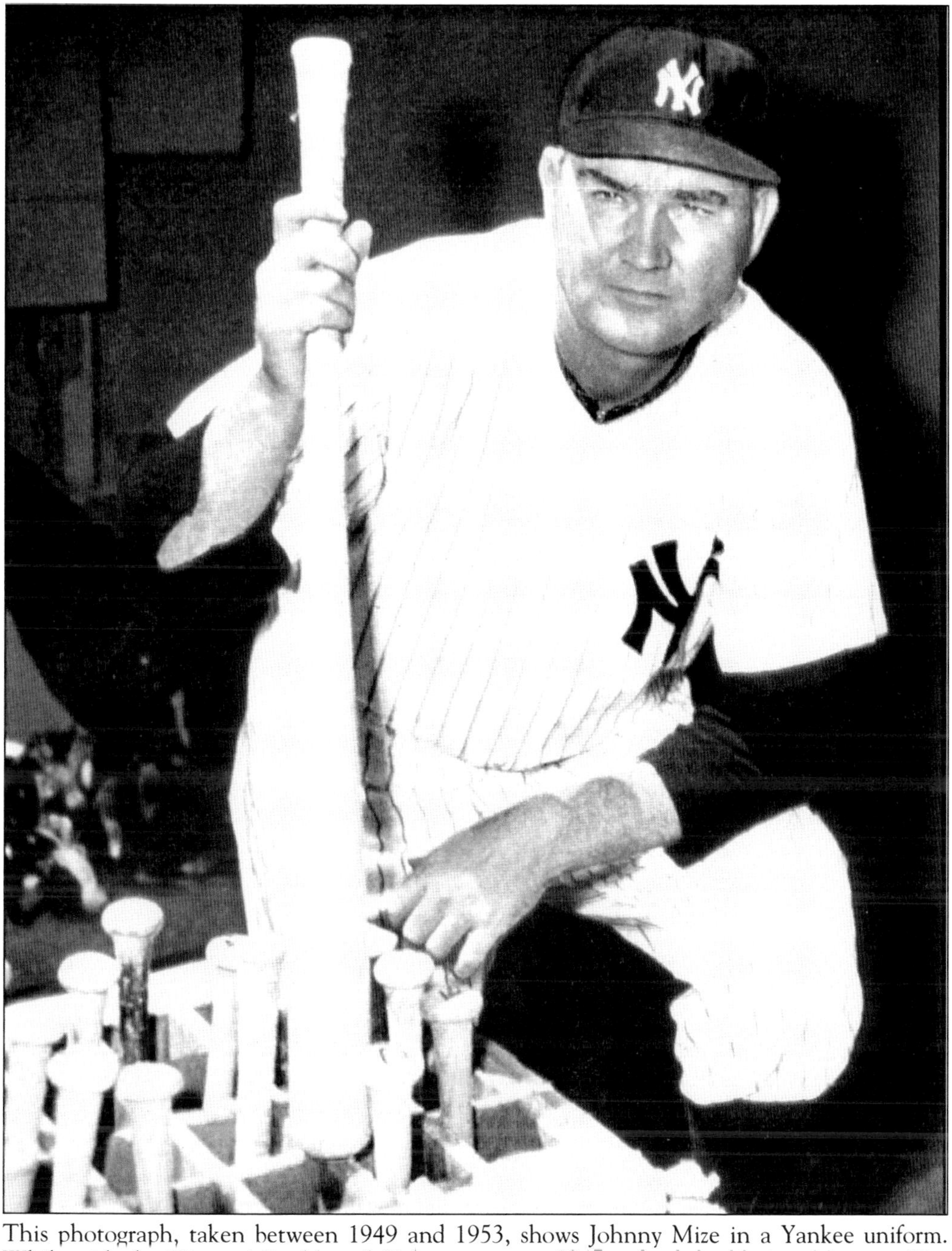

This photograph, taken between 1949 and 1953, shows Johnny Mize in a Yankee uniform. While with the Giants, Mize blasted 51 home runs in 1947 to lead the National League. The only other year he came close to that number was 1940, when he hit 43. Nearing the end of his career when he joined the Yankees, Mize was not able to duplicate his slugging feats for the American-Leaguers.

Frank Crosetti

Career 1932–1949 all in New York

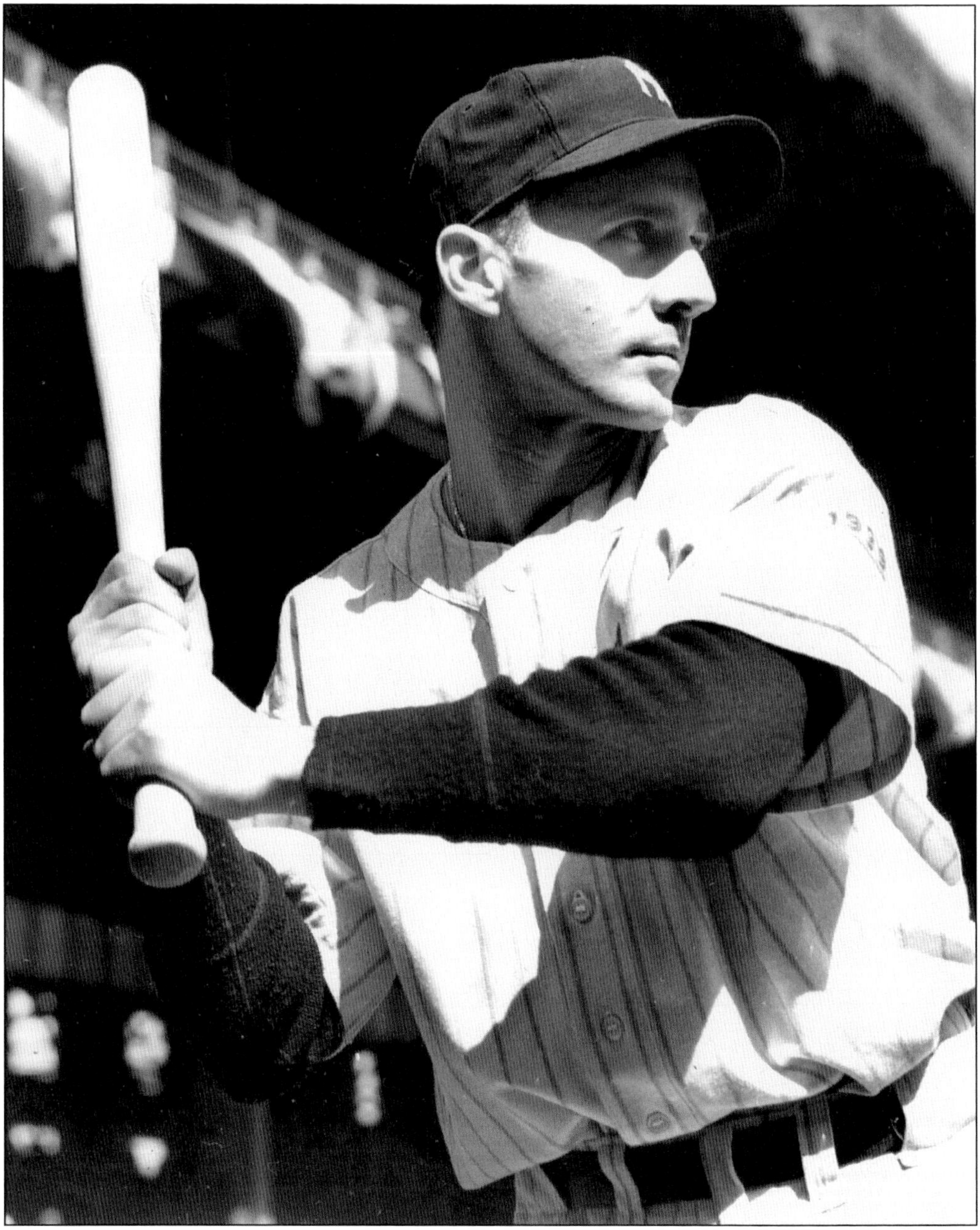

"The Crow" played 1,516 games at shortstop for the New York Yankees, covering 17 years in the Bronx. Frank Crosetti earned some unusual batting records: he set the mark for number of at-bats during a 154-game season with 757 plate appearances in 1938, and he was the American League hit-by-pitch champion in eight seasons. Crosetti was selected for the All-Star team in 1936 and 1939, and he played in 29 games in seven World Series for the mighty Yanks. After he retired from the field, Crosetti served as third-base coach for the Pinstripes for 20 more years.

Nick Etten

Career 1938–1947 New York 1943–1946

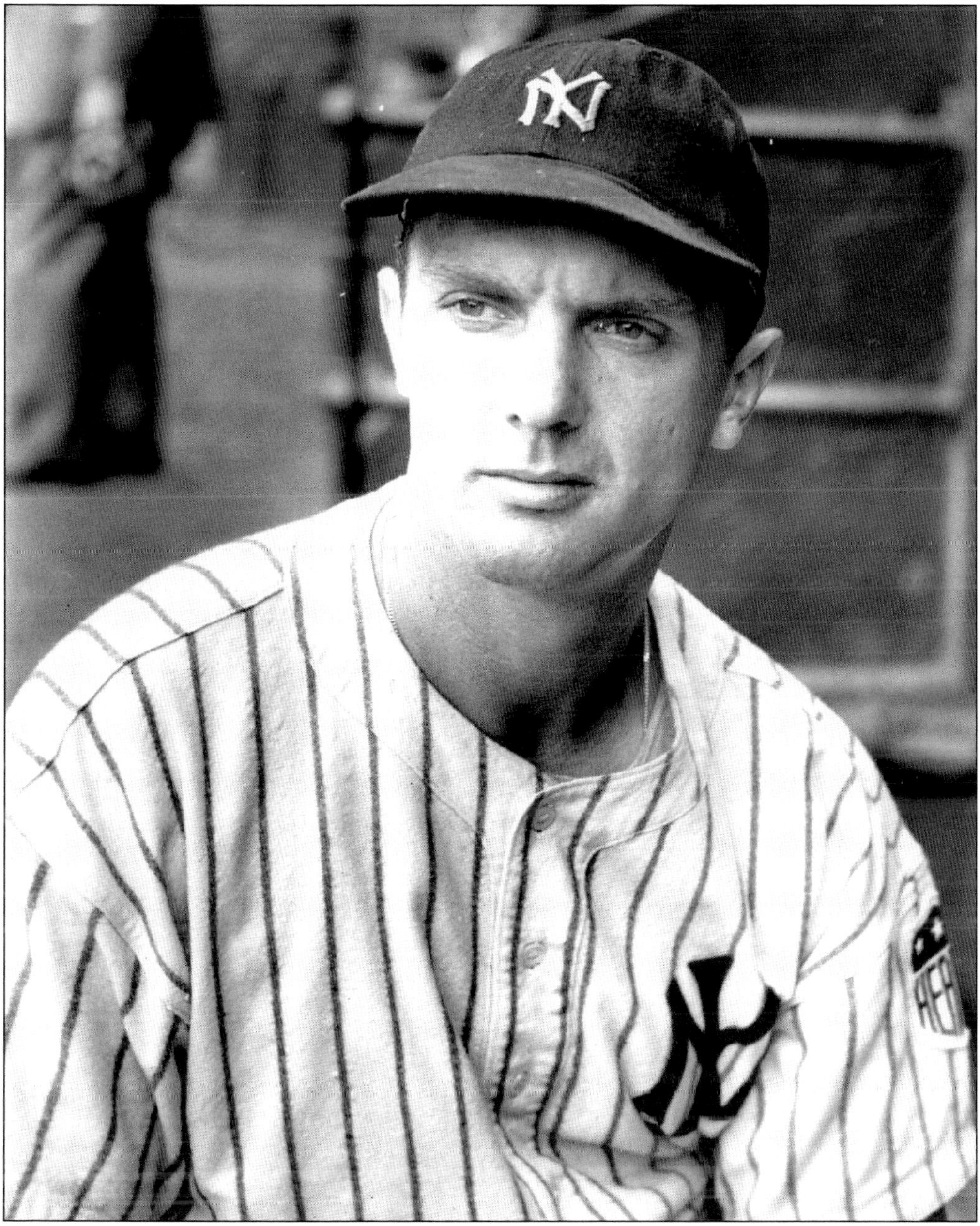

Nick Etten had the ecstatic experience of being traded from the last-place Philadelphia Phillies in the National League to the champion Yankees in the American League. The first baseman responded well, knocking in 107 runs in his first season with New York, 1943, and racking up league-leading totals of 22 home runs and 97 RBIs in 1944. He again topped the league in 1945, when he drove in 111 runs. But when World War II ended and the regulars who had gone to fight in Europe and Asia returned, Etten's major-league career was over.

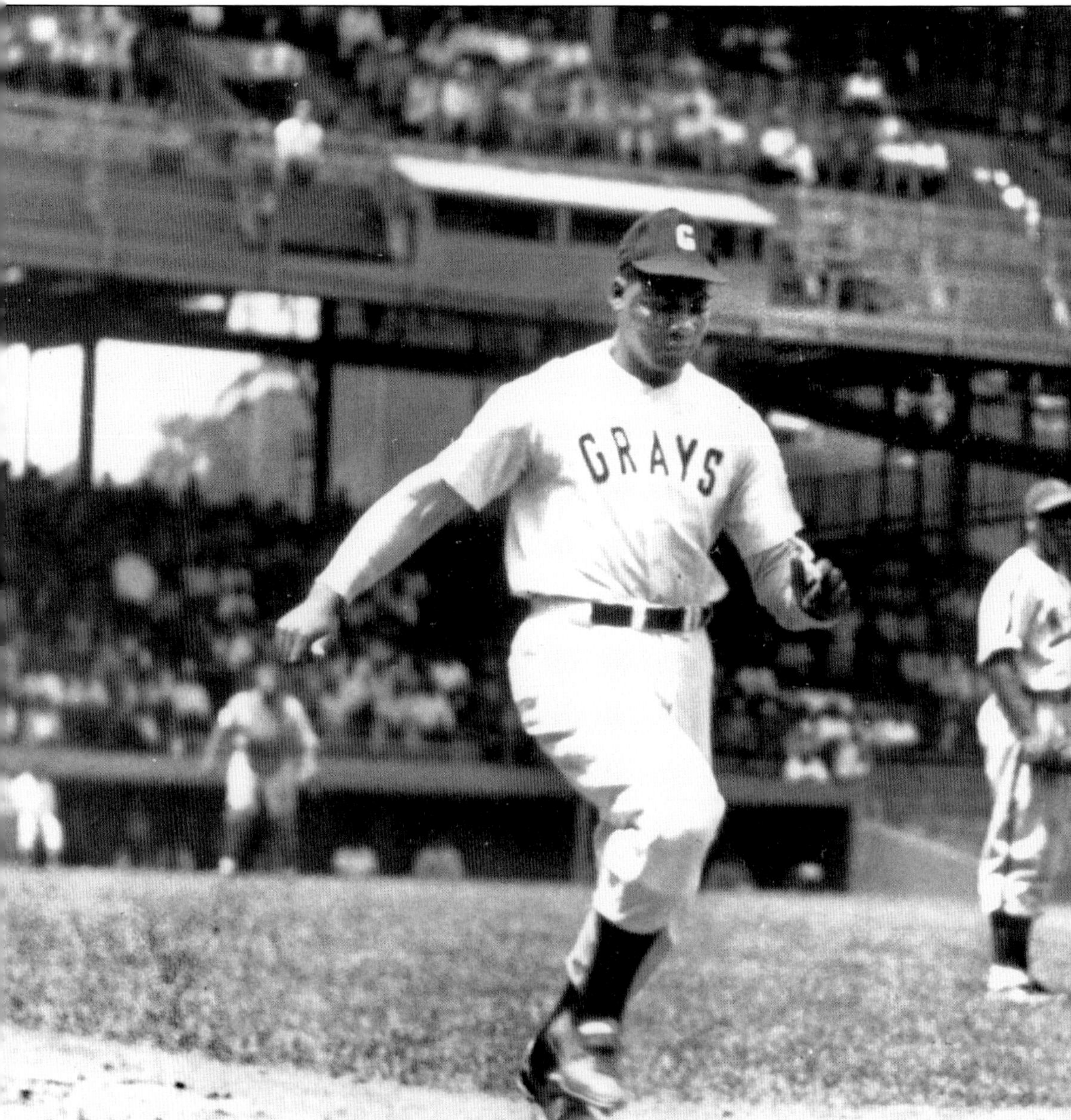

The marvelous action photograph above was taken in 1940 in Griffith Stadium in Washington, D.C., the alternate home field of the Homestead Grays. (The team split its home schedule between Washington and Forbes Field in Pittsburgh.) A caption on the photograph identifies Buck Leonard as the Grays player running toward first base and James Stark as the first baseman for the New York Black Yankees. Negro League teams used this ballpark in Washington for

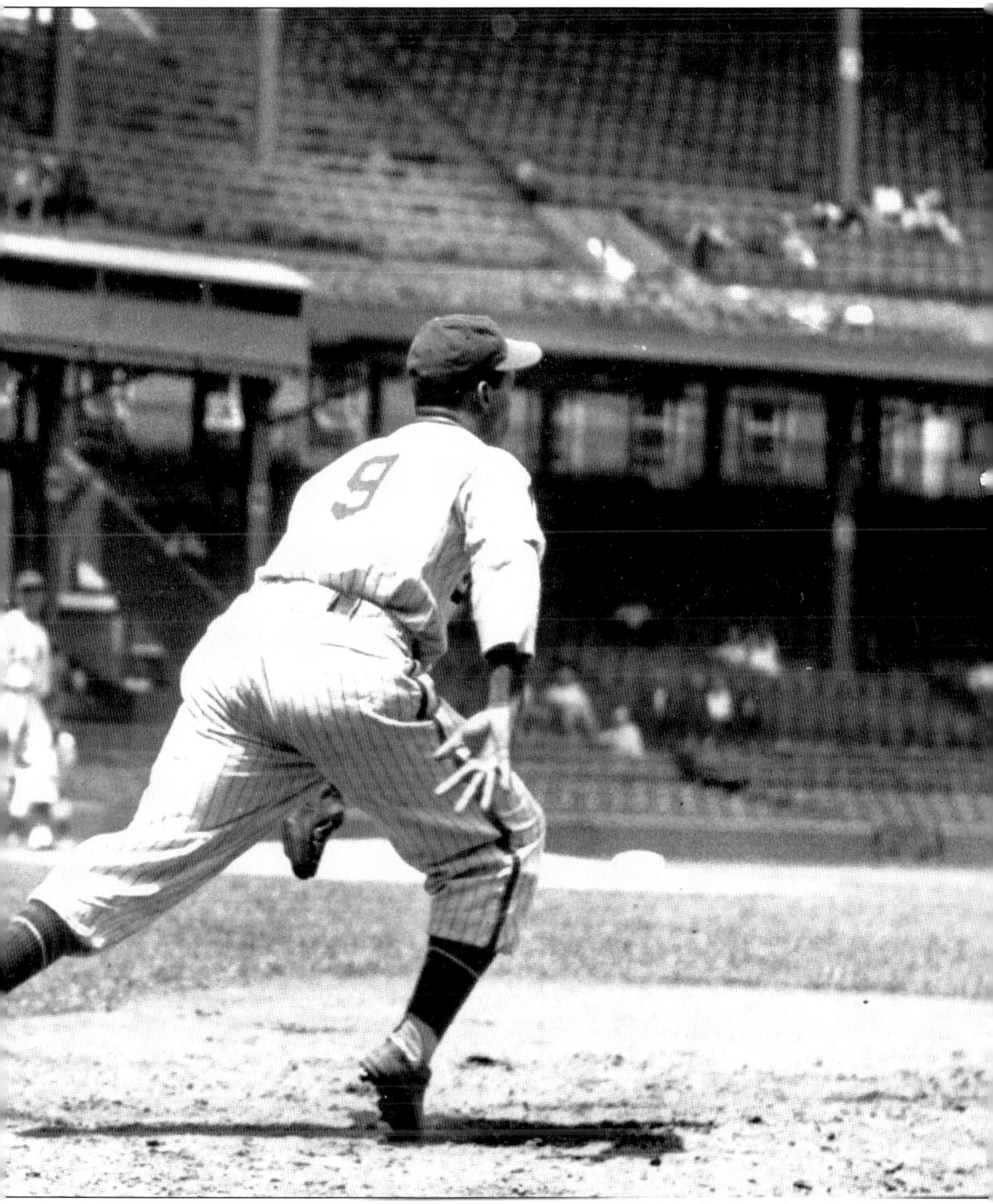

decades whenever the Washington Senators were out of town. The Black Yankees had no chance of keeping up with the Grays, who finished that season with a 28-13 record compared to the Yankees' 10-22 mark. The Grays were like the white Yankees in the American League, as they won seven consecutive pennants in the Negro National League. In sharp contrast, the Black Yankees usually occupied the cellar. The league was dismantled after the 1947 season.

Phil Rizzuto

Career 1941–1956 all in New York

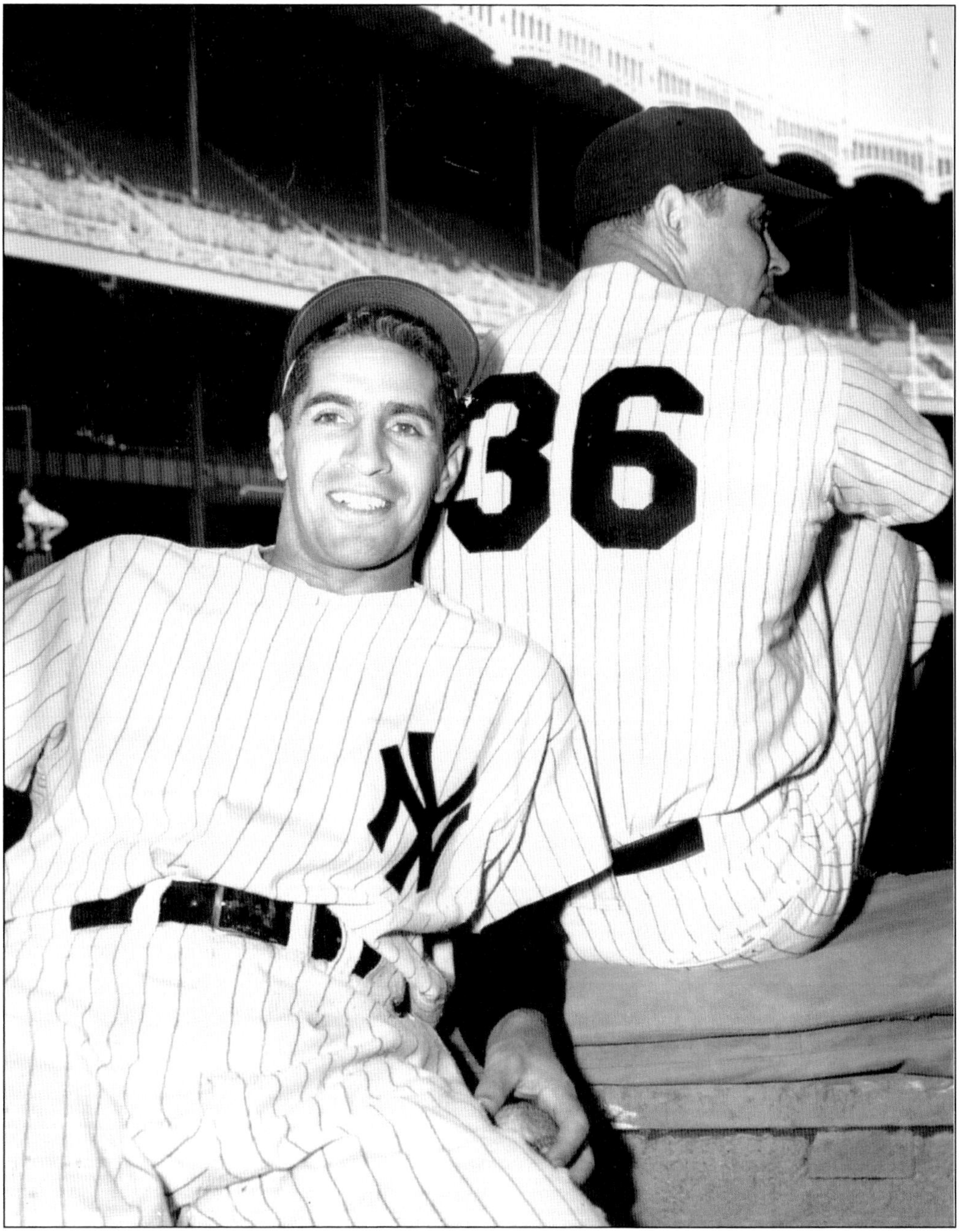

Phil Rizzuto was known as the Scooter; he was quick on the base paths and lithe at the shortstop position. In his career, Rizzuto stole a total of 149 bases for the Yanks and scored 877 runs. He was a master of bat control and was one of baseball's best bunters. Rizzuto was immediately put into the starting lineup after arriving at Yankee Stadium in 1941, and he stayed there through 1954.

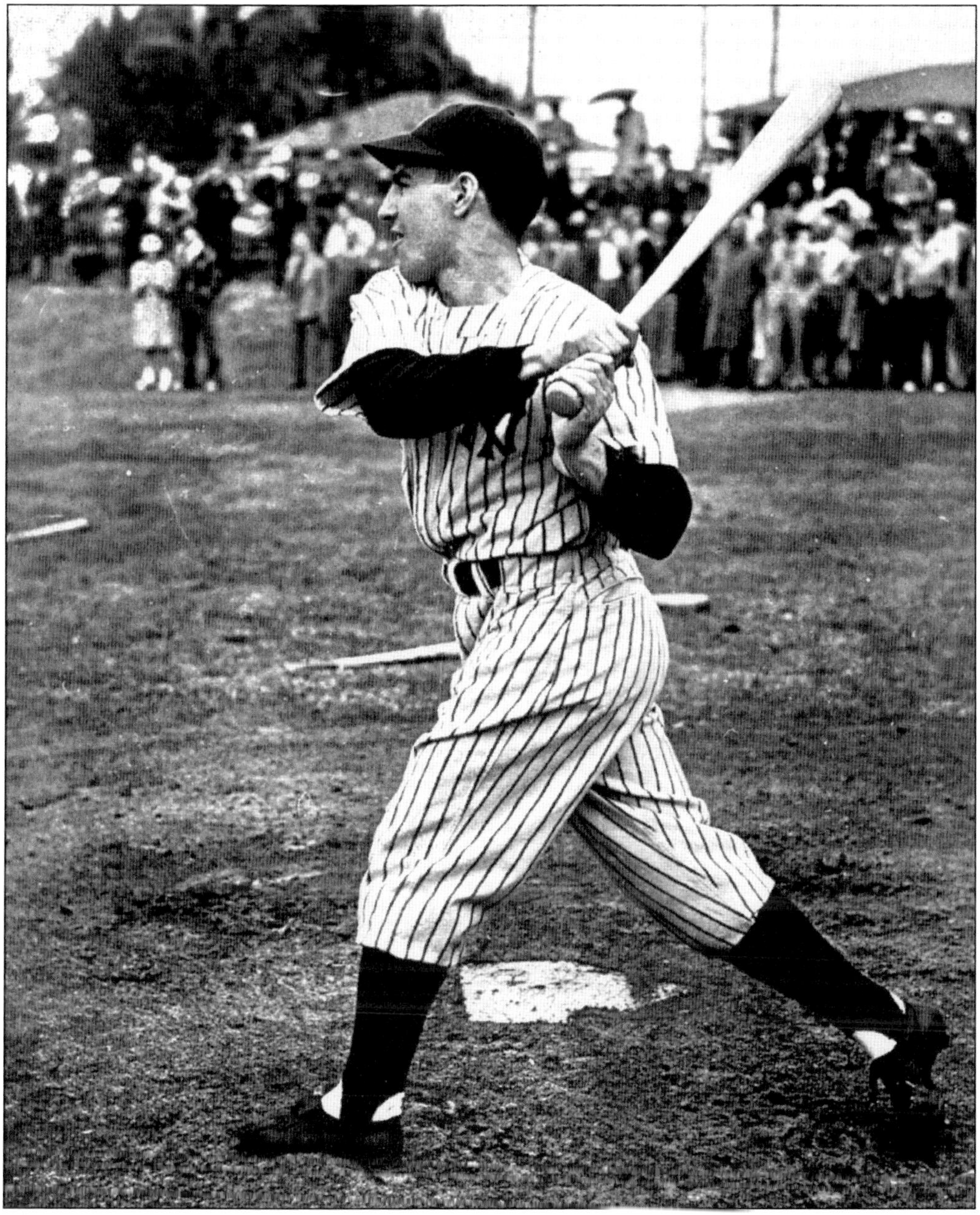

The years of 1949 and 1950 were Phil Rizzuto's finest, and he was moved into the leadoff position in the lineup. His breakout season came in 1949, when he put up numbers far better than any in previous years. That season, Rizzuto scored 110 runs, collected 169 hits, drove in 65 runs, batted .275, and stole 18 bases. He got stronger in 1950, when he reached 200 hits for the only time in his career, scored 125 runs, knocked in 66, hit .324, and earned a slugging percentage of .439, his highest. Rizzuto served as a defensive backup in his last two years in the majors, but he was never out of the New York spotlight. Right after leaving his spot on the infield, he was hired as a color announcer for the Yankees' radio broadcast team. His ubiquitous face (an advertisers' favorite in New York City) and humorous use of language made Rizzuto an amusing celebrity.

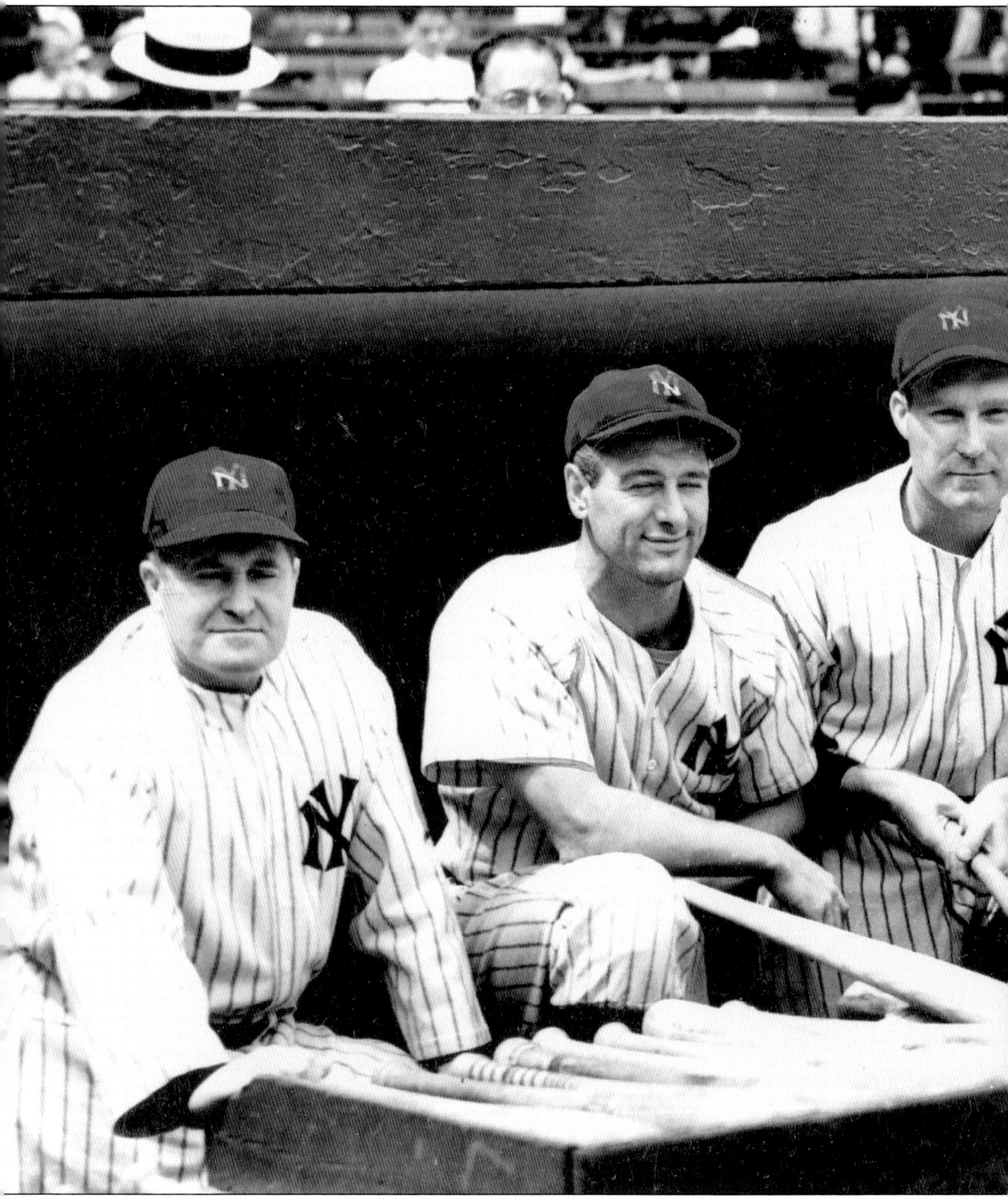

Photographers loved to pose Yankee groups in the dugout. This is one of Joe McCarthy's crews checking out the lumber. McCarthy had the skills to handle some of baseball's biggest egos. Often exasperated by the antics of Babe Ruth, McCarthy was clearly happy when the Babe moved to the Boston Braves in 1935. Five times McCarthy's Yanks won more than 100 games, and they notched 98 and 99 wins in two other seasons. He and his coaches were able to fashion flag-winning clubs in eight seasons. And the Yankees finished second in 7 other campaigns

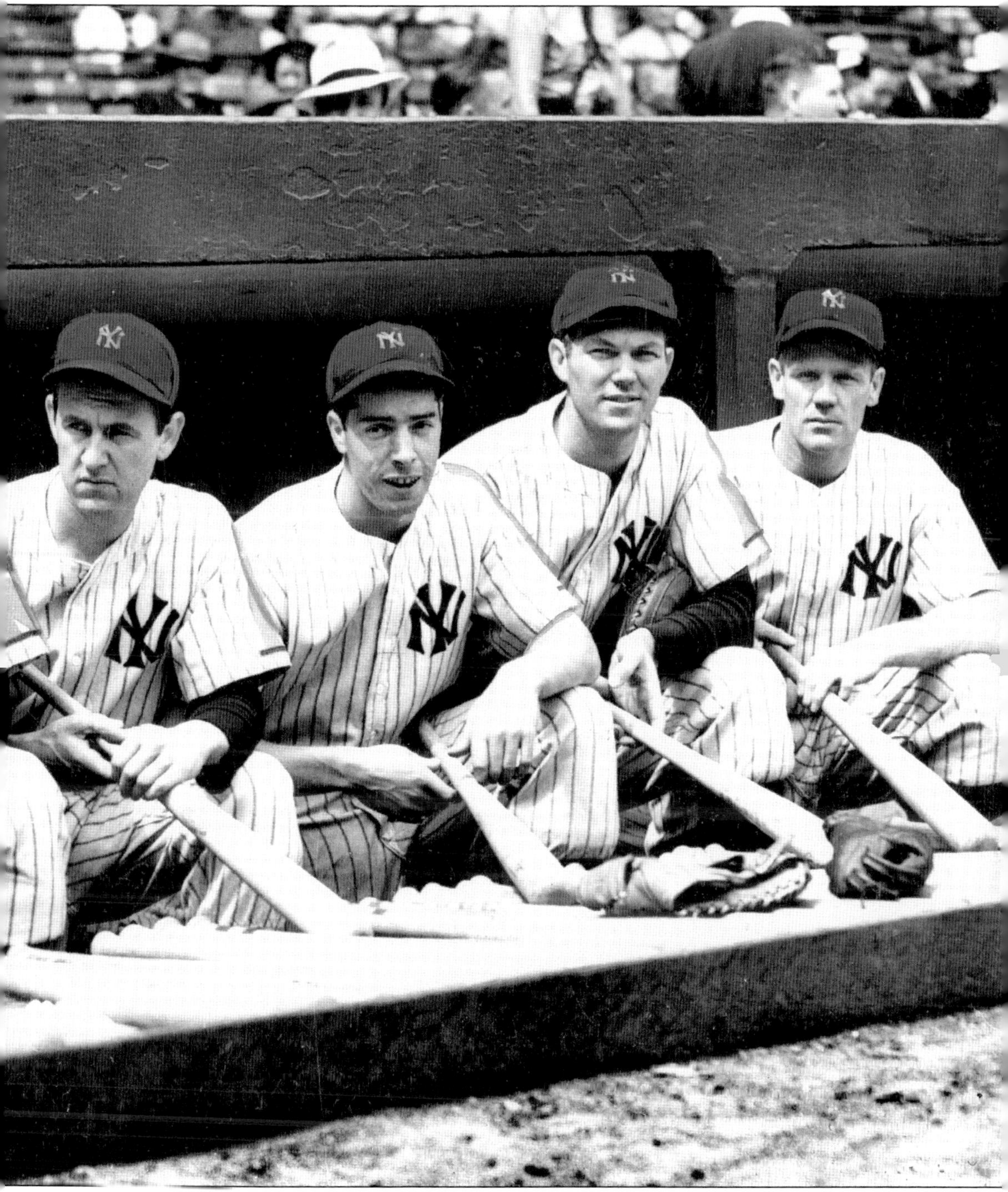

among the 19 that McCarthy managed in New York. Hitting was a team specialty, as this photograph wishes to convey. Even the Yankee pitchers included in this photograph could hit, especially Red Ruffing, who had a .267 lifetime batting average. From left to right are McCarthy, Lou Gehrig, Ruffing, Lefty Gomez, Joe DiMaggio, Bill Dickey, and Red Rolfe. One of Gomez's few memorable hitting feats came in 1933, when he drove in the first run ever scored in an MLB All-Star Game.

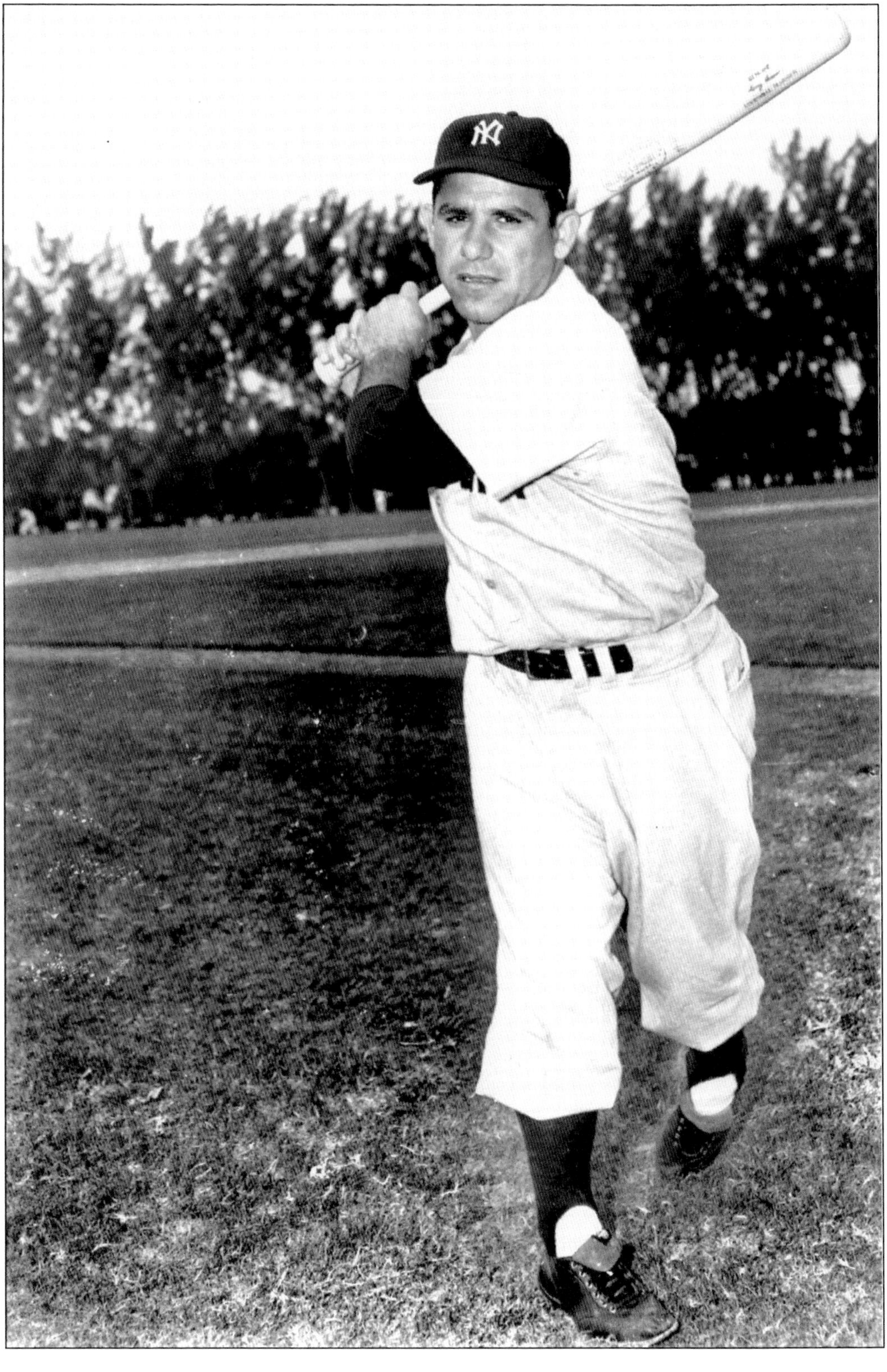

Yogi Berra

Career 1946–1965 all in New York

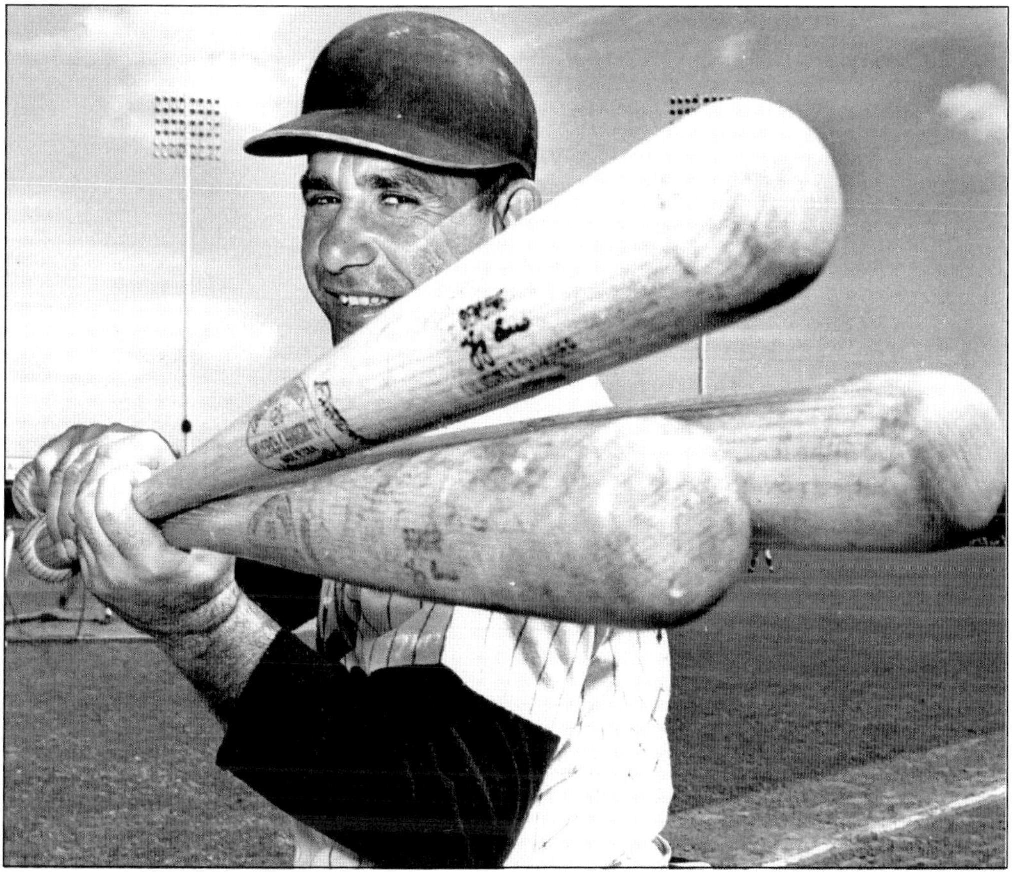

Lawrence "Yogi" Berra is one of the most famous ballplayers of the 20th century. His name got him a lot of attention, but he would still be unknown had he not been a consummate catcher and hitter. Berra was nearly impossible to strike out; no matter where a pitch was thrown, he could hit it. After World War II, Berra spent one year with Newark in the minors. He was on the Yankee roster by the end of the 1946 season. Berra hit 30 home runs in both 1952 and 1956, setting an American League record for catchers. His record total of 306 career home runs stood until Carlton Fisk passed him in the early 1990s. Yogi received Most Valuable Player honors in three separate years: 1951, 1954 and 1955. He caught for the American League in the All-Star Game for 15 straight years, from 1948 to 1964. Berra's World Series accomplishments are legendary. He played in 75 games over 14 postseason classics, hit 12 homers, scored 41 runs, and collected 39 RBIs. He was a world champion during most of his career in New York.

Tommy Henrich

Career 1937–1950 all in New York

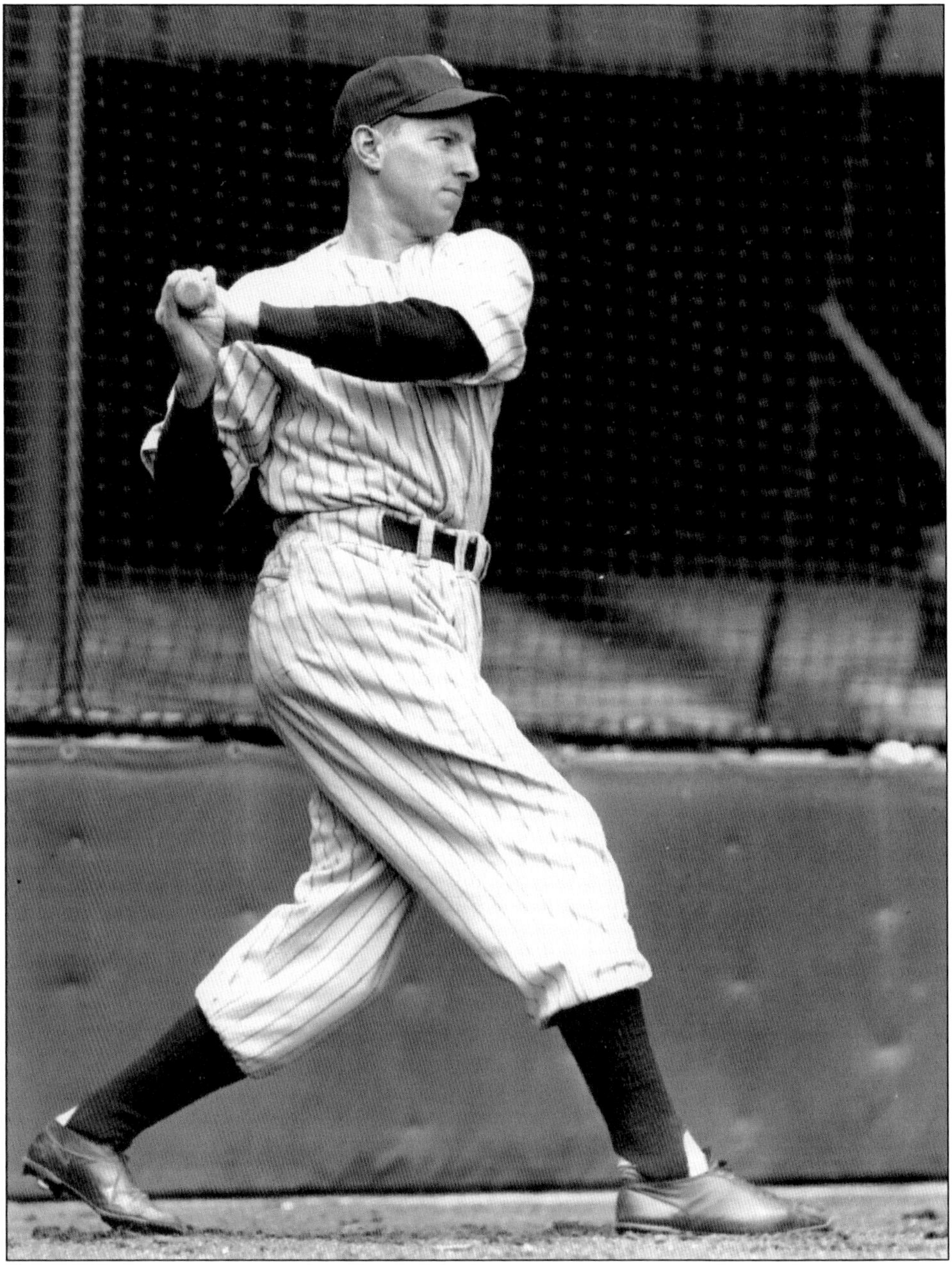

Tommy Henrich never appeared in a major-league game in anything other than a Yankee uniform. Playing the outfield with Joe DiMaggio and Charlie Keller, Henrich completed a trio that was one of the best of its era. A clever base runner as well as a hitter, Henrich twice led the American League in triples, and in 1938 he scored more runs than anyone else, crossing the plate 138 times. He could hit home runs, too, knocking out 31 in 1941, 25 in 1946, and 24 in 1949. The 1949 season was his most important for the team, as he scored 90 runs and had 85 runs batted in.

Don Mueller

Career 1948–1959 New York 1948–1957

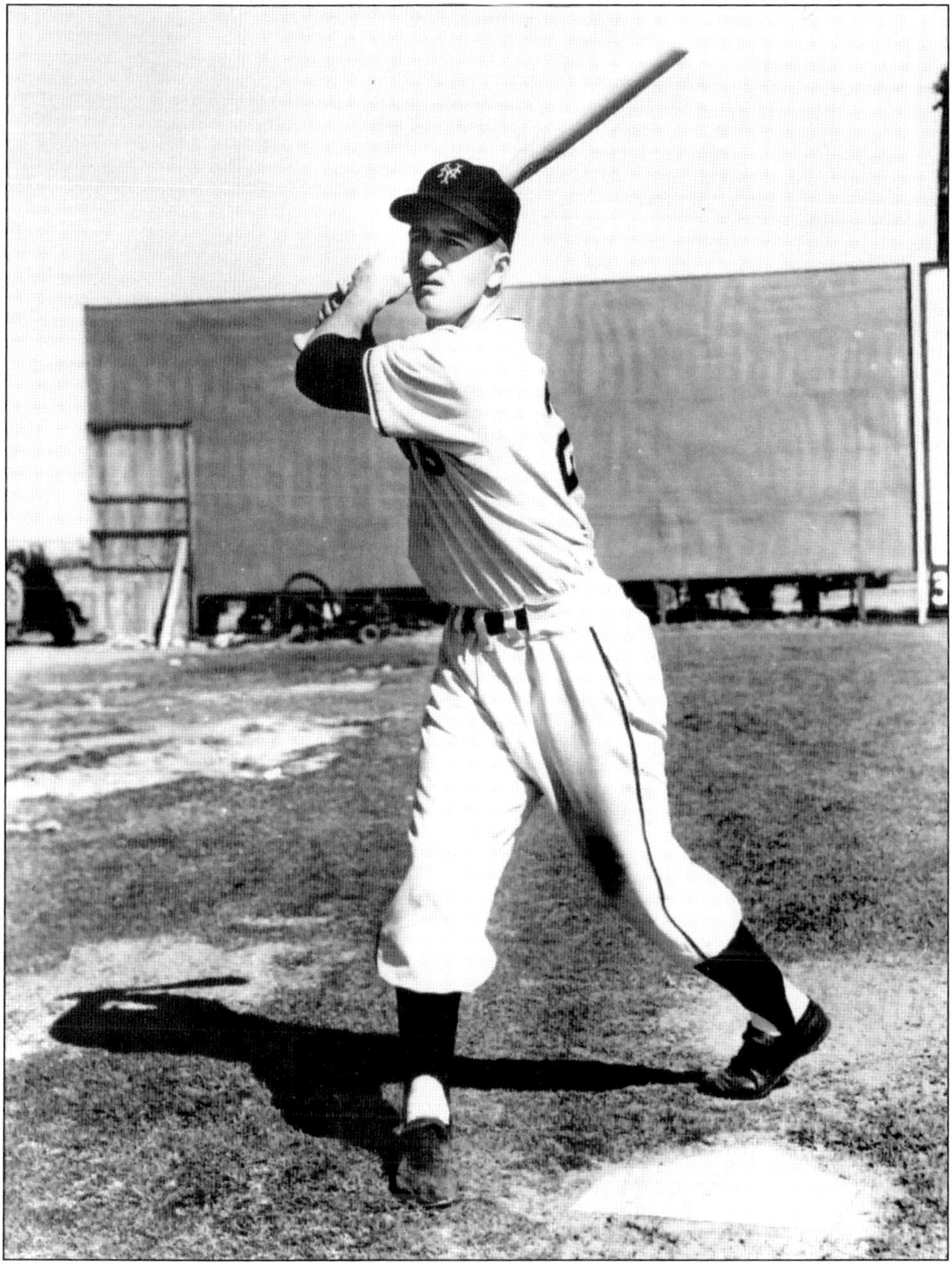

While Tommy Henrich was impressing fans with his outfield play, Don Mueller was putting on a show for the Giants' faithful back in Manhattan. He came up to the big leagues at the end of the 1940s, and by 1950 he was a starting right fielder in the Polo Grounds. In 1953, his career came to full flower, as he finished fifth in the National League batting race with a mark of .333. Continuing to improve the next season, Mueller raised his average to .342 and led the league in base hits with 212. Mueller saw World Series action with the Giants in 1954.

FLASH GORDON

CAREER 1938–1950 NEW YORK 1938–1946

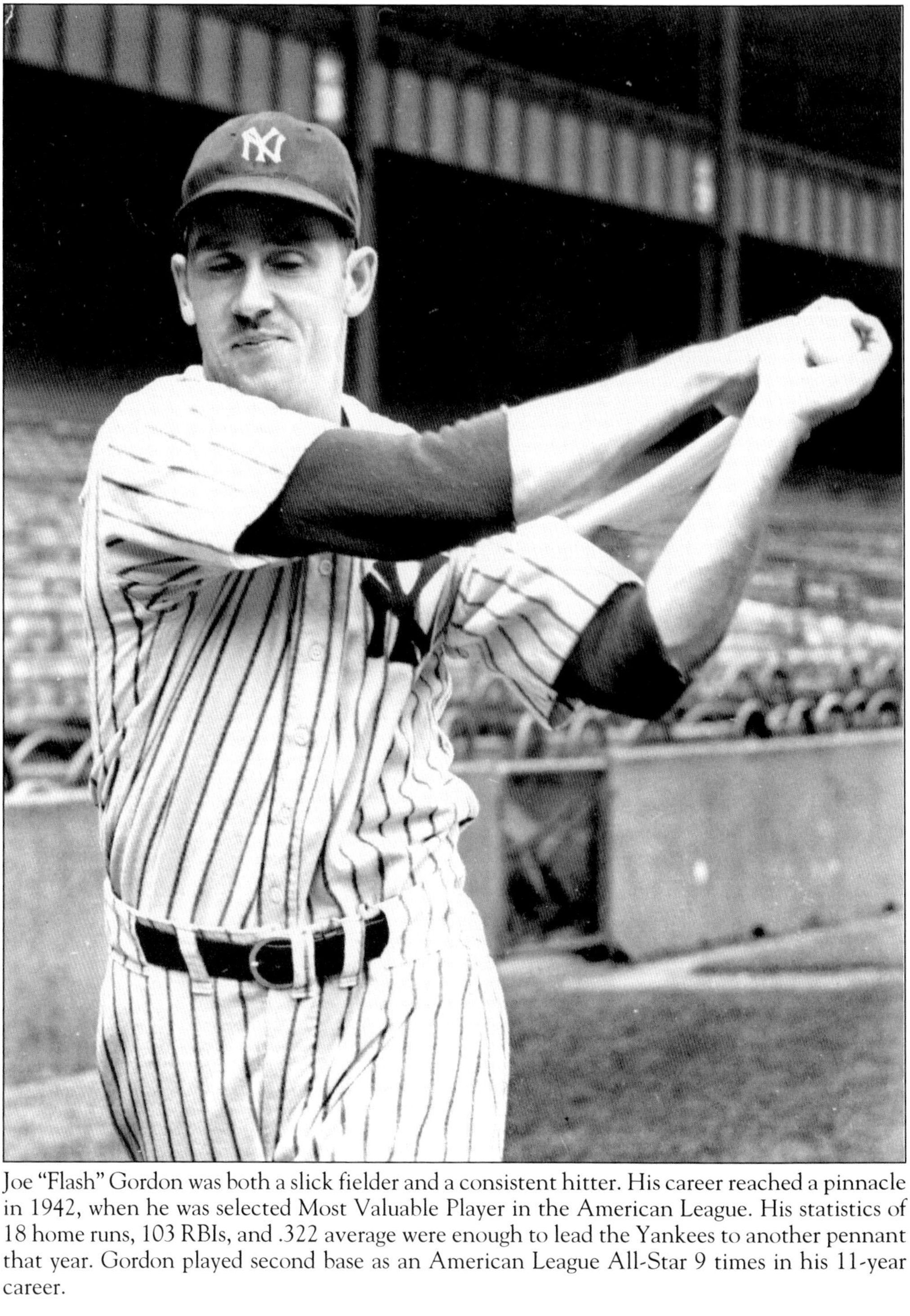

Joe "Flash" Gordon was both a slick fielder and a consistent hitter. His career reached a pinnacle in 1942, when he was selected Most Valuable Player in the American League. His statistics of 18 home runs, 103 RBIs, and .322 average were enough to lead the Yankees to another pennant that year. Gordon played second base as an American League All-Star 9 times in his 11-year career.

Sid Gordon

Career 1941–1955 New York 1941–1949, 1955

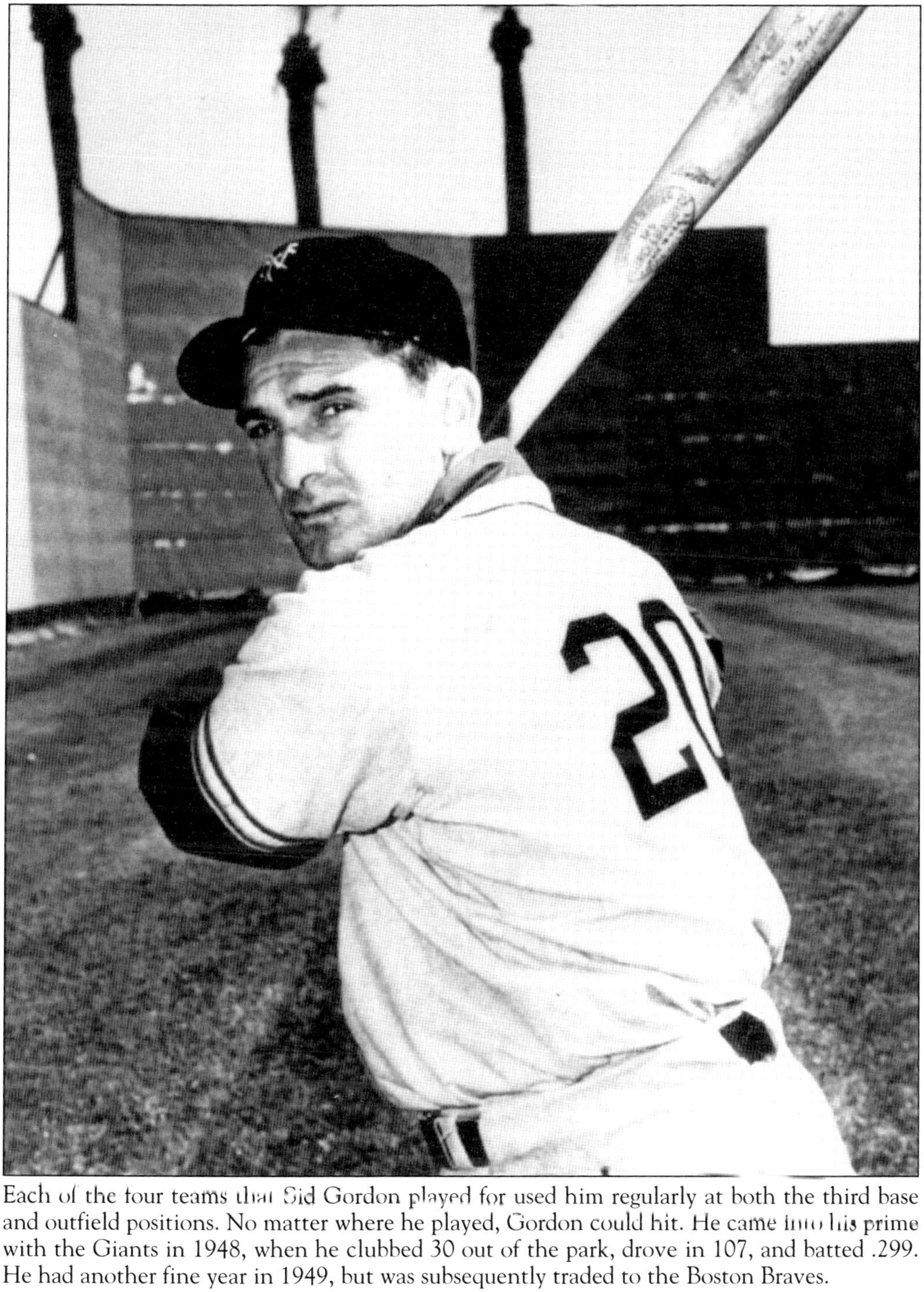

Each of the four teams that Sid Gordon played for used him regularly at both the third base and outfield positions. No matter where he played, Gordon could hit. He came into his prime with the Giants in 1948, when he clubbed 30 out of the park, drove in 107, and batted .299. He had another fine year in 1949, but was subsequently traded to the Boston Braves.

Monte Irvin

Career 1937–1956 New York 1949–1955

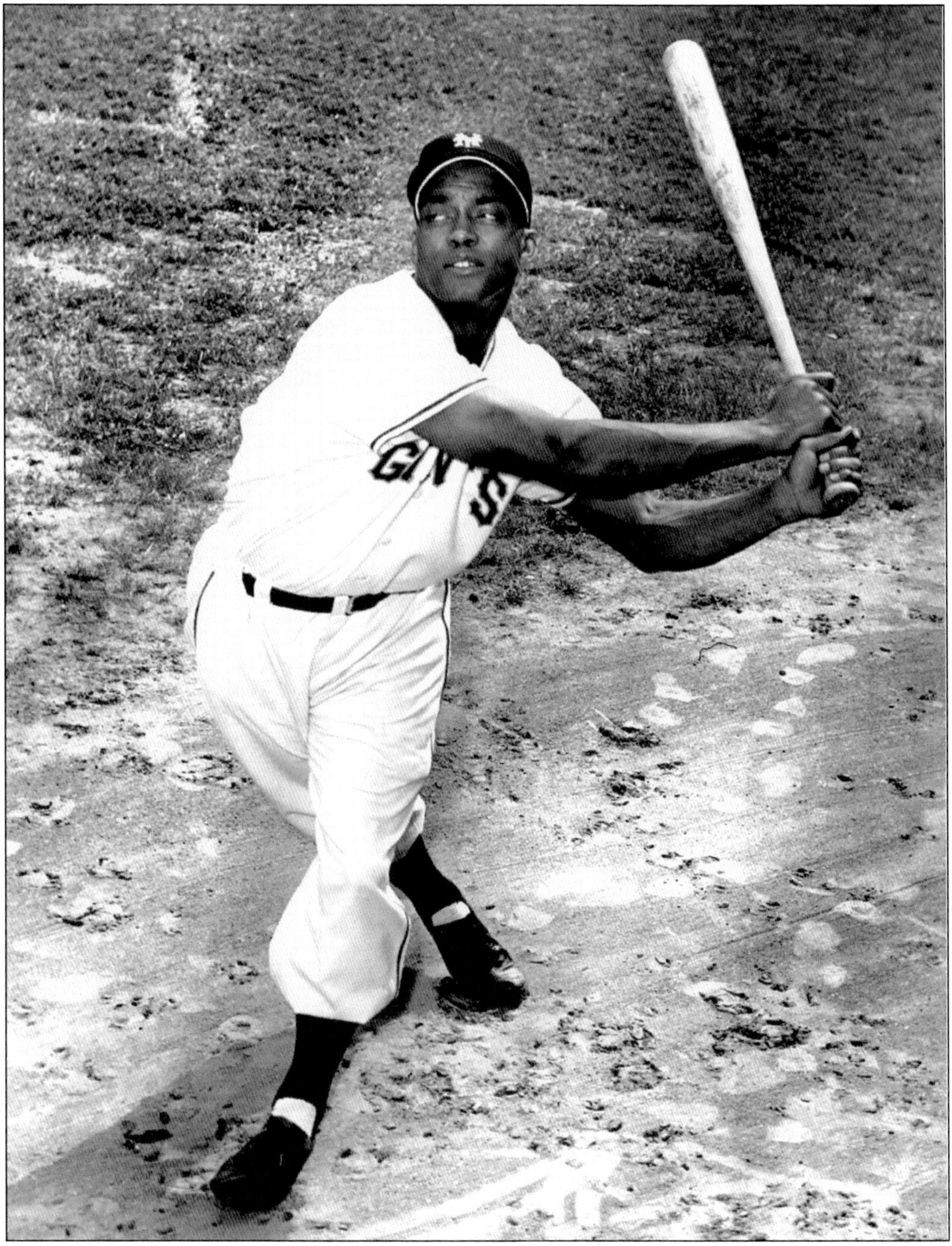

Monte Irvin was one of those players whose historical timing was very fortunate. He lived in two worlds, playing professional baseball in first the Negro National League and then the integrated National League with the Giants. In addition, he played winter ball in Cuba, Mexico, and Puerto Rico, which gave him a broad perspective on baseball across the Americas.

From 1937 to 1948, Monte Irvin played infield and then center field for the Eagles of Newark, New Jersey. The Giants obtained Irvin after a contractual snafu, and in 1949 he was monitoring center field in the Polo Grounds. By 1951, Irvin led the league in runs batted in with 121. His top batting average with the New Yorkers was .329 in 1953. The image below shows Irvin in the Giants dressing room, helping out Willie Mays (right) with a treatment, while manager Leo Durocher (center) looks on.

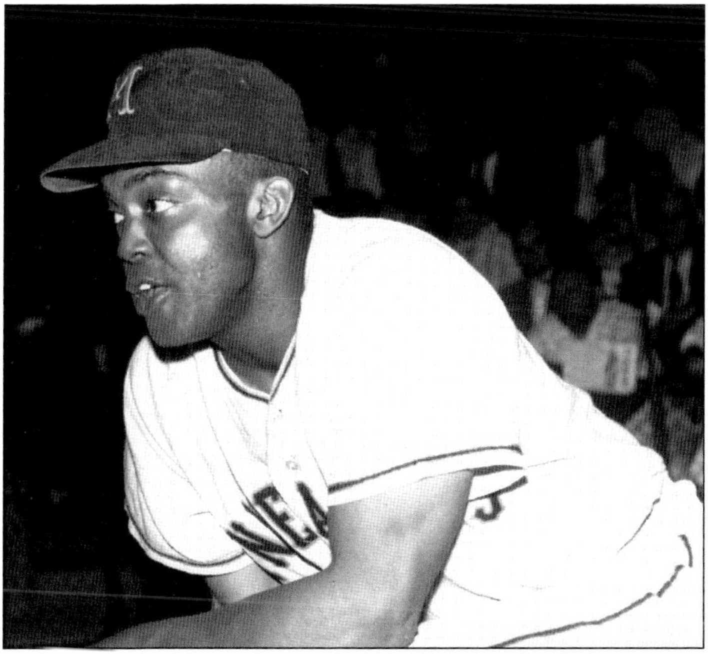

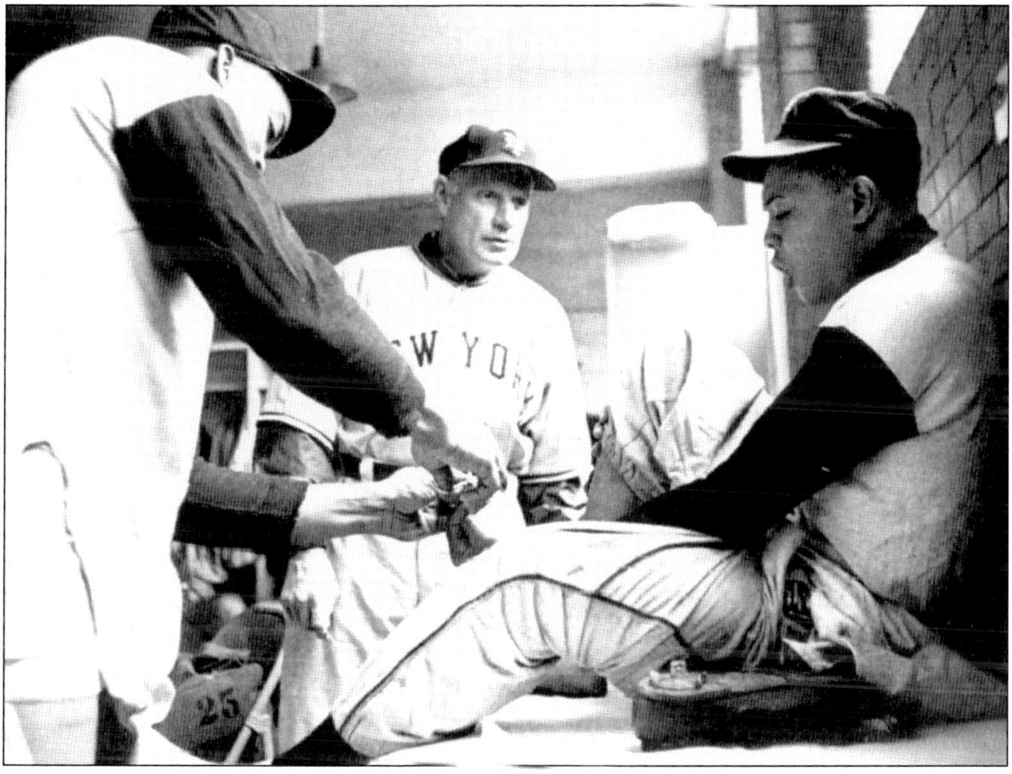

Hank Thompson

Career 1943–1956 New York 1949–1956

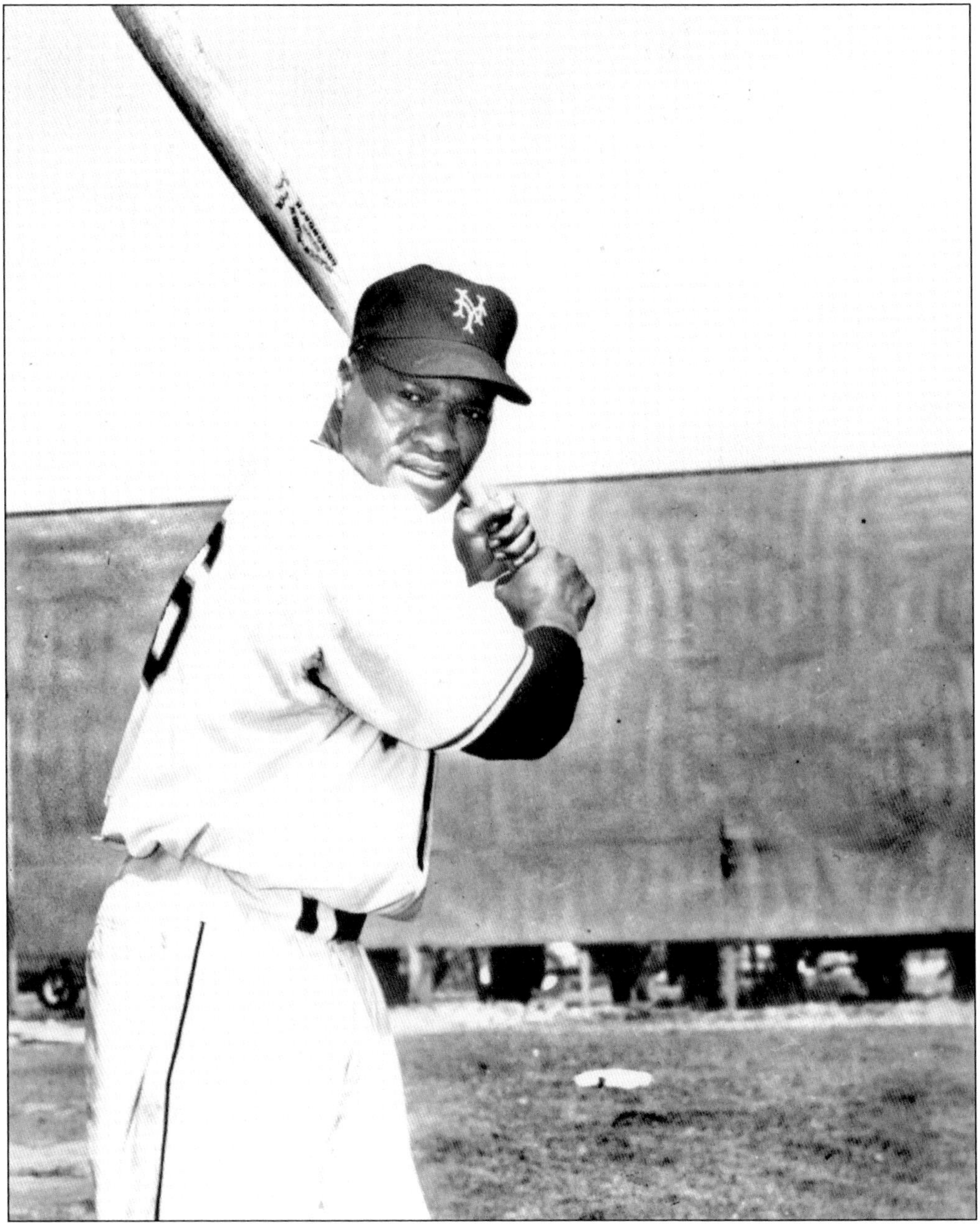

Hank Thompson's career also spanned the period before and after baseball segregation. Like a double Jackie Robinson, Thompson was the first black player for the St. Louis Browns and the New York Giants. He had some excellent seasons while playing third base and outfield in the Polo Grounds. Thompson put up his best numbers in 1953, with 24 home runs, 74 RBIs, and a .302 average. He helped the Giants win pennants in 1951 and 1954, and enjoyed competing in nine World Series games.

Charlie Keller

Career 1939–1952 New York 1939–1949, 1952

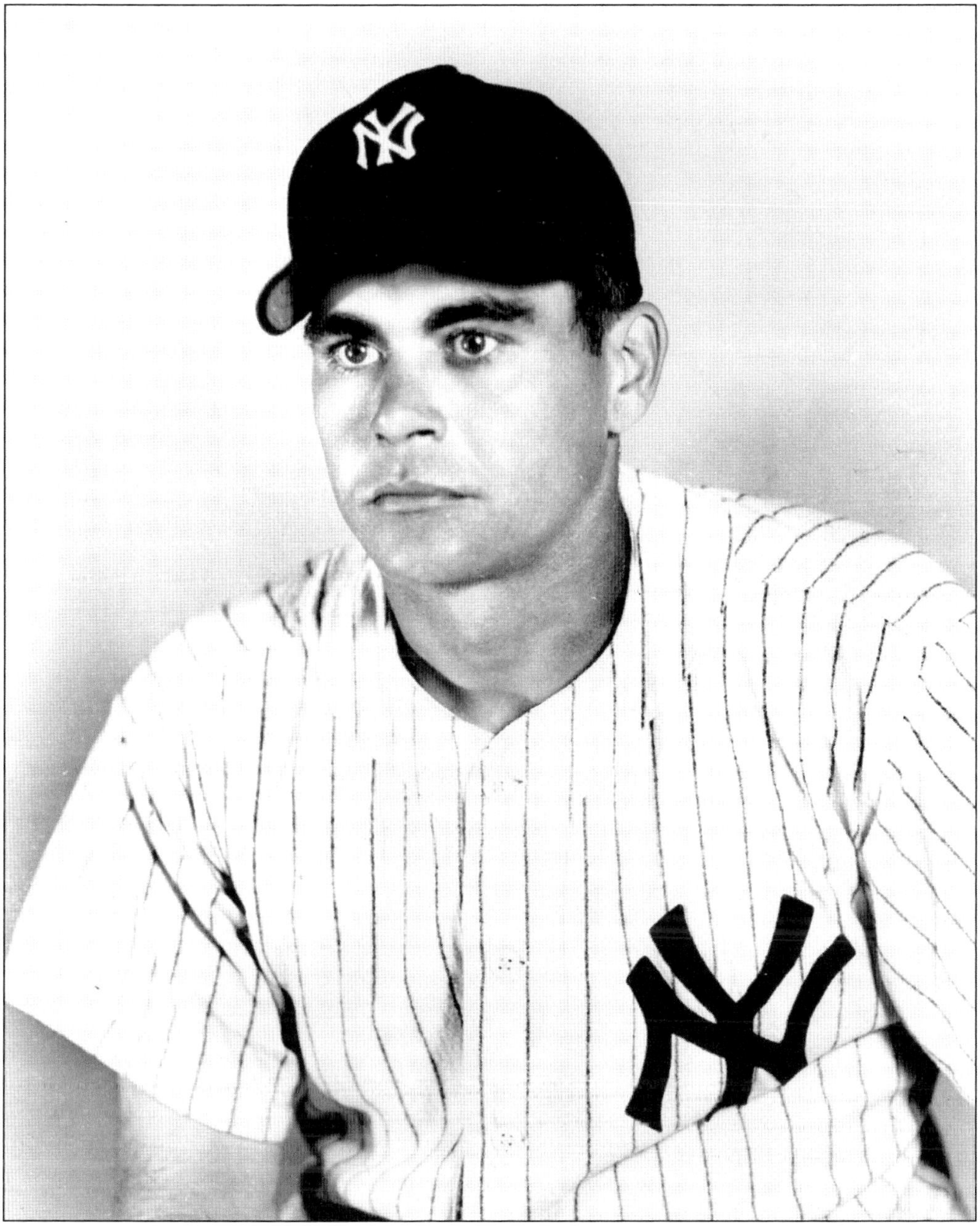

The statistics make it clear that Charlie Keller's best major-league years were early in his career with the New York Yankees. He was named to five All-Star teams during the 1940s, and he covered the outfield in four World Series, where he batted .306 and knocked in 18 overall. In 1941, Keller scored 102 runs, drove home 122, and finished with a .298 batting average. He also had a keen batting eye: Keller had more than 100 walks in five different years and led the American League in two of those seasons.

Bobby Thompson

Career 1946–1960 New York 1946–1953

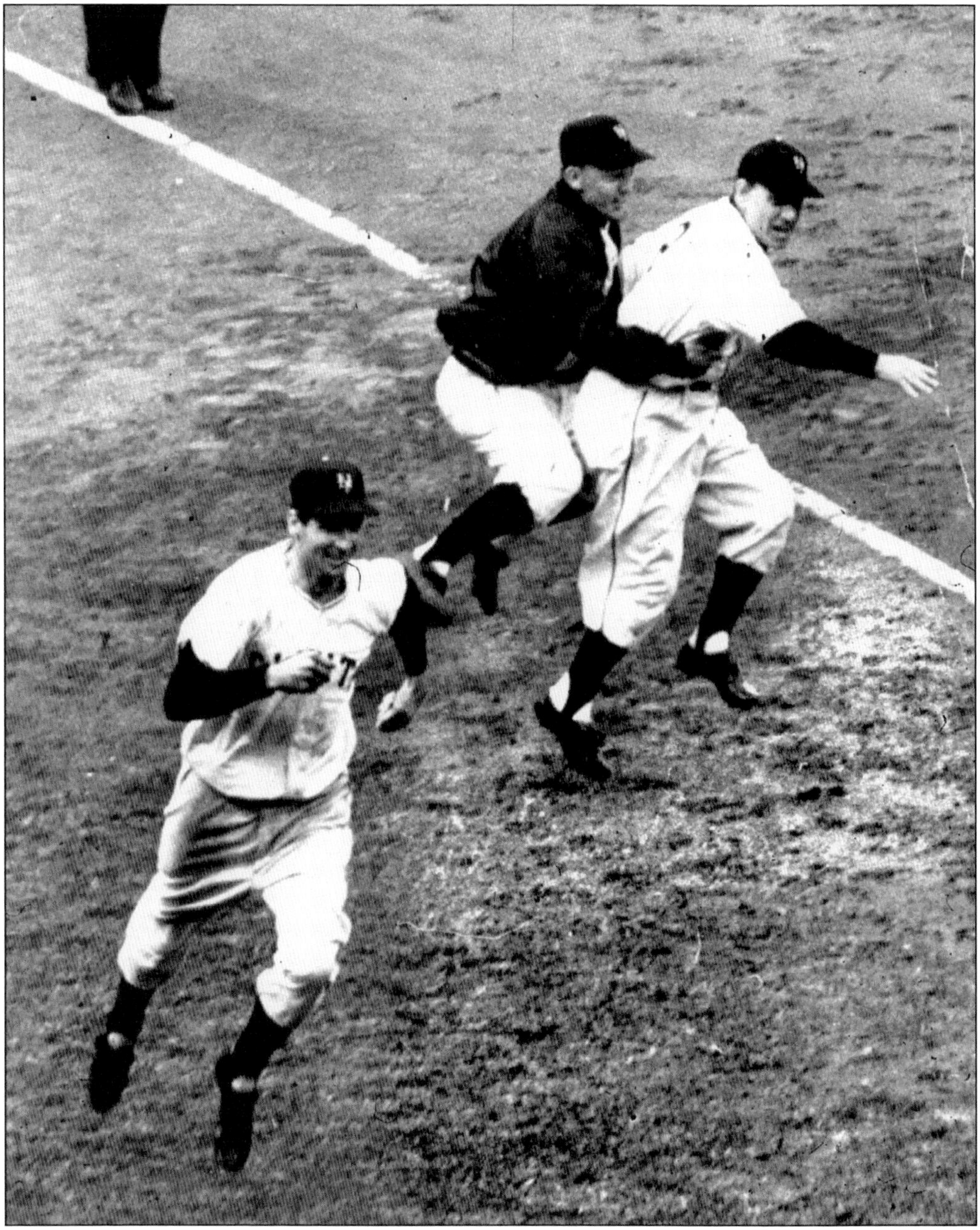

What a joyous time it was in Manhattan when Bobby Thompson's ninth-inning home run, with two men aboard, cleared the wall in a 1951 playoff game against the Brooklyn Dodgers. Above, Thompson romps home to clinch the pennant for the Giants after jubilantly touching third base. This was without a doubt Thompson's most glorious moment, but he had a few others that were memorable as well. He played in the All-Star Game three times, and over his 15-year career had 264 home runs among his total 1,705 hits.